THE PRESS AS OPPOSITION
THE POLITICAL ROLE OF SOUTH AFRICAN NEWSPAPERS

THE PRESS
AS OPPOSITION

The Political Role of South African Newspapers

by

ELAINE POTTER

ROWMAN AND LITTLEFIELD
TOTOWA, NEW JERSEY

First published in the United States 1975
by Rowman and Littlefield, Totowa, N.J.

Library of Congress Cataloging in Publication Data

Potter, Elaine.
  The press as opposition.

  Bibliography: p.
  Includes index.
  1. Press and politics—Africa, South. 2.
Africa, South—Politics and government—
1948–   I. Title.
PN5477.P6P6   1975   301.16'1   74-28037
ISBN 0-87471-445-1

Printed in Great Britain by
Cox & Wyman Ltd
London, Fakenham and Reading

Contents

5

CONTENTS

Preface

The unique character and contradictions of a White minority-ruled South Africa in the context of Black Africa has attracted considerable study, and an extensive literature on South Africa has developed. Little attention has been focused, however, on the role of the South African press in the political system and on the complex relationship between the press and the Government. This study is a first attempt to fill this gap. It would have been possible to inspect a small part of the subject in minute detail but the paucity of literature in the field seemed to justify a broader examination of the political role of the press in South Africa.

There are in South Africa two quite different types of newspapers. On the one hand there is an English language press which uniformly opposes the Government, its ideology and its supporters, who now constitute a majority of the White population. On the other hand, the Afrikaans language press, which fails to compete with the English press for readers, is an integrated part of the National Party and the governmental machine.

The central argument which I develop in this book is that between 1948 and 1968 the English language press became an 'external' opposition, whilst the Afrikaans language press, as an institution within the ranks of Government, constituted an 'internal' opposition. I chose to begin the study in 1948 as it was in that year that the National Party came to power. Twenty years later, the National Party was facing the first major split in its ranks, largely as a result of the ferment created by the Afrikaans press. The English press' extensive deprivation of political information and the Nationalist government's unresponsiveness to pressures from outside its own ranks, underlined the importance of the growth of the Afrikaans press as an internal opposition, as much as it moulded the English press' development during these twenty years of Nationalist rule.

Since then South Africa has not changed appreciably. The Nationalist government are still in power and the impotent United and Progressive Parties persist. There have been some changes in the ownership structure of English language newspapers and the two major Afrikaans Sunday newspapers have merged. The English language press has been confronted with further threats to its existence but, as I demonstrate in the book, the government already has all the power it needs to suppress any newspaper if it so chooses. The most recent threats are part of a consistent pattern (discussed at some length in the book) whereby legislation and threats of legislation against the press are used by government to persuade the press to exercise self-censorship.

The emergence in the last few years of Black leaders in the so-called Homelands has emphasized rather than detracted from the role played by the English language press. The best known of the Black Homeland leaders, Chief Gatsha Buthelezi, told me, when I saw him in Nongomo a year ago, that he relied very extensively on the English language press, for all its limitations, to communicate his ideas. Since then, he has formalized this relationship by writing a regular column in South Africa's biggest morning newspaper, the *Rand Daily Mail*.

This study is the product of many years research for a D.Phil thesis undertaken at Nuffield College, Oxford. I must record my gratitude to the large number of journalists, editors of English and Afrikaans language newspapers, newspaper proprietors and politicians, who gave so much of their time in interviews and informal discussions. I regret the necessity to consign them to anonymity; where possible in the text I have named my sources, though for obvious reasons I have deliberately sought to obscure the identities of others.

I cannot adequately express my gratitude to Professor Max Beloff of All Soul's College, Oxford, who acted throughout as my university supervisor. I could not have completed the study without his unstinting intellectual support and encouragement, despite differences of political opinion. I am deeply indebted to him.

I must also record my gratitude to the Warden and Fellows of Nuffield College for electing me to a studentship and enabling me to undertake my research. My thanks go also to the Astor Foundation who generously provided me with funds to visit the International Press Institute in Zurich, and, with Nuffield College, financed my research in South Africa.

I am indebted to David Butler, my College supervisor, who provided me with invaluable advice. Finally, a special thank you to my husband David, for his unfailing support and patience and for reading the manuscript with a soberingly critical eye.

February 1974   E.P.

Introduction

The primary function of the Press–and the source of any influence it might have–is communication. It is through the communication of attitudes, ideas and information that the Press performs all its other functions. This is not to say that communication is the sole prerogative of the modern mass media; on the contrary, they are only one of the many sources from which individuals in society acquire attitudes or information about their environment. However, by enlarging the personal experience of great numbers of individual men, and imposing a uniform picture of their society upon them, the Press effectively alters the environment. Thus the kinds of structures which perform the specialist communication function (and for the purpose of this study, the newspaper Press) are a significant barometer of the society of which they are an integral part.

Two quite different types of mass communication structures developed in South Africa after 1948: on the one hand there was a Press which was a co-ordinated agency of a centralized party and Government, and part of the Government's extensive communication network; on the other hand, there was a Press which was independent of Government and which as a matter of general principle believed its independence to be a necessary prerequisite for its functioning.

The differences between the two structures, of Afrikaans and English-language Press, were fundamental. They both reflected, and in some measure helped to maintain, the existing divisions within South African society. The differences in their basic orientations, their relationships to the economy and the polity, their audiences and their intentions were most clearly evidenced in the style and content of the two newspaper groups. In theory the mass media are capable of assisting national development and the integration of disparate elements in society, but in order to do so, the Press at least would require the implicit support of Government and other institutions within society. In South Africa the rigidly entrenched hierarchy of exclusive racial groups has ensured the continuing divisions within society. But the enforcedly divided nature of society and the racially exclusive character of most of its institutions has placed the Press in a unique position. For it was after 1948 one of the few racially non-exclusive institutions in society, in the sense that all racial and linguistic groups had access to it.

The power of the Press, derives from the fact that people read it. This truism acquires an added dimension in the South African context. For, through its accessibility to all groups including those who were not a part of the political system at all in that they were not permitted to participate directly or indirectly in the political process, the Press acquired a unique character in the system. While four-fifths of the population could neither vote nor engage in any kind of collective bargaining, even for economic purposes, they could read the newspapers.

Accessibility is not in itself a significant measure of the relevance of the Press as a multi-racial institution. Its peculiar pertinence in the South African context was dependent on the existence of two types of mass communication structures, and the marked differences in the contents and intentions of their newspapers. If the Press had merely served to communicate Government imperatives and attitudes, it would have been simply another agency for encouraging conformity to existing political ideas. It was the existence of an English-language Press which was not only independent of Government but opposed to it (and as such, posed an alternative view of society) which gave significance to the fact that newspapers were available to and read by members of all racial groups.

Thus the impact the Press may have is dependent in the first instance on who reads the newspapers and what the content of those newspapers is. It is necessary, for the purposes of explaining in what sense audience is relevant to this study, to distinguish two types of audiences over whom the Press might exert any kind of influence, namely a mass public and a political public.[1] By political public is meant those members of society who are, through their membership of particular institutions, in a position to have effect on political policies, as for example, members of the Government. The mass public are those who are primarily recipients of political information rather than being directly concerned with the creation of Government policies.

This study is not concerned directly with the impact of the Press on the mass public, but rather with its role within the political system as determined by its relations with the political public and governmental structures within the system. Thus the emphasis on the

---

[1] This useful distinction is borrowed from C. Seymour-Ure, in *The Press, Politics and the Public* (London: Methuen & Co. Ltd., 1968).

audience as a determinant of the political role of the Press in South Africa does not stem from any claims about the actual impact of the Press on its audiences, but is rather a statement about the nature of the political system itself. Further, the Presses' audiences are important because Government attitudes to the two Presses, which helped to determine their respective roles were in large measure a response to Government beliefs about the impact of a newspaper on its readers.

The central argument of this study is that between 1948 and 1968, the English-language Press came to function as an 'external' opposition and that in the performance of all its other more 'traditional' political functions such as, for example, its role as 'watchdog' or representative of minority (or majority) opinion, or interest articulation, it generally reinforced its primary opposition role. The Afrikaans-language Press on the other hand, served primarily as a channel for 'political outputs' and initially was concerned with the integration and mobilization of a single group within the totality. But, during the twenty years under observation, the Afrikaans Press too began to function as an opposition, but as an 'internal' opposition and with very different intentions and consequences from those of the English-language Press in its role of 'external' opposition.

Some new perspectives on the structuring of power in South Africa can be gained by an analysis of the style and content of political communication through the Press and of the factors which affected the manner in which the two newspaper media performed their various roles. As in the last analysis it is the content of newspapers which determines their political roles, it is necessary to know not only what that content was but what factors governed their choice of content.

It is difficult to know which feature of a newspaper is a consequence of which pressure. Rather the style and the content are a product and compromise of frequently competing forces. However, by isolating individual factors which undoubtedly affect the character of a newspaper and examining them closely, it is possible to describe the framework within which the Press had to operate and to suggest the likely effects of such a framework.

What then are these factors? First, there is the political system itself within which the Press functioned and of which it was an integral part. In Chapter 1 the protagonists are introduced, pointing very briefly to the significant features in the histories of the competing groups who came either to dominate or be dominated in the political system. The main political issues, conflicts and alignments which occurred between the creation of the modern South African state in 1910 and 1948, when the Nationalist Government came to power, are

11

traced. The chapter is concluded by asking what changes occurred after 1948, what effects those changes had on the workings of the political system and with what consequences for the Press.

In Chapter 2 the Presses' own political histories, which have moulded their various traditions, are described. The question then is how important have those traditions been in determining the way in which the Presses defined their own roles? And what effect have their definitions had on the performance of their roles? Chapter 3 asks in what way the financial structure of the Press and its relationship to the economy affected first, the internal working of newspapers and second, the attitudes of newspapers to society and to governmental structures within it.

The fourth chapter examines newspaper readership. Because this study is not concerned with the actual impact of the Press on its readers, questions about audience interest, that is, which parts of a newspaper were read by whom, are not dealt with. Rather, a detailed analysis of newspaper readership provides a substantiated explanation of governmental attitudes to the Press, which, it is argued, stem directly from Government's beliefs about the consequences of political communications.

In Chapter 5 the nature and variety of governmental pressures on the Press—through a Press Commission of Inquiry, a Code of Conduct, and a very extensive body of legislation—are discussed. In this chapter an attempt is made to discover what Government pressures, in all their forms, have tried to achieve and with what effect. Are the pressures then a result of a coherently worked out Government policy or are they simply a response to specific political crises or needs? In what way and how often does Government actually use its extensive powers against the Press? And how does the Press respond?

Chapter 6 examines the working relationship between the Press and the Government, and poses the question of how political information is transferred from Government to the Press. The answers are, of course, conditional, for the chapter is based very extensively on interviews and the conclusions cannot be substantiated with documentary evidence. The aim was not to describe random events but to detect wherever possible continuing processes. Thus the kinds of questions which are discussed in the chapter are: how easy is it for the English-language Press to get access to governmental information? What is the nature of the relationship between members of the Afrikaans-language Press and members of the Government, how does this relationship affect the access of Afrikaans journalists to political information and what use does the Afrikaans Press make of that information? What impact does the Press make on Government?

INTRODUCTION

The key question of the final chapter, Chapter 7, is to what extent and why both English and Afrikaans-language Presses came to constitute the opposition in South Africa after 1948. The answer to this question is to be found in the actual content of the Press. Accordingly, the last chapter is devoted to an analysis of what the newspapers said between 1948 and 1968 through the selection of a few relevant events and issues during those years.

1

Politics and the Press

The Protagonists

The South African nation today is a conglomerate of peoples of different races, cultures and origins. The predominant group in terms of population were the Africans or Blacks, who in 1968, out of a population of 19,167,000 comprised the majority at 13,042,000 people.[1] The ruling group since 1948 has been the Afrikaners, a people of mainly Dutch origin who comprised 59 per cent of the 'White' population of 3,639,000. The remaining Whites are almost exclusively English-speaking and while they have originated predominantly from Great Britain and are frequently referred to as English South Africans, they have been formed by immigration from many other European countries. Amongst the remaining population, two groups are of particular importance. In 1968, the Coloureds, originating from a slave population from Asia and other parts of Africa and bred through miscegenation, numbered 1,912,000 while Asians, mainly from India, comprised 574,000 of the population.

This great spread of people, diverse in heritage and culture, forms the modern South Africa. It is from this diversity that the tensions in South Africa spring and to consider the operation of the modern state in South Africa, it is essential briefly to examine the origins and present roles of the constituent groups.

The Afrikaners emigrated to the Cape of Good Hope in the middle of the seventeenth century. For some time the Cape had been an important stepping stone on the sea route between Europe and the East, but no European power had considered it worthy of colonization or economic exploitation. The new Dutch settlers found abundant farming land populated only very sparsely by a nomadic African people, the Hottentots (later assimilated into the Cape Coloured community). They formed self-contained agriculturally based units free of any hegemony from Europe.

The settlers developed in their isolation a fierce independence and

---

[1] From the South African Government Bureau of Statistics news release dated February 10, 1969.

the beginnings of an indigenous new culture. By the end of the eighteenth century, the Afrikaners as they already called themselves, had established a philosophy and way of life which was uniquely theirs. Isolated from civilized Europe, the Boers (farmers) survived because of their independence and their capacity to meet their needs from the farm. These traditions of independence, doggedness and introversion have been perpetuated and are cherished by the modern Afrikaner.

The strategic importance of the Cape in the sea routes of the world led Britain to an interest in the Cape at the end of the eighteenth century. After an earlier temporary occupation, and spurred by the threat of other nations occupying the Cape during the Napoleonic Wars, Britain finally occupied the Cape in 1806. Confrontation with the Boers was almost immediate. For the first time, the Boers found alien and external laws applied, ownership of land had to be registered, and the new ideas of a liberal Europe were introduced to the distant and isolated Cape. But the British were not only a great naval power, they were also a colonial power, and a new wave of settlers from Britain entered the Southern Cape of Africa. Particularly after the upheavals of the Napoleonic wars, immigrants from Europe also arrived but immigrants who were quite alien to and who threatened the Boer way of life. The new settlers were the beginning of the English-speaking South African group. They were townsmen concerned with commerce and trade, international in their links with Europe. Whereas the Boer lived in the country the new settlers lived in the town; whereas the Boer was occupied in farming, the immigrants were concerned with business and trade; whereas the Boer had developed an aggressive dislike of control by government and was culturally cut off from Europe, the English brought administrative reforms and retained, however tenuously, their cultural links with Europe.

It was also during the seventeenth and eighteenth centuries that the third major group, the most populous group of peoples, were being established in Southern Africa. From other parts of Africa, the African tribes were migrating to what is in present-day South Africa, the Transvaal, Natal and the north-eastern Cape. It was at the Fish River in the east that the two nations, of Afrikaners and of Africans met.

To escape the twin enemies of Afrikanerdom in the Cape– organized British Government and the growth of racially egalitarian ideas–the Afrikaners in the 1830s started the 'Great Trek' into the hinterland of South Africa. Between 1836 and 1846 nearly a quarter of the Afrikaners living in the Cape Colony 'trekked' to even greater isolation to find new farmlands and to preserve their identity, language and culture. They created two new Boer republics in what became the Orange Free State and the Transvaal where for a short while at least they remained unfettered to continue their way of life. The Constitutions of the two republics, though they differed in some respects, entrenched inequality between White and non-White but the social and economic homogeneity of the White citizens of the republics were reflected in the 'democratic' nature of their Constitutions in so far as they governed the activities of White members of the society. The republican tradition thus became firmly established in Afrikaner thinking.

The Anglo-Boer War between 1899 and 1902 marked the final defeat of the old Boer republics and probably did more to unite Afrikanerdom and to foster an Afrikaner nationalism than any other event in South African history. British Imperial policy after the war–particularly attempts to anglicize the Afrikaners in the ex-republics–did nothing to quench the rising spirit of Afrikaner nationalism. Furthermore the war and the period of reconstruction leading to Union, helped unite the Boers in the Cape with those in the ex-republics.

After Union in 1910 two main themes dominated the policies of all parties: the position of the Union in relation to Great Britain and the Empire, and the issue of race relations.[1] At the root of the constitutional question was the power struggle between the English and the Afrikaners, which up until 1948 overshadowed the Native issue. Initially the main concern of both language groups was the possibility that one or the other of the groups would enforce its own cultural and political pattern on the whole society.

General Louis Botha, an Afrikaner and a moderate, became the first Prime Minister of the Union. He included in the cabinet of his South African Party (SAP) the Afrikaners and the moderate English; in opposition were the exclusively English-speaking Unionists and four members of the weak Labour Party. Botha's Government pursued a policy of conciliation between English and Afrikaner but it soon became clear that a large number of Afrikaners in the Free State and Transvaal particularly, did not support his 'one-stream' policy, which aimed at the development into one nation and people of the English and Afrikaners. Thus, just two years after Union, General J. B. Hertzog, already known for his introduction of compulsory bilingualism in the Orange Free State, broke with Botha, and

---

[1] D. W. Kruger (ed.), *South African Parties and Policies, 1910–1960* (Cape Town: Human and Rousseau, 1960).

formed the National Party in 1914. Hertzog's 'two-stream' policy was based on the belief that Afrikaans and English-speaking South Africans should develop separately, nurturing their own cultural and linguistic traditions. In external affairs, the National Party stood for a 'South Africa first' policy, which expressed the belief that the interests of South Africa should come before those of Empire. The great upsurge of nationalism which accompanied Hertzog's break from Botha became increasingly attractive to greater numbers of Afrikaners when South Africa entered the Great War–'Britain's War'–in 1914. The effects of South Africa's participation in the war were evident in the results of the 1915 election. On the one hand the strength of anti-British, anti-Botha Afrikaners was confirmed, while on the other hand, the total support of the all-English Unionist Party for Britain in the war, served to underline the unswerving loyalty of most English-speaking South Africans to Britain. Botha's party was returned as the major party but an administration was only formed with the help of the Unionists.

By 1920 the Nationalists, with exclusively Afrikaner support, succeeded in winning more seats than the SAP now under the leadership of General J. C. Smuts, who took over on Botha's death in 1919. Even with the support of the Unionists, with whom Smuts was forced to form a coalition Government, Smuts could only muster a majority of four. Realizing that electorally he stood to gain more in the English-speaking cities, Smuts was (unwillingly) prepared to risk losing rural Afrikaner support and in 1921 the SAP and the Unionist Party fused. This confirmed more and more Afrikaners in their opinion that a Nationalist movement was the only way to ensure their survival. Despite the changing alignments which occurred after 1921, the opposing forces in the political arena subsequently were more or less permanently defined: an exclusive Afrikaner Nationalist Party arraigned against a coalition formed from a decreasing number of Afrikaner moderates and virtually all of the English.

The constitutional and race issues were to some extent subordinated to social and economic issues in the ensuing years. The SAP came to represent the urban industrial interests and the wealthier farmers, while the Nationalists, representing the rural and urban Afrikaner proletariat and the new Afrikaner intelligentsia,[1] formed an electoral pact with the English-speaking party of White labour, namely the Labour Party. The Nationalist–Labour pact was victorious and governed the country between 1924 and 1933. Hert-

[1] Sheila Patterson, *The Last Trek* (London: Routledge & Kegan Paul, 1957) p. 99.

zog's victory in 1924 was a major landmark in the rise of nationalism as a political force in South Africa and it was during Hertzog's administration, in 1925, that Afrikaans, as opposed to Dutch, became one of the two official languages of South Africa.

Hertzog, as Prime Minister, returned from the Imperial Conference of 1926 with a document which set out the new sovereign status of the Dominion parliaments, and which was later enacted in 1931 as the Statute of Westminster. With this document he attempted to persuade Afrikaners that South Africa had really achieved independence from Britain. But already there were murmurs from the more extremist groups in the National Party that Hertzog had abandoned his republican ideals in order to appease the Labour members of the Pact Government, as it was called. Hertzog in fact still believed that a republic was the most suitable form of Government for South Africa but that it could not be implemented until the English were ready for it. The breach between Hertzog and the extremists (the Malanites) widened still further when Smuts and Hertzog finally reunited again in a widely approved coalition Government in 1933.

With the fusion movement under way, Dr Daniel Malan and most of the Cape Nationalists broke away in 1934 to form the Purified National Party and Afrikanerdom once again split in two as it had done in 1912. In Natal, the devolutionists led by Col. C. Stallard, fearing a surrender to Hertzog, splintered from the SAP to form the Dominion Party which opposed South Africa's independent status, and pledged itself to maintain the British connection. With the two irreconcilable extremist elements out of the way, Hertzog and Smuts joined together again in June 1934 to create the United South African National Party or United Party (UP), a party representing the spirit of Union, of English–Afrikaner co-operation, and respect for the dominion ties with Britain and the Commonwealth. In the 1938 election, the Malanites succeeded in winning twenty-seven seats, but the 'one-stream' and most of the 'two-stream' Afrikaners stayed loyal to Hertzog in the United Party.

The Second World War brought the Constitutional question back into the forefront of political argument and Hertzog, refusing to fight what he regarded as Britain's war, resigned. Smuts once again became Prime Minister and formed his war cabinet with the support of the Labour and the Dominion Party. It was not long after rejoining Malan's purified Nationalists in the newly constituted 'Herenigde Nasionale of Volksparty' (HNP) in 1940 that Hertzog found he was equally not at home within a party which had begun to think in terms of domination by the Afrikaners. Hertzog's policy throughout his career, was based on the assumption that co-operation between

19

English and Afrikaners must be co-operation between equals, which was only possible when the Afrikaners had been rehabilitated. Malan on the other hand held that the Afrikaners would never get co-operation from the English, that in any event co-operation with the English was a danger to the existence of Afrikaner culture, and that as soon as possible a simple parliamentary majority should proclaim a republic. Hertzog withdrew from the HNP and with his long-time supporter, N. C. Havenga, founded the Afrikaner Party. However he had lost most of his supporters to Malan and in the 1943 election the Afrikaner Party did not win a single seat. Malan and his successors, however, modified their republican policies and when the Republic was created it came about in Hertzog's way, through a referendum of the White population, although with the support of only 51 per cent of the electorate.

1948 and After

The 1948 victory of the 'Herenigde Nasionale of Volksparty' was particularly significant in that it created the first all-Afrikaner government and ensured the final defeat of the old-fashioned National Party. The purified nationalists who would not toy with the notion of co-operation with the English, had proved their dominance. Hertzog, a nationalist of the old, traditional National Party, could find no place in the new. Prior to 1948, compromise had been an essential prerequisite for securing political power; the victory of an all-Afrikaner Nationalist party did away with the need to compromise.

Victory of united Afrikaner nationalism determined where the new emphasis for policy would lie. Prior to 1948, the primary battleground was the Afrikaner–English conflict. But by 1948, both because the Afrikaners had in a sense settled the Afrikaner–English issue and because the political demands of a growing number of urban, educated Africans were being heard, the main area of controversy lay in policies on race.

The popularity of the National Party's policy of enforced racial segregation together with their anti-Indian, anti-Communist propaganda and their uncompromising appeal to Afrikaner nationalism, was evidenced in the election results. Significantly, voting according to national origins and sentiments was very apparent. Between them, the National Party and the Afrikaner Party won virtually all seats in the predominantly Afrikaans-speaking areas. According to Gwendolen Carter, only about 20–25 per cent of the Afrikaans-speaking section of the electrorate voted for the United Party although United Party candidates were equally divided between those who were

English and those who were Afrikaans-speaking.[1] The HNP on the other hand did not have a single English-speaking candidate in the election and for the first time in South African history, only one sector of the dominant White group constituted the Government.

The Nationalist control of Government in 1948 was tenuous, but in the subsequent decades by manipulating the machinery of Government and by winning additional electoral support they clearly established their political dominance. Through the loading of rural constituencies, the abolition of Native Representatives, the elimination of the Cape Coloureds from the common roll, the disproportionate representation of South-West Africa, and the intensive indoctrination of their supporters,[2] the Nationalists steadily became more powerful. Their total triumph of political victory and power was achieved finally in the creation of the Republic in 1961. In the elections of 1953, 1958, 1961 and 1966, the Nationalists increased their majorities acquiring control of more than two-thirds of the seats in the House of Assembly. This was in spite of the fact that at most 55 per cent of the electorate voted for them. It has been suggested that the electoral system is such that even if 60% of the electorate supported the Opposition the Government would win.[3] Thus in 1948, the NP–AP coalition received 40 per cent of the votes and seventy-nine seats, while the UP received 50 per cent of the votes and only sixty-five seats. Urban concentration of supporters, the traditional loading of rural constituencies and the constant activity of the delimination committee all worked against the UP.

The history of the National Party to 1968 illustrated the victory of the extremists over the less extreme: after 1948 the leadership of the National Party passed into the hands of successively more extreme nationalists; from Malan to Strijdom, to Verwoerd and Vorster, marking a shift in the balance of political power from the Cape to the Transvaal.

The United Party's shock electoral defeat in 1948 and the subsequent death within two years of its two most important leaders, Smuts and his deputy J. H. Hofmeyr, left the party in great confusion. While in office it was possible and even profitable to include both White English capitalists and anti-Nationalist Afrikaners, to propagate the Commonwealth connection and yet retain a 'republican' clause, in opposition the competing interests the party represented

[1] Gwendolen Carter, *Politics of Inequality* (London: Thames and Hudson, 1962), p. 36.

[2] See Pierre van den Berghe, South Africa, *A Study in Conflict* (Berkeley and Los Angeles: University of California Press, 1970), p. 103–4.

[3] R. Farquharson, 'South Africa', in D. E. Butler (ed.), *Elections Abroad* (London: Macmillan & Co., 1959), p. 229.

was one of its greatest weaknesses. From 1953 to 1959, four minority groups representing viewpoints to the left and right of the United Party, broke away to form new groups. Despite these fissions, the United Party's greatest political disadvantage remained the broad middle-of-the-road coalition of interests it historically represented. In appeasing its 'centre', the UP has invariably alienated both 'right' and 'left'.

Increasingly after 1948, the UP moved nearer to the policies of the National Party in an effort to make itself more acceptable to the White electorate as the custodian of all White interests (as opposed to exclusively Afrikaner interests). Yet despite its continued claims to represent the interests of all White South Africans, and despite the fact that a majority of its members in Parliament were Afrikaners, the United Party essentially became an English party, dependent on the minority White group for its support. At the most, 15 per cent of the Afrikaans population continued to give their support to the United Party.[1]

In opposition, the loose and sometimes ambiguous structure and policies of the party made it wholly unequal to the task of opposing the tightly knit, self-conscious and exclusive National Party, which succeeded in persuading the 'Volk' that it alone was their true political representative.

The Decline of Opposition: Causes and Effects

There was between Government and Opposition very broad agreement over a wide range of issues. Prior to 1961, the main difference between the UP and NP was over South Africa's relationship with Britain and the Commonwealth. The UP traditionally advocated close ties with Britain while Nationalists wanted, and finally achieved, a republican form of government outside the Commonwealth. The UP's tacit, if reluctant, acceptance of the Republic and the severance of Commonwealth links left it with very few policies fundamentally distinguishable from those of the National Party. By depriving English-speaking South Africans of their international connections, the Republic paradoxically brought the two language groups closer together than they had ever been before. On the major issue of post-1948 politics, namely race policy, the two parties were in fundamental agreement: both were deeply committed to a policy of White supremacy and they differed only in the practical details of policy implementation. Thus while the Nationalists talked of apartheid or

---

[1] This figure is suggested by T. Karis, 'South Africa', in Gwendolen M. Carter (ed.), *Five African States* (Ithaca: Cornell University Press, 1963), p. 530.

race separation, the Opposition spoke of 'race federation' or 'White leadership with justice' along traditional lines.

Thus the differences between the two major parties were to be found not so much in their policies as in their ability to formulate and to articulate policy, in their approach to political action—both in terms of internal party structure and to the winning of votes—and finally, in their attitudes to constitutional procedures.

The UPs inability to compete with the Nationalists was due as much to the growing similarity of its policies to those of the Government party, as to the differences that existed between the two parties. The UPs failure to produce significant alternative 'Native' policies stemmed from the fact that the UP was a White party and was as surely committed to White supremacy as the National Party. But it also failed because it was a conservative, pragmatic, loosely organized party, dominated by expediency and a lack of concern for political theory. Opposed to it was a tightly knit hierarchically structured, ideological party which claimed to be the sole representative of a whole nation. It was the very flexibility of the UP with its willingness to deal with social and political problems on a day-to-day basis, which enabled the Nationalists, with their simple, rigid and theoretically comprehensive political idea of apartheid, to claim to be the only reliable guardians of White (and Afrikaner) civilization in South Africa.

Paradoxically it was the United Party which had a unitary organizational structure, while the formal structure of the NP was decentralized. The powerful provincial parties of the NP drafted their own constitutions, directed their own organizations and had their own annual party congresses. The UP's national organization was much stronger than the NP's Federal Council which outside of Parliament was the NP's most powerful national body. A more important difference in the organization of the two parties, was that the NP, as the political arm of Afrikaner Nationalism, made continual demands on and use of its members, while the UP, resembling a coalition of groups rather than an integrally organized body, tended to create its machinery afresh for each election and made few demands on a largely passive membership.[1] Party congresses, for example, cannot generate the same enthusiasm as Government party congresses, where rank and file can, or believe they can have some influence on Government policy. Because it was not in office, the organization in the case of the UP was relatively more important than it was for the Government party.

[1] R. Farquharson, op. cit., p. 259.

The third important distinction between the UP and NP was their attitude to constitutional procedures. The distinction is significant not only in revealing the differences in orientation of the two parties, but in highlighting the conflicting traditions within the NP itself. In 1910 South Africa took over the parliamentary traditions of the Cape based as they were on the British model of parliamentary democracy, rather than adopting the Transvaal republican model which had not survived long enough to develop anything more than an empirical type of constitutionalism. Thus from the outset two rival ideas of Parliament co-existed, though in fact the British idea dominated as both Natal and the Orange Free State were spiritually closer to the Cape than to the Transvaal. The Transvaal republicans held that British parliamentary democracy was not suited to the Afrikaner's temperament and that anyway it was unworkable in a heterogenous society which lacked a common language and culture.[1]

Broadly speaking the UP adhered to the British concept, while the Nationalists harked back to the Transvaal republican model. Sheila Patterson distinguishes two persistent and conflicting trends in Afrikaner political thinking: the 'authoritarian' and 'libertarian' traditions, which reflect the conflict within the 'Volk' between the 'patriarchal or leadership principle' and the 'desire for liberty and equality'.[2] Broadly the two opposing views were expressed along provincial lines, with the authoritarian tradition being expressed by the Transvalers and the libertarian tradition by the Cape Nationalists. The two schools of nationalist thought confronted each other on two fundamental issues; first, in their attitude to Afrikaner–English relations; and second, in their attitudes to democratic processes. The libertarians believed in co-operation with the English and respect for the democratic process while the authoritarians wished to dominate or absorb the English and were essentially opposed to the processes of democracy.

The increasing dominance of the authoritarian wing of the NP made its impact on the workings of the political system. South Africa's 'constitutional crisis' revealed the conflicting traditions within the NP as well as highlighting one of the most clear-cut differences between the UP and NP.

In 1951 the Nationalists, in implementing their apartheid policy, sought to remove the Cape Coloureds from the common voters roll. At the time of union it was agreed that each province should maintain its own franchise provisions and in order to safeguard the Cape's

[1] L. Marquard, *Peoples and Policies of South Africa* (London: Oxford University Press, 1969), p. 194.
[2] Sheila Patterson, op. cit., p. 77 et seq.

multi-racial franchise, a special 'entrenched' clause was added to the South African Act of Union. It ensured that the Coloureds could not be removed from the voters roll unless a two-thirds majority of both Houses of Parliament, sitting in joint session, passed a Bill nullifying the entrenched clause. However, in 1951 the Nationalists, by a simple majority in the Lower House, passed the Separate Representation of Voters Act 2 (No. 46 of 1951) which removed the Coloureds from the common roll.

The Act was immediately referred to the Courts to test its validity and a long struggle between Parliament and the Judiciary ensued. Finally in 1956, after two attempts at winning a two-thirds majority in a joint sitting, the Government acted by enlarging the Senate and 'packing' the law benches, so that the Coloureds were 'constitutionally' removed from the common voters roll.

At the time the Nationalists argued that the sovereignty of Parliament, as proclaimed by the Statute of Westminster in 1931, made the entrenched clause procedure no longer binding. Further, they claimed that parliamentary sovereignty was being practised in accordance with the principles of majority rule, and that by implementing apartheid it was merely carrying out the 'will of the people'.

Malan and Havenga had for a period attempted to settle the issue in a more strictly constitutional manner, despite the initial attempt to remove the Coloureds by a simple Act of Parliament. But under pressure from the more extreme wing of the party and finally under the leadership of Strijdom, the Nationalists revealed as Marquard has said, 'a curious mixture of respect for the letter of constitutional forms and a disregard for their spirit', and an 'impatience with the legal and legislative safeguards that a parliamentary system is presumed to provide'.[1]

The United Party revealed its deep-seated attachment to the British concept of constitutional principle and to the conventions of parliamentary democracy. The most consistent aspect of the Opposition's argument against removing the Coloured voter was based on a plea for Constitutional observance and the party was all along less concerned with the primary issue of the rights of the Coloureds. (It was not until 1957 that the party pledged itself to replacing the Coloureds on the common roll.)

It is perhaps strange that in a country, where four-fifths of the population are by the consent of the competing White groups excluded from participation in the political system, attitudes to constitutional principles and democratic processes can be a source of

---

[1] Marquard, op. cit., p. 195.

conflict within the ruling group. It becomes less strange when, in the words of Pierre van den Berghe, it is realized that the South African state 'preserves its dual character of a democracy for the *Herrenvolk* and a racialist colonial regime for the non-Whites'.[1] However, the democratic forms of Government which were (with the partial exception of the Cape franchise prior to 1956) the exclusive prerogative of the Whites, were gradually eroded after 1948. The two party, bicameral traditions of Westminster, were effectively replaced by a one-party system of Government, since only one party won elections while a declining Opposition party became a permanent Opposition.

The permanency of the Opposition and the permanency of Government changed the nature of both parties. The acquiescence of the Opposition in the system on which the Government's legitimacy was founded, in addition to the fundamental agreement about principles, left the Opposition without purpose or policy and it became a minority party with diminishing relevance. Even within the framework of White politics, it ceased to be a political Opposition; it offered no credible alternative to the Government.

The prolonged domination of a single party, whose attitudes to the political system were in any event equivocal, resulted in the system becoming less and less responsive to larger and larger groups in society, including groups within the White sector. Within Parliament itself, consultation between Government and Opposition virtually ceased, despite the increasing areas of agreement between the two parties. The Nationalists did not show contentious legislation to the UP before introducing it to the House (as the UP did when in office) and consultation through the regular channels, such as party whips, took place infrequently. The speaker of the House was elected without consulting the Opposition. It has been suggested that one reason for the Nationalists' refusal to consult the Opposition is that the 'compromise inherent in any two-party system has inevitably been construed as collaboration and even treason, and leadership has passed to the men who could produce the purest form of Nationalism'.[2] The effect of Nationalist manipulation of the democratic procedures of Government was to diminish the importance of Parliament as a legislature or as a debating chamber. It is arguable that after 1948, Parliament merely served to ratify the private and caucus decisions of the Government and this impotence arose partly as a result of Government methods and partly because of the United Party's failure to oppose.

[1] Pierre van den Berghe, op. cit., p. 86.
[2] Sheila Patterson, op. cit., p. 104.

Press as Opposition

The emergence of a single dominant party, the failure of the institutional Opposition, the diminishing importance of Parliament as a debating chamber in which alternative views might be discussed and the exclusion of the African from the political system all helped to define a unique role for the South African Press. Within the ranks of the National Party and Government, the Afrikaans Press functioned increasingly as the opposition; while the English-language Press assumed the function of an external opposition.

The Afrikaans Press as an opposition within the ranks was concerned primarily about the methods of Government and not with any of the principles upon which Government was based. The English Press on the other hand, though an opposition organized independently of Government, became an opposition by default, for in the final analysis the 'real' opposition in the country was the African. It was the total exclusion of the African from constitutional politics in South Africa which cast the English-language Press in the role of the opposition.

This may be explained by the fact that almost all White constitutional politics after 1948 were concerned with the voteless Black opposition. In the first decade of Nationalist rule, and before the Nationalists had become obviously unbeatable, the Opposition and Government parties vied with each other to become accepted as the real custodians of White interests. Equally, whichever party was least militantly opposed to the African was manoeuvred quickly into the position of appearing to represent him. However, as the UP declined as a political force in the country and the Government ceased to feel threatened by its opposition, the English Press increasingly became identified with the African opposition, which challenged not so much the Government of the day, as the socio-economic system as a whole. It was perhaps inevitable that once the English–Afrikaner power struggle had been settled by an Afrikaner nationalist victory, the 'real' alternatives–an exclusive White polis or 'majority rule'–would be faced. As a White-owned, traditionally English-oriented Press, South Africa's English-language Press had vested interests in maintaining the *status quo*, and yet it was without exception opposed to the Government and to its apartheid policy. It went much further than the UP, which it once supported unanimously, in its opposition to apartheid. The English Press was identified increasingly as the opposition by the Government, and through a growing and positive

27

vision of itself as the sole institutional representative of the African, the English Press, within the limits of the political system itself, functioned as an external opposition.

The decline of Parliament as an arena of political debate was due not only to the failure of the institutional opposition but also to the fact that the specialized media of communication partially usurped this parliamentary function.[1] But it was the English-language Press alone, which through a self-conscious policy attempted to provide a platform for a wide variety of opposing political ideas. In giving publicity to such opposing ideas—whether through letter columns or news or feature articles—the English Press merely entrenched itself more firmly as an external opposition. The spectrum of 'alien' ideas, to which the Afrikaans Press was prepared to expose its readers remained extremely narrow, but individual newspapers did from time to time allow their columns to be used as forums of genuine if limited debate. Once again, however, the emphasis was on intra-party conflict rather than with an extension of the debate to include genuinely alternative viewpoints.

The decreasing responsiveness of the political system to demands made upon it from interests or groups outside of party or govern-mental structures, ensured the political impotence of the English Press in directly influencing Government policy, except insofar as it did so inadvertently through 'publicity'. The Afrikaans Press, on the other hand, as an 'internal opposition' both in the sense of reflect-ing and instigating conflicts within the party, held an extremely powerful position, particularly as fewer and fewer groups within the society were consulted or conciliated.

Since the Press had functions other than those of opposition it was not capable of wholly replacing a specialist, institutionalized opposi-tion within the political system. On the other hand, the Press had advantages over an institutional opposition for neither was it com-pelled to win votes (though, of course, it had to win readers) nor was it essential for it to propound consistent or thorough-going alternate ideologies or policies, for its aims were not to constitute on alternative Government. The Afrikaans Press took advantage of its relationship with the National Party and with Government and of the failure of the institutional opposition to fulfil this function by replacing it on an *ad hoc* basis within the confines of power politics, though never with the intention of unseating the Government. As an institution within the White 'democracy', the English Press was able, by

---

[1] c.f. Ionescu and Madariaga in *Opposition* (London: C. A. Watts & Co. Ltd., 1968), p. 103 et seq.

articulating what it saw as the interests of the African, to extend the boundaries of the political system. At the same time it opposed by being a constant and harsh critic of Government and Government leaders.

2

A Brief History of the Press

The Presses' own political history has been particularly important in moulding its traditions which have dictated the functions that the media have come to perform in modern South Africa. Individual newspapermen have sometimes been influential in shaping the traditions of single newspapers or newspaper groups; in other cases the institutions (political party, economic or cultural organizations) to which newspapers have been affiliated have been the most important sources of change in the development of a newspaper's traditions.

Most South African newspapermen share an acute consciousness of the traditions of their newspapers, both as individual newspapers and as a collective part of the English or Afrikaans newpaper groups. None would be able to define tradition in any other than the most general terms, but they acknowledge that a newspaper's traditions are contained in the attitudes and values for which it has stood and has embodied in the past, as much as in their present interpretation of those values.

Thus any study of the contemporary Press must take that Presses' origins into account. In the South African context where the newspapers, with a fairly remarkable consistency, have revealed the aspirations and the visions of the two competing White groups and only very rarely found common cause, the need for historical perspective is essential to an understanding of the tensions which have arisen in such a heterogenous society.

In South Africa, as in Canada and Australia, the Press initially had to do battle with the colonial authorities. But whereas in the other colonies a truly indigenous Press, emphasizing regional and local interests developed, the first South African newspapers took a more imperialistic line. They not only modelled themselves on Fleet Street but right up until the 1920s imported most of their journalists to ensure that the model closely resembled the original.[1] Thus whilst the English-language Press indeed had to overcome the hostility of

[1] See, for example, Francis Williams, *The Right to Know: The Rise of the World Press* (London: Longmans, 1969) and Henry Mayer, *The Press in Australia* (London: Angus and Robertson, 1964).

the colonial authorities, the Press was not born out of a struggle for freedom, nor to meet the needs of immigrant masses. Rather, it asserted itself on the grounds of the right to run a business for profit. In the Cape the Press spoke for commercial and financial interests and later in the Transvaal for the White 'uitlander' mining interests. As Francis Williams has said, these newspapers did not

> 'establish themselves as independent forces, sympathetic to, but not controlled by the expanding commercial interests in their society. . . . They were the direct instruments of financial and commercial power springing fully armed into the arena: the ancillaries of commerce, not its mentors'.[1]

In contrast, the Afrikaans Press–which came much later than the English Press–was filled with evangelical zeal and kindled the flame of a cause. The Afrikaans newspapers differed both in content and form from their English-language counterparts. Where the English newspapers were dominated by commercial and managerial demands and where printers were sovereign the Afrikaans Press was always subservient to the cause of 'taal' (language) and 'Volk' (people) and later of the National Party.

Regardless of the interests they historically represented or opposed neither the English nor the Afrikaans Press could remain untouched by events outside South Africa, or by changes in the political power-balance within. The English Press particularly was affected by the climate of the international Press which by the second half of the nineteenth century had established Press freedom as one of its basic tenets. It could not fail to develop an existence which was independent of its promoters and to assume obligations to groups other than its shareholders. The Afrikaans Press like the Afrikaner, was never touched by the liberalism sweeping Europe in the nineteenth century. Prior to the South Africa Act (which entrenched Dutch as an official language) and Hertzog's 'two-stream' policy, there was no genuine Afrikaans Press. Most of the publications aimed at Afrikaner readers were written in High Dutch, the language of literature, of officialdom, State and Church. The Afrikaans, as distinct from the Dutch-language Press, only really began to grow in the 1920s as an element in the growth of Afrikaner nationalism as a political force in South Africa.

The First Newspapers

Until 1823 the only publication in the Cape Colony was the Government sponsored *Cape Town Gazette*, but in that year the

---

[1] Francis Williams, op. cit. p. 48.

printer George Greig rallied the support of the poet Thomas Pringle, one of the 1820 settlers, James Fairbairn, whom Pringle invited to the Cape from England, and the clergyman Abraham Faurie, to set up the bilingual *South African Commercial Advertiser*. In setting out the prospectus of the newspaper for Lord Charles Somerset, then Governor of the Cape, Greig promised an apolitical uncritical, uncontentious medium of communication. As Greig conceived of the paper, its primary task was to supply news of trade and commerce, to act as an advertising medium and to publish literary material.

Greig's original application was rejected by Somerset, but Greig discovered that the law prohibiting publication without prior authority, applied only to periodicals and not to newspapers. Thus the first issue of the paper appeared on January 7, 1824, and immediately Greig and his associates established that their policy was vigorously to support the liberty of the Press and harmonious race relations; a stance which largely defied the paper's original prospectus.

Shortly before publication of the eighteenth issue, the Government demanded to see the proof sheets before printing. In particular, Somerset was incensed by the publicity the *South African Commercial Advertiser* was providing to the court proceedings of libel actions brought by the Governor, against those who had accused him of acting corruptly in the administration of the colony. The eighteenth issue was published but with an addenda: that until the position of censorship had been clarified, the *South African Commercial Advertiser* would cease publication. Within three days Greig had been given a months notice to leave South Africa and orders had been issued that the paper should be closed.

Before his departure for England, Greig issued a pamphlet entitled 'Facts Connected with the Stoppage of the *South African Commercial Advertiser*', in which he defiantly affirmed his refusal to publish a newspaper under conditions of pre-publication censorship. In England Greig made representations to the Colonial Secretary about the *Advertiser* affair which resulted in permission being granted for him to return to the Cape and resume publication.

It was not long, however, before the *South African Commercial Advertiser* was banned for a second time, once more as a result of Somerset's influence, for publishing extracts from an article in the London *Times* which were critical of a local official. On this occasion leading citizens of the colony raised the money for Fairbairn to return to London and plead the Presses' case. One and a half years later, in October 1828, Fairbairn returned to the Cape and the *South African Commercial Advertiser* resumed publication for the third time. Fairbairn brought with him the promise from the Colonial Secretary that a Press ordinance, based on the law of England, would be introduced in South Africa.

The Press ordinance of 1828 stated that 'printers and publishers who were prepared to deposit £300 as personal surety and a like amount guaranteed by friends, might publish newspapers on 1d stamped sheets paid for in advance at the Capetown Stamp Office, subject to the law of libel as interpreted by the Judges'.[1] It was known as the freedom charter for the Press of South Africa, and stimulated the birth of a number of newspapers in both English and Dutch. By 1830 a blueprint of what was later to be peculiarly significant in the political history of South Africa and South Africa's Press, could already be said to have been devised. In that year a Dutch-language newspaper, *De Zuid Afrikaan* was started in opposition to the *South African Commercial Advertiser*. Fairbairn, as editor of the *South African Commercial Advertiser*, had for some time been interested in race relations. He was closely associated with the liberal missionary, Dr John Philip, who was renowned in the colony on account of complaints he had made to London about the brutality of the Boers towards the slaves. Fairbairn believed that the rights of all races and classes in South Africa should be safeguarded and was also a staunch protagonist of increasing Press freedoms and responsible Government. P. A. Brand, a Dutchman of slave-owning stock, started *De Zuid Afrikaan* with the avowed purpose of opposing the *South African Commercial Advertiser* on all these issues. He determined to expose 'humbugs' and amongst the first of these were a free Press and the missionaries.[2] In the succeeding years *De Zuid Afrikaan* helped to keep literary Dutch alive amongst the rural Boers. In the 1870s *De Zuid Afrikaan* amalgamated with J. H. Hofmeyr's newspaper, *Volksvriend*, and was to become more closely drawn into the struggle for 'taal' and 'Volk'.

In the meantime Hofmeyr, one of the most important leaders of the Cape Dutch community, and a central figure in the growth of the Cape Dutch Press, started his own newspaper, *Het Volksblad* in 1849. Hofmeyr stressed the importance of retaining separate 'racial' identities while maintaining harmonious relations between the two White groups in the Cape, a view which combined with the language question was to bring him into conflict with other sections of Afrikanerdom.

[1] As cited in Eric A. Walker, *A History of Southern Africa* (London: Longmans, Green & Co., 1957, first published, 1928) p. 162–63.

[2] Theo Cutten, *A History of the Press in South Africa* (Johannesburg: The National Union of South African Students, 1936).

When the Cape was granted responsible government in 1854 English became the sole language of Parliament with the result that the Dutch-speaking Boers, who constituted an overwhelming majority of the Cape's White population, were markedly under-represented in the Cape legislature. It was not until the 1870s when *De Zuid Afrikaan* and Hofmeyr's *Volksvriend* merged that the claims of the Dutch language began to be heard.[1] An influential group of Afrikaners led by Hofmeyr and the Cape Dutch Church, supported the continuation of High Dutch as a literary language, whilst opposed to them were the 'Genootskap van Regte Afrikaners' (Society of True Afrikaners) whose objects were 'to stand for our language, our nation and our people'. In accordance with these objects the society, which was founded in 1875, created a newspaper to propagate its views. In 1876 *Di Patriot* the first Cape Dutch or Afrikaans-language newspaper appeared. Both *Volksvriend* and *Di Patriot* recognized the importance of language to group survival and the creation of a nation. But the Genootskappers believed that Afrikaans, the spoken language, should be the instrument whereby the nation was created, and not as their powerful opponents held, the literary language, High Dutch. Thus *Di Patriot* set out not only to perpetuate Afrikaans as a spoken language and to represent the interests of the group, but to create a literature and a written form for the spoken language of the Boers, Afrikaans.

Expansion and Growth

The second half of the nineteenth century saw the development of newspapers in Natal and the Republics as well as the establishment of most of the important English-language papers in existence today. In Natal scores of newspapers were started, beginning with *De Natalier* in 1844, which was edited by an ex-editor of *De Zuid Afrikaan*, C. E. Boniface. *De Natalier,* which opposed the Government, had ceased publication by 1846. In the same year it was replaced in this largely English stronghold by *The Natal Witness,* originally a bilingual paper but later an English-only paper.

In Durban in 1854, G. Robinson started the *Natal Mercury and Commercial Shipping Gazette,* known today as the *Natal Mercury* and Durban's only morning newspaper. Sir John Robinson, the son of G. Robinson, took over the editorship of the neswpaper from his father. Sir John was one of the prime movers for responsible Government in Natal and the colony's first Prime Minister. The *Natal Mercury* was a fiercely loyal, imperialist newspaper and later helped

[1] Sheila Patterson, op. cit., p. 52.

to create the all-English Dominion Party. After Union the paper continued to concern itself with the defence of provincial, English, and for a long time, British interests.

The Orange River colony never developed a multiplicity of newspapers as was the case in the Cape and Natal and after the establishment of its first newspaper in 1850, nearly twenty years elapsed before a second newspaper appeared. The colony's first newspaper, *The Friend of the Sovereignty and Bloemfontein Gazette,* changed its name to *The Friend of the Free State* with the acquistion of independence for the Free State in 1854. It was published both in Dutch and English (until 1894 when it was published in English only) with the avowed aims of furthering the national well-being and the interests of all, regardless of race or colour. In 1899, with the outbreak of the Anglo-Boer War, *The Friend* changed hands when Lord Roberts, who led the British troops in Bloemfontein, took it over. The Military Governor sent for the then editor of *The Friend,* Arthur Barlow, and asked him to continue to edit the paper under instruction from the British rulers. Barlow, who had supported the Boers against the British, refused. When a few weeks later the Argus Group began printing *The Friend* for the British, Barlow protested against the use of the paper's name to propagate pro-British views. The result of this was the establishment of a new Argus Group newspaper, the *Bloemfontein Post*, which the authorities issued with the help of British war correspondents, amongst whom was Rudyard Kipling. Kipling edited the paper until the troops were evacuated from Bloemfontein.

After the South African War, Barlow restarted *The Friend* under a new company with Abraham Fischer, later Prime Minister of the Free State, General J. B. M. Hertzog and other leading Free State political figures on the board. *The Friend* gave its support to the Afrikaner party, *De Oranje Unie,* the Free State equivalent of Het Volk, Botha's party in the Transvaal. In opposition to *The Friend in* the early 1900s stood the *Bloemfontein Post.* It was less popular than *The Friend* in this largely rural and Afrikaans area and its war-time record was no assistance in winning a wider readership.

It was not until 1915 that the *Bloemfontein Post* finally yielded and was incorporated with *The Friend.* Political conditions had changed quite considerably since the post-war years which helped to make the merger possible. Hertzog had splintered from Botha and Smuts to form the National Party and in the 1915 elections, the National Party had won almost every seat in the province. Shareholders in the company owning *The Friend* represented equally the South African Party and the Nationalists and the latter were attempting to win control of *The Friend* to acquire an organ for the party in the Free State. Both

The Friend and the *Bloemfontein Post* were then supporting Botha. Largely to stave off a Nationalist takeover, the Friend Newspapers Ltd. agreed to pay a nominal fee for the takeover of the *Bloemfontein Post* while the Argus Company became the group's London advertising agency. From that moment the Argus Group began acquiring shares in *The Friend*, although it was not until 1947, after the death of the major shareholder and the then editor D. M. Ollemans, that the Argus Group obtained a controlling interest in the newspaper.

The first newspaper in the Transvaal was a Dutch-language newspaper introduced more then twenty years after the Great Trek. *De Oude Emmigrant*, as it was called, did not survive for very long, and it was not until 1874 that the first important Transvaal newspaper appeared. *Die Volkstem* was started in Pretoria as a Dutch-language newspaper. Before Union, *Die Volkstem* under the editorship of J. F. Celliers represented the Boer point of view and strongly opposed the annexation of the Transvaal. However, it was more the Cape than the Transvaal Boer view which *Die Volkstem* expressed. Celliers was one of an influential group of Transvaal Afrikaners with Cape affiiliations, who were opposed to the Transvaal Boers as epitomized by Kruger and Krugerism.[1] After Union, *Die Volkstem* supported the South African Party's 'one-stream' policy and loyally followed Smuts and not Hertzog after the split. In 1922 the paper began to appear in Afrikaans and in 1951, by then a weekly, it closed. No Afrikaans daily which failed to stay with the National Party, survived. Despite *Die Volkstem's* relatively moderate political stance, in opposing annexation the paper came into conflict with the British administrators. Theo Cutten cites a letter written by Sir Theophilus Shepstone, then administrator of the Transvaal to a colleague, in which he said:

> 'Up to this moment there has been but one Dutch newspaper in Pretoria and that has uniformly devoted itself to creating disaffection and ill-feeling towards everything English. From being the oldest paper and being published in Dutch at the seat of Government, it is universally read by the Boers who, being extremely ignorant, are correspondingly credulous and settle any doubtful point by saying: "Does it not say so in the *Courant*."'[2]

The important point to be made about this characterization of the Boers and this interpretation of the Dutch-language newspaper, is that it was an attitude which persisted amongst English-speaking

---

[1] See Sheila Patterson, op. cit., and J. S. Marais, *The Fall of Kruger's Republic* (Oxford: Clarendon Press, 1961).
[2] Theo Cutten, op. cit. p. 54.

South Africans. It was also a view shared by the English Press for a very long time and one which perhaps still persists today. Equally though, the Afrikaners held the English Press responsible for being hostile towards everything Afrikaans.

Birth of the Argus Empire

By far the most important papers of the early years were the newspapers of Cape Town, from whence South Africa's greatest modern newspaper empire has originated. In 1857 the *Cape Argus* was born when the Oxford-educated MP, Bryan Henry Darnell, approached the prominent Cape Government printer (and MP), Saul Solomon, who agreed to print the newspaper. The paper set out its aims:

> 'to secure free expression for the opinions of all, with view to reconcile rather than to stir up party differences. Its reviews of public measures will be written with moderation and care, it will advocate neither the one side nor the other of any great question on mere party grounds . . .'[1]

Darnell was intensely pro-British, supported the Governor and strongly opposed the claims for full responsible government. Before very long he sold his shares in the *Cape Argus* to his editor, Richard William Murray, another Englishman who shared his political bias. An economic recession forced Murray to sell half of his interest in the paper to the so-called 'negrophilist' printer, Solomon. Solomon was not only classed as negrophilist, but he favoured responsible government, and opposed separation of the eastern and western parts of the colony which was being demanded by the English settlers in the east. Murray and Solomon clearly could not survive together for long. After selling his stake in the *Argus* to Solomon in 1863, Murray departed for Grahamstown to start another newspaper, *The Great Eastern*, with the specific purpose of supporting the then Governor and High Commissioner, Sir Philip Wodehouse.

Under Solomon the *Cape Argus* prospered and increased its circulation, almost all its staff were brought out from England, and it became the first newspaper to use the new telegraph facilities. In 1872 full self-government was conferred on the colony and for this the *Cape Argus*, under Solomon, was perhaps in some measure responsible. In 1877, Solomon appointed Francis Joseph Dormer as editor of the *Cape Argus* and before long Dormer had modified the pro-Native and particularly the anti-British Government policy of the paper. Within a few years Dormer's influence over the newspaper

[1] L. E. Neame, *Today's News Today* (Johannesburg: Argus Printing and Publishing Co., 1956).

had increased and eventually Solomon, in financial difficulties, sold out to him. Dormer, who alone did not have the capital to take over the newspaper, was backed financially by Cecil John Rhodes, whose influence set the paper on a new course. The only paper prepared to speak for the Africans was effectively gone.

With the change of ownership the *Cape Argus* published a notice reviewing past policy and stating its own policy for the future, which was clearly one of more moderation than had previously been the case. The notice read:

> 'While abating to some extent the intense devotion to one idea which may perhaps have militated against the usefulness and popularity of the *Cape Argus* in the past, it is its fixed determination to support none but such measures as, being based upon the eternal principles of justice, tend to the advancement of those over whose destinies it is the mission of South African colonists to preside; ... we refer to the subject of Native policy because it is the only one which in this country, should offer any difficult problems for solution ... It should never, and we trust will never be a question how White men of different nationalities should live together in the presence of barbarian tribes.'[1]

While it was true that Solomon's policies were not universally popular in the colony, a more important factor in the decreasing popularity of the *Cape Argus* was the advent of the *Cape Times* in 1876. The *Cape Times* was the country's first daily newspaper and was sold as a penny paper, unlike the *Cape Argus* which cost threepence. By 1880 the *Cape Argus* had itself changed from a tri-weekly paper to a daily and reduced its price to one penny. The *Cape Times*, conservative in Imperial politics but progressive in South African matters, soon became one of the leading papers in the country and by 1968 was one of the few remaining 'independent' newspapers (non-group affiliated).

The formation of a public company, the Argus Printing and Publishing Company in 1866 was a landmark in the history of the Press in South Africa. It marked the end of independent editor-owners and the beginning of managerial newspapers. Amongst the original subscribers to the company was the young Cecil John Rhodes (through a nominee) who, having made his fortune in the Kimberley diamond mines, was searching for outlets for his political ambitions. Other subscribers broadly represented the professional and commercial life of Cape Town.

[1] Neame, ibid., p. 21.

In the meantime gold had been discovered on the Rand, Johannesburg was beginning to grow, and Dormer was looking northwards for the company's expansion. The *Eastern Star*, the newspaper started in Grahamstown by two brothers, Thomas and George Sheffield, moved to Johannesburg in October 1887. When Dormer arrived in Johannesburg, a year after the discovery of gold, there were already seven journals in the town and instead of continuing with his plans to start a new Argus Company newspaper, he succeeded in taking over the *Eastern Star*. Thomas Sheffield became one of the directors of the re-formed Argus Company while George Sheffield acted as temporary secretary to the company. The newspaper changed its name to the *Star* and in 1889 it was expanded from a tri-weekly to a daily evening paper. At the opening of the new *Star* building in October 1899, Dormer revealed his very clear foresight in assessing the future newspaper industry of South Africa. In a speech, Dormer suggested that the newspaper of the future in South Africa was the evening newspaper and that this idea had prompted him to buy the only existing evening newspaper on the Rand. This proved to be quite true. Throughout South Africa, unlike Britain, evening newspapers have invariably maintained a circulation dominance over their morning competitors.

By 1895 gold and other mining interests were conspicuously over-represented in the Argus Group's shareholding. The major shareholders in the growing mining companies were also major shareholders in the Argus Company. They included Rhodes, Barney Barnato and Solly Joel.[1] The mining and commercial impetus of the company's origins were to leave a lasting stamp on the company's future policies. Equally they were to give the company's newspapers an advantage over all their competitors. Argus Group newspapers were benefited with business and management expertise, which from the beginning put them on a sound financial footing, and ensured the optimum facilities and techniques of modern newspaper production.

The policies of the *Star* were moderate in tone, not hostile to the Republic and opposed to the British Government's annexation of the Transvaal. Dormer insisted on maintaining friendly relations with the Kruger Government in Pretoria and began a regular correspondence with the State Secretary. In 1889 he informed the State Secretary that an Afrikaans graduate of Cape Town University had been employed by the *Star* to pay particular attention to matters concerning the Dutch people. From that date the *Star* was received regularly in the offices of the Kruger administration and advertisements

[1] Press Commission of Inquiry Report, Part I, p. 58.

from the Republican Government were published frequently in the paper.

But the *bonhomie* between the *Star* and the Kruger administration was not to survive the decade and was never to be re-established. In 1895 Dormer resigned both as editor of the *Star* and as managing director of the Argus Company. The sympathetic coverage given to the Kruger Government was due entirely to Dormer. Under a new editor, the *Star* switched its support from 'progressive Republicanism' to the newly formed Transvaal National Union (TNU). The TNU was demanding Government reforms particularly in the existing limited franchise which excluded the 'uitlanders'.

Already in 1896 the Transvaal *Volksraad* (legislature) had passed a Press law which required that the names of printers and publishers be disclosed, and gave the President (with the consent of the Executive Council) the power to prevent publication of material which might be dangerous to the order and peace of the Republic, or to good morals. In no way intimidated by the law, the editor of the *Star* persisted in a highly critical policy towards the Government. On March 24, 1897, the *Star* was banned. The banning order stated that for three months circulation of the newspaper was prohibited on the grounds that the contents were dangerous to the peace and quiet of the Republic. The board of the Argus Group promptly recalled Francis Dormer to edit *The Comet*, an evening daily looking remarkably similar to the *Star*. Thomas Sheffield, who was now managing director of the Argus Company, was not content to let matters rest but took their case to court. The judges concurred with the claim of the defence that the law only made provision for suppressing matters after publication and gave no power to prevent matter being printed in the future. The *Star* reappeared the following afternoon.

Shortly after the Jameson raid in which the *Star* was held to be deeply implicated, members of the Transvaal National Union and including Frederick Hamilton the editor of the *Star*, were tried. Hamilton left South Africa after the trial and was replaced by an editor whose criticism of the Kruger Government was even more forceful than before. The *Star* ensured the permanent hostility of the republicans although the confrontation between the English-language Press and the Afrikaner Republicans was not to take place for another fifty years.

The South African War halted publication of the *Star* once more; in this case for over two years, and after the war the Colonial Secretary appointed the Argus Company as printing advisers to the Government Printing Works. So close had the association between Milner and the Argus people become, that Milner virtually selected the *Star's* ninth editor. Shortly before his return to Britain, Milner lobbied strenuously to have his private secretary, Geoffrey Robinson, (later Geoffrey Dawson, editor of the London *Times*) appointed as editor. Milner succeeded and earned a staunch supporter lodged securely in South Africa's most powerful newspaper. Even after Milner's departure Robinson continued to support him in his opposition to full responsible self-government for the Boer ex-Republics.

The *Star* supported the Progressive Party in the first Transvaal Parliamentary elections and before his departure to *The Times* in 1909, Robinson had given much coverage and encouragement to the Unionist movement. The *Cape Argus*, too, under the editorship of a member of the Cape Parliament, Edmund Powell, was supporting the Progressives. It is interesting to note that in the early 1900s the Argus Company stated that its policy on important political issues 'be as indicated from time to time in the leading columns of the *Star*, and all publications of the company, unless specially authorized to the contrary by the Managing Director, are to follow the lead therein given in all matters of a political nature which are of more than local importance'.[1]

This did not mean however that editors were discouraged from applying their individual preferences to the policy of the newspaper. When for example Powell was relieved of his post, his successor, Ernest Glanville, was far less interested in party politics and refrained from giving the Progressive Party such unequivocal support. Nor did he follow the *Star's* editor in his fight for unification but gave his support to Federation.

Contraction

It was not until 1902 that one of South Africa's most important English daily papers was established in the Transvaal. The *Rand Daily Mail* owed its inception to the enterprise of a businessman, Freeman Cohen, and to its first editor, the fiction writer Edgar Wallace, who was then the Johannesburg representative of the London *Daily Mail*. Under Wallace's aegis a circle of provincial and foreign correspondents were gathered around the paper providing it from the beginning with a more 'popular' and international flavour than its competitors on the Rand. After the death of Freeman Cohen, the paper was acquired in 1905 by Sir Abe Bailey. Sir Abe, who already had established himself as a mining magnate and who was elected to Parliament in 1908, formed a private company, the Rand Daily

[1] L. Neame, op. cit., p. 109.

Mails Ltd., in which he was the largest shareholder. Bailey, like Cohen before him, took little active interest in the newspaper's affairs and in 1904 he leased the paper to a three-man syndicate: George H. Kingswell, an Australian journalist who became its general manager, Ralph Ward Jackson, an ex-cavalry officer who came to edit the paper and A. V. Lindbergh, chairman and founder of the Central News Agency, the major newspaper distributing agency.

In 1906 Kingswell, Jackson and Lindbergh started a Sunday newspaper, the *Sunday Times* which together with the *Rand Daily Mail* was the founder of popular journalism in South Africa. The *Sunday Times* adopted a less serious tone than most of its contemporaries and from the beginning was financially very successful. The *Rand Daily Mail* and the *Sunday Times* worked in close association with each other although a single company was not formed until 1955, when the South African Associated Newspapers (SAAN) Company, the second largest newspaper group in the country, came into being. From 1915 onwards, the 'Rand Daily Mails Ltd. and Sunday Times Syndicate Ltd. either singularly (*sic*) or jointly took a number of steps to eliminate their competitors ...'[1] The Rand Daily Mails Group and the Argus Group were to assert their dominance by absorbing rival newspapers, sometimes jointly, sometimes in conjunction with other existing newspapers, thus ensuring the elimination of serious rivals, the contraction in the numbers of newspapers and the concentration of ownership in fewer and fewer hands.

The first steps were taken in May 1915 when the Rand Daily Mails Ltd. took over and absorbed the rival morning newspaper, the *Transvaal Leader* whilst the Sunday Times Syndicate absorbed the rival Sunday paper in Johannesburg, the *Sunday Post*. This left the *Rand Daily Mail* as the only morning newspaper and the *Sunday Times* as the only Sunday newspaper published in Johannesburg. The owners of the *Transvaal Leader* and the *Sunday Post*, the Cape Times Ltd., were given shares in the two takeover companies. However, the Bailey interests soon acquired the *Cape Times'* shareholdings in the *Rand Daily Mail* and *Sunday Times*.

Also in 1915, John Martin, one of the most important figures in English-language South African newspapers, became the general manager of the Argus Company, and at an early stage revealed his expansionist visions for the group. After acquiring holdings in *The Friend* he turned his sights to the only province where the company held no interest, Natal. By December 1918 the Argus Company had bought out the *Natal Advertiser* (later the *Daily News*), a daily pub-

---

[1] From the SAAN submissions to the Press Commission Report, 1962, p. 7.

lished in Durban. On acquiring the *Natal Advertiser* the Argus Group extracted a promise from the sellers that they would not start a newspaper for fifteen years. They also reached an agreement with the *Natal Mercury* about publishing times and advertising rates. John Martin then looked to Kimberley where the company began buying shares in the only morning newspaper, the *Diamond Fields Advertiser*. In 1922 the Argus had obtained a controlling interest in the newspaper which, when it was founded in 1878 had been the most important in the city. The *Diamond Fields Advertiser* was run like all Argus Group newspapers, receiving the benefits of features, telegraphic and overseas news, which it would not have been able to afford as an independent newspaper.

By 1920 the Rand Daily Mails Ltd., the Sunday Times Syndicate and the Argus Company had entered into an agreement not to publish newspapers in competition with each other, an agreement still in force in 1968. In 1929 the *Rand Daily Mail* and the Argus Group together purchased the *Pretoria News*, the main evening daily in Pretoria, with the Argus Group retaining the majority shareholding. The acquisition of the *Pretoria News* gave the Argus Group, which already owned newspapers in the legislative and judicial capitals, a foothold in the administrative capital.

The existing newspaper owners began consolidating their interests on other fronts too. As early as 1910, the Argus, the *Rand Daily Mail* interests and the *Cape Times* formed a partnership with the British news agency, Reuters, to establish the Reuter South African Press Agency. The partnership took over the selling of Reuters news to the South African Press and also collected South African news for sale in South Africa and for Reuters World News Service. In 1932, a news sharing service, the South African Morning Newspaper Group, was formed to help existing non-Argus newspapers compete with the extensive news gathering facilities of the Argus Group. The members of the morning group included the *Rand Daily Mail* (and later the SAAN newspapers) the *Cape Times* and the *Natal Mercury*.

After this period of consolidation no serious rivals emerged until 1934, when for the first time the established Press was faced with serious competition from interests outside mining. In 1934, I. W. Schlesinger, a theatre and cinema magnate who already controlled the commercially run African Broadcasting Company, entered the newspaper field. In 1934 Schlesinger started the *Sunday Express* in Johannesburg and the *Sunday Tribune* in Durban; in 1937 he started publishing daily newspapers in those towns, the *Daily Express* and the *Daily Tribune*. In addition Schlesinger established a news agency, (known as 'Africopa') to rival the South African Press Association (SAPA) which had been formed in 1932 from the Reuter South African Press Agency. In response to this unaccustomed competition, many of the established newspapers altered and improved their styles and layouts. But in 1939, the *Rand Daily Mail*, the *Sunday Times* and the Argus Group bought out Schlesinger's entire newspaper interests. It has been suggested that the strongest pressure was put on Schlesinger by the South African Jewish community. They apparently argued that the English-language Press was sympathetic to the Jews at a time when the rest of the world was not, yet Schlesinger, the most powerful member of the Jewish community, continued to oppose and antagonize that Press.[1]

The *Daily Tribune*, the *Daily Express* and the *Sunday Tribune* were closed. The profitable *Sunday Express* was maintained under the joint ownership of the rival groups. Shortly after the outbreak of the Second World War, the *Rand Daily Mail* and the *Sunday Times* acquired the Argus Group's shares in the *Sunday Express* to ensure that no rival newspaper in the Sunday field existed and to absorb overflow advertising from the enormously successful *Sunday Times*. The Argus Group retained the *Sunday Tribune* which they restarted after the war and which today is Natal's only Sunday newspaper. Schlesinger undertook to refrain from participating in the newspaper or news-agency business for fifteen years. After the sale of the Schlesinger Press interests, not more than one English morning and one English evening daily was published in any South African city. The last take-over occurred in 1959, when SAAN acquired a controlling interest in the two Port Elizabeth dailies, the *Eastern Province Herald* and the *Evening Post*, making the *Evening Post* the only evening daily newspaper not owned by the Argus Group.

The Afrikaans Press: Emergence and Contraction

When the English-language Press was beginning its period of contraction, the Afrikaans-language Press was only really beginning to grow. As outlined earlier, there was, broadly speaking, no Afrikaans Press before the time of Hertzog's 'two-stream' policy and the language provisions in the constitution of 1910 which guaranteed equal language rights for English and Dutch and made provision for Afrikaans.

From the start the Afrikaans Press was linked inextricably to the cause of Afrikaner nationalism. In its earliest years, the years of *Di*

---

[1] H. Lindsay Smith *Behind the Press in South Africa* (Cape Town, Stewart, 1947), p. 136.

Patriot, it was associated with Afrikaner nationalism in the broadest sense – with the language movement, the development of group consciousness and Afrikaner culture. But with the establishment of the first daily newspaper, using both Dutch and Afrikaans as a medium of expression, the Afrikaans Press became associated with a very much narrower and more emotional idea of nationalism, centred on the creation of a political party. A variety of Afrikaans newspapers were initiated in sympathy with Hertzog's cause when he broke with the South African Party in 1912. But it was not until 1915 when the National Party itself was formally established that the Nationalists founded a true party organ. In that year Dr D. F. Malan, a Dutch Reformed Church minister at Graaf-Reinet, left the pulpit to edit *De Burger*, the new daily newspaper established in Cape Town and to lead the Cape National Party.

The Cape Nationalists experienced great difficulty in raising the necessary capital for their newspaper venture and were unable to find a printer willing to print *De Burger*. However, the *Transvaal Leader* had closed down in 1915 and the newly formed company, Nasionale Pers Beperk (NPB) bought the equipment from the *Cape Times*.

After 1915 *De Burger* increasingly used Afrikaans as the language of written communication, although it was not until 1922 that the paper changed its name to *Die Burger*, stopped using Dutch altogether and wrote its first leader in the newer language, Afrikaans. Just two years after creating *Die Burger*, NPB acquired a second newspaper, this time in the Orange Free State where the Nationalists had been so successful in the previous elections. *Die Volksblad* as the new NPB bi-weekly was called, also used Dutch and Afrikaans as media of expression and like *Die Burger* switched to Afrikaans exclusively in 1922. In 1925 *Die Volksblad* became a daily. NPB then made an unsuccessful attempt to penetrate Natal, starting *Die Afrikaner* which ceased publication in 1932. In 1937 NPB bought the last of its existing daily newspapers, *Die Oosterlig* in Port Elizabeth, which remained the smallest and least successful of NPBs ventures.

While the initial impetus of the Nationalist movement was centred around the Cape, the necessity of establishing a National Party mouthpiece in the Transvaal was recognized. Also in 1915, *Die Vaderland* was started in Pretoria as a bi-weekly under the editorship of a Boer General, General J. C. G. Kemp. Kemp was followed by Harm Oost who like Malan at *Die Burger*, remained editor until 1924 when he entered Parliament. In 1931 *Die Vaderland* was taken over by a new company, Afrikaanse Pers Beperk, and the signatories to the Memorandum of Association included the then Prime Minister General Hertzog, General Kemp, N. C. Havenga, E. G. Jansen, Dr

Albert Hertzog, and O. Pirow. All except for Dr A. Hertzog (the Prime Minister's son), were members of General Hertzog's cabinet.

Thus not surprisingly *Die Vaderland* supported Hertzog in the coalition Government and later in the fusion United Party Government, while the NPB newspapers stayed loyal to Malan when he went into opposition in 1933. In 1936 *Die Vaderland* moved to Johannesburg as a daily to provide the United Party with an Afrikaans-language newspaper. A year later *Die Transvaler* came into being, 'born from the political need of the National Party to have a newspaper in the Transvaal to put forward its views'.[1] Malan already had the support of *Die Burger* in the Cape and *Die Volksblad* in the Orange Free State, and at this stage the National Party had only a single MP in the Transvaal, Strijdom. Thus in 1936 the Voortrekkerpers Beperk was incorporated and funds were raised to start *Die Transvaler* as a morning daily in Johannesburg. Dr H. F. Verwoerd, then a professor of sociology at the University of Stellenbosch, became the first editor of *Die Transvaler*. In addition to editing the newspaper Verwoerd was expected to canvas throughout the Transvaal for subscribers and to recruit new members to the National Party.[2] The first directors of Voortrekkerpers Beperk, included the leaders of the National Party in the Cape, the Transvaal and the Orange Free State, the chairman and general manager of NPB and a representative of the Natal National Party.

In *Die Transvaler's* first issue on October 1, 1937, Verwoerd declared in an editorial that the newspaper had a mission to serve the 'Volk' and to ensure that the voice of 'sublime nationalism' be heard. *Die Transvaler* put great emphasis on topics of race and republicanism and the first issue carried a report of a speech warning that too many Jews were flowing into the country. *Die Transvaler* was already proving more militant and extreme than the Cape Nationalists, including Malan, had intended.

Further changes in the Afrikaans Press came about as a result of political realignments in 1939 when the United Party Government split over South Africa's participation in the war. When Hertzog and Havenga formed the Afrikaner Party, only *Die Vaderland* of all the Afrikaans-language newspapers, gave the old Boer general its support. *Die Transvaler* and the NPB newspapers were with Malan and the rising politician, Strijdom. Some measure of unity was achieved for the 1948 elections when the Afrikaans Press joined together to support the election of an all-Afrikaner Government. By 1951 the Afri-

---

[1] Press Commission Report, Annexure IV, p. 430.
[2] See Alexander Hepple, *Verwoerd* (London: Penguin, 1967).

kaner Party had merged with the National Party but it was not really until 1962 that *Die Vaderland* was to be drawn wholly back into the fold. In that year a new company Afrikaanse Pers (1962) Beperk was formed to incorporate both *Die Vaderland* and the major Afrikaans Sunday newspaper, *Dagbreek*.

In 1947 Marius Jooste the advertising manager of *Die Vaderland* resigned from the newspaper and took with him the then editor Willem van Heerden one of the most respected political commentators in the Transvaal. Van Heerden and Jooste were financed by English business capital and mining interests and together they created *Dagbreek*, with the intention of producing a politically independent Sunday newspaper. By the end of their first year *Dagbreek* had acquired Die Afrikaanse Pers Beperk's unsuccessful Sunday venture *Sondagnuus* which they incorporated. Already by 1951 many of the shares in the company were placed in the hands of Transvaal Nationalists, and *Dagbreek* became more openly a Nationalist supporting newspaper. In 1962 Afrikaanse Pers made a second unsuccessful attempt to produce a Sunday newspaper in competition with *Dagbreek,* only this time Afrikaanse Pers were in financial difficulties. Amidst speculation that the Argus Group of NPB might attempt to take over Afrikaanse Pers, *Dagbreek* succeeded in bringing about an amalgamation between the old Afrikaner wing of the party and the Transvaal wing of the National Party. *Dagbreek* and *Die Vaderland* came together.

The final episode of this history of the Press occurred in 1965. In 1965 NPB could no longer be stalled and the Cape Nationalists launched *Die Beeld* their own Sunday newspaper in the Transvaal.[1] *Die Beeld* was created in the face of fierce opposition from the Transvaal Nationalists and as will emerge later in this study, was to mark another turning point in alignments within the ranks of Nationalist Afrikanerdom.

A study of the South African Press would not be complete without at least a brief reference to the non-White Press and the other major medium of communication, radio. South Africa's non-White Press has been excluded from this study as in its present form it has had no special relevance. Although there have been African controlled newspapers[2] the African Press today is controlled and financed wholly by

---

[1] After 1968 *Die Beeld* was amalgamated with *Dagbreek*, though the spirit (and many of the staff) of *Die Beeld* rather than *Dagbreek* survived the merger.

[2] See A. J. Friedgut, 'The Non-European Press' in Ellen Hellman (ed.) *Handbook on Race Relations in South Africa* (Cape Town: Oxford University Press, 1949, published for the South African Institute of Race Relations) pp. 484–510.

White interests, though frequently staffed and edited by Africans. In 1931 a non-profit making company, the Bantu Press, was established on the initiative of two White South Africans to increase the scope of non-White publications and to guide their political and commercial development. Their first venture was *Bantu World* which as *The World* became a daily and is today the largest of the non-White newspapers. Bantu Press quickly assumed control of the major surviving African newspapers and it was not long before the Argus Company bought its way into Bantu Press. In the 1950s the Anglo-American Corporation provided the Argus Company with substantial funds with which to acquire further control in Bantu Press.

It was impossible for any independent African newspaper to survive the competitive power of the White-controlled Bantu Press, and indeed this was the intention. The only rival in the field of publication for non-Whites has been the Government. Afrikaanse Pers published *Bona* as an 'educational' magazine for Africans for circulation particularly among the schools. Afrikaanse Pers also purchased *Imvo* and *Zonk* from Bantu Press and Voortrekker Pers published *Our Own Mirror*, formerly published independently in Natal under the name of *Eletha*.

Perhaps the best known of the South African publications for Africans was the politically open-minded magazine *Drum*. The magazine was controlled by Sir Abe Bailey's son J. R. Bailey in the 1950s and aimed at the urbanized African. But by 1965 *Drum* had dwindled into a supplement of the other Bailey paper, *Post*, a bi-weekly aimed at the non-White market. One of the few non-White owned newspapers to survive has been run by the more affluent Indian community in Natal. *Indian Opinion* as the journal is called was founded by Mahatma Gandhi in 1906 and although financially independent it has pursued a closely conservative political line.

Those newspapers which in the past had an influential African readership, such as the Communist inspired *New Age* and its phoenix-like followers which differed only in name are no longer in existence.[1] A South African underground Press has been virtually non-existent. Sporadic attempts at distributing mimeographed leaflets and papers have been made though with little continued success since the legal penalties and the difficulty of distribution have made an underground Press inoperable.

The fact that in 1968 South Africa was probably the only developed country in the world not to have television, greatly increased the

---

[1] See Brian Bunting, *The Rise of the South African Reich* (Harmondsworth: Penguin, 1964).

48

significance of the other media of communication. South Africa's refusal to introduce television was the result of Nationalist fears about the effects it might have on the non-White population and, most importantly, fears of producing a cultural imbalance weighted in favour of English-speaking South Africans and against the Afrikaans culture. The theory was that South African television would initially at least have to rely heavily on television programmes from English-speaking countries. It seems that some of these problems have been overcome as television is going to be introduced within the next few years.

South Africa's radio network is Government controlled and this in turn has highlighted the uniqueness of the English-language Press in the country. The South African Broadcasting Corporation was established as a statutory body in 1936 and was modelled on the British Broadcasting Corporation. It took over Schlesinger's African Broadcasting Company and provides four programmes: English, Afrikaans and African programmes (in seven languages) and a commercial channel. Increasingly its news and current affairs programmes have been subject to propaganda. The violence of its attacks on the English-language Press and on individual newspapers frequently has not been matched even by the Afrikaans newspapers. The corporation long ago abandoned any pretence at upholding the principles of its charter to act as an impartial public body, and has been used extensively – both inside and outside South Africa – to disseminate the views of the National Party Government.

3

The Ownership Structure of the Press

The concentration of ownership observed in the previous chapter resulted in the emergence of four dominant newspaper groups, namely the Argus Group, South African Associated Newspapers (SAAN), Nasionale Pers and Afrikaanse Pers, and between them they controlled thirteen of the eighteen daily newspapers and all five Sunday newspapers. The Argus and SAAN Groups together owned nine of the thirteen English-language dailies (all the evening and four of the eight morning newspapers) and all the English Sunday newspapers. In 1968 these nine dailies between them accounted for 77·0 per cent of the total circulation of all the English dailies published in South Africa.[1] Nasionale Pers, the larger of the two Afrikaans Press groups, but considerably smaller than either Argus or SAAN, owned three of the five Afrikaans dailies and one of the two Afrikaans Sunday newspapers. In 1968 the dailies belonging to the group accounted for 8·0 per cent of the total annual circulation of all dailies and 45·0 per cent of the annual circulation of all Afrikaans-language dailies.

In addition to the concentration of newspaper ownership and the collusion between existing proprietors to keep independently motivated newspapers out of the industry, there were other important factors contributing to the maintenance of the *status quo*: distribution was monopolized through the Central News Agency (CNA) and the South African Press Association (SAPA) limited the distribution of agency news to its members. SAPAs shareholders were the proprietors of the English and Afrikaans-language newspapers.

SAPA was created in 1938 by the owners of existing newspapers to provide the South African (and Rhodesian) Press with a country-wide news gathering service, and after 1939 SAPA was the only news agency in the country. The SAPA franchise system permitted the shareholders to grant or withhold permission for any would-be newspaper to make use of the agency's services. Furthermore, a three-

[1] This calculation is based on the Audit Bureau of Circulation figures for June–December, 1968.

quarters majority of votes was required for any alteration in membership, and as the English Press could control 87·4 per cent of the votes at a general meeting it has been able to regulate access to the service. The CNA was the only concern undertaking the distribution of newspapers in South Africa. The CNA monopoly not only militated against the emergence of new newspapers but discriminated against existing ones, giving preferential distribution to English-language newspapers by the negotiation of separate and discriminatory contracts with individual newspapers, the charging of higher prices, and the insistence that Afrikaans-language newspapers be loaded on the distribution vans before their competitors, allowing English-language newspapers to print later than the Afrikaans Press.[1] The reasons for this lie mostly in its history. CNA Ltd. was incorporated in 1903 and initially distributed the newspapers of the Cape Times Ltd. and of the Argus Group. The owners of the *Cape Times* and the Argus newspapers became major shareholders in the CNA and since the CNAs incorporation always appointed a director to its board. SAAN too, since its formation in 1955, appointed a director to the CNA board. The two founders of the CNA, M. Davis and A. V. Lindbergh, were also shareholders in the *Rand Daily Mail* and the *Sunday Times*. Lindbergh's descendants had shares in SAAN and the CNA.

There can be little doubt that the CNAs virtual monopoly of newspaper distribution and its vested interests in the financial success of a substantial percentage of the country's newspapers contributed to the demise of independent newspapers and operated to the disadvantage of the Afrikaans Press. The complex interconnections between the CNA and other newspaper interests is demonstrated in a simplified table, Table 1. When looked at in conjunction with Table 2, which reveals the interlocking of SAAN newspaper interests with other newspaper interests, it can be seen that the majority of the country's newspapers had a vested interest in protecting each others privileges.

This concentration of ownership is by no means unique to South Africa nor indeed to the newspaper industry. It has been a feature of business enterprises in most developed countries and the tendency in the newspaper industry has been for fewer and fewer groups to control an often declining number of newspapers.[2] In South Africa, concern about the monopolizing tendency of newspaper ownership was expressed by diverse interests. In 1946 the South African Society of Journalists (SASJ), representing working newspapermen,

[1] The Press Commission Report, Annexure XII, p. 82 et seq.
[2] See for example, R. B. Nixon, 'The Problems of Newspaper Monopoly' in W. Schramm (ed.) *Mass Communications* (Urbana: University of Illinois Press, 1960). p. 241–50.

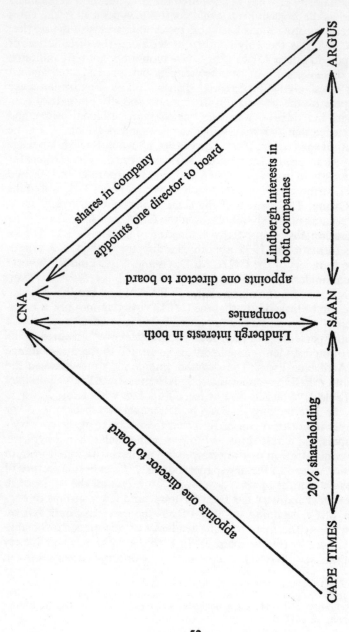

Table 1 Connections between the CNA and Newspaper Companies

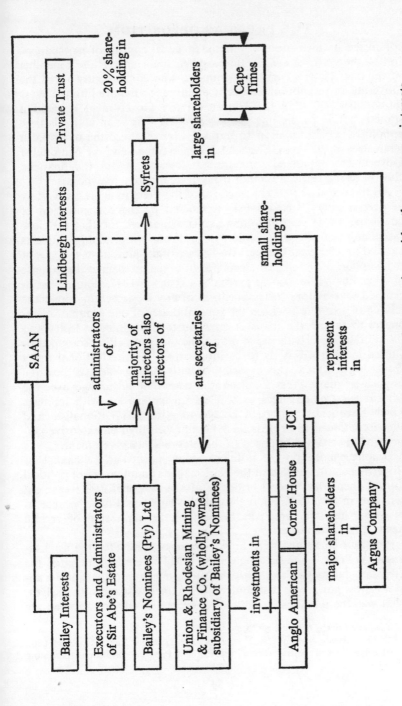

Table 2 Major shareholders in SAAN, and their connections with other newspaper interests

conducted its own inquiry into the financial control of newspapers. In 1948 the SASJ briefed Dr Bernard Friedman, an MP and a member of the then United Party Government, who consequently asked the Government to appoint a Select Committee to inquire into the Press monopolies. In 1950 the National Party Government debated a similar motion to the one proposed by Dr Friedman and this time appointed a Commission to inquire *inter alia* into the monopolist tendencies of the Press. The SASJ, Dr Friedman and the Nationalist Government expressed very similar concerns about the financial control of the Press, although from quite different viewpoints.

All three agreed that the freedom of the Press to express a variety of diverse views was seriously hampered by the concentration of newspaper ownership in so few hands. All agreed too that the close association of the English-language Press with mining interests worked to their disadvantage. In the case of the journalists this meant that support for mining interests was imposed on them at the expense of a genuine public service journalism. Thus in 1947, Lindsay Smith claimed that 'Before the publication of any items bearing upon the mining industry, it has been the general policy of one group of newspapers to submit the items in question to the mining industry and should they clash with the mining policy they are either scrapped or altered in such a way as to be inoffensive'.[1] In the National Party Government's view, this association with mining interests gave the English-language Press a substantial economic advantage over the Afrikaans-language Press as well as an association with interests which historically had been hostile to Afrikaner nationalism and which continued to express their hostility through an extensive network of newspapers opposed to the Nationalist Government.

Despite changes in the political realm—particularly a change of Government after 1948 and the Nationalist's maintenance of political control thereafter, liberal critics[2] and the Nationalist Government persisted in their belief that the English-language Press, because of its ownership structure, was preventing the expression of certain views in its newspapers.

It cannot be refuted that mining interests dominated the English-language Press, quite as much as political interests dominated the Afrikaans-language Press. But the more important question to answer is how power was distributed within the newspapers themselves: what was the relationship between owners and editors, between the

[1] Lindsay Smith, op. cit., p. 73.
[2] See Rosalynde Ainsley, *The Press in Africa* (London: Victor Gollancz Ltd., 1966) for a 'liberal' assessment of the English Press' commitment to mining interests.

commercial or political ethic of proprietors and the journalistic ethic of newspapermen. And to what extent a distinction between the two functions was made and at what points they confronted each other.

The Press Commission of Inquiry concluded that 'The persons who control the companies and company groups owning the major urban newspapers are in fact the persons who ultimately determine the policies of the major urban newspapers in the Union'.[1] In the sense that owners determine the general principles upon which their newspapers are run, this conclusion was undoubtedly true. But it is necessary to know what kinds of decisions newspaper owners made and under what circumstances they chose to exercise their influence. One of the most important areas of ownership influence on editorial policy was the owners' selection of an editor. The owners could, by careful selection of senior editorial staff, ensure the perpetuation of general principles. Second, owners could exert influence on editorial policy by controlling the financial policy of a newspaper-by determining to what extent newspapers were run primarily for profit or politics and making decisions about the allocation of resources. Lastly, owners could exert influence by direct editorial intervention, whether for commercial or political motives.

Lord Thomson, in giving evidence to the British Royal Commission on the Press said that he ran his newspapers as businesses and looked to them to produce profits. As such, he claimed he would not interfere with the editorial functioning of his newspapers. Lord Beaverbrook on the other hand, claimed that his newspapers were run for propaganda purposes. But he went on to say that to ensure that he could continue to make propaganda, his newspapers had first to sell.

In South Africa the English and Afrikaans-language Presses roughly paralleled the Thomson–Beaverbrook distinctions, but with one significant difference. The Afrikaans Press was never prepared to sacrifice political commitment for the cause of circulation. This remained true throughout the twenty years of this study although Nasionale Pers' experiment with *Die Beeld* suggested that profit and propaganda were not necessarily incompatible.

Within the English-language Press the theory that owners control the policies of their newspapers did not take account of two important facts. First, that the structure of modern newspaper ownership in South Africa was such that business administrators rather than Press Lords predominated, and the large scale organizations of necessity demanded a greater sharing or delegation of functions than was required in earlier years. Second, there was the strength of journalistic

---

[1] Press Commission Report, 1962, Volume 1, Chapter 1, p. 7.

traditions and the fact that by their function, editors and not owners of newspapers, had to make decisions about what to put into newspapers every day.

Newspapers are very individual properties and each has its own peculiar internal organization relating to the particular individuals who work within it at any time. However, by observing the formal structure of ownership it is possible to make some generalizations and to distinguish the newspapers belonging to any one group from those belonging to any other group. More specifically it is suggested that the type of financial control defines the relationship between owners and editors, a relationship which in turn defines the type of editorial influence of newspaper owners.[1]

Hence it is to the ownership structure of the newspapers that this chapter now turns. Each newspaper group is dealt with separately, beginning with an explanation of the formal organization of ownership and followed by a discussion of the effects of ownership on the group's newspapers.

The Argus Group

The Argus Group was in 1968 the largest newspaper group in Africa, with interests throughout Southern Africa. In South Africa itself, the group owned three daily newspapers, one Sunday, and controlled three dailies and three periodicals. In addition, the group had major interests in Bantu Press (Pty) Ltd. which gave it an influence in one African bi-weekly and two weekly papers owned by Bantu Press.

(a) Financial Structure

Control of the Argus Printing and Publishing Co. Ltd., the parent company of the group, was vested in the Argus Voting Trust which until 1958, was in effect the sole policy-controlling body of the group. The Trust was formed in 1931 at a time when there was a threat of French investors gaining control of the Central Mining and Investment Corporation Ltd., by the directors of the corporation, who were the majority shareholders in the Argus Group. The purpose of the Trust was to ensure that the votes, conferred by the shares held by the corporation in the Argus Printing and Publishing Company

---

[1] Very much more detailed research is needed in the area of this study, particularly as the ethical, social and political values of the individuals involved is so relevant to the choices they make. This chapter is extensive rather than intensive and suggests a line of approach rather than offering a comprehensive examination of the relationship between those most intimately involved in the policy-making processes of newspapers.

Ltd., would always remain in the hands of those favourably disposed to the British interests in the corporation. The trustees were given full and complete power to frame the rules governing the operation of the Trust. On November 1, 1943, they recorded that the object of the Trust was to ensure that the newspapers under the control of the Argus Company were to: '(a) maintain an honest, responsible standard of journalism . . . solely concerned with the public interest; (b) help towards the advancement and development of the Union and Rhodesia within and as part of the British Commonwealth; (c) further the cause of racial co-operation and follow a sympathetic and benevolent policy in matters concerning the welfare and progress of the non-White population; and (d) let the earning capacity and circulation of the newspapers be governed by a continued adherence to the standards of journalism, production and general policy that have been observed hitherto and have placed the newspapers concerned in their present position of public esteem and financial strength'.[1]

The Trust, which effectively created a policy-making triumvirate (there was a statutory maximum of three trustees), ensured the continuation of its objects by ruling that the existing trustees alone would decide on any successors. From 1910 to 1951 all the directors of the Argus Company were drawn from the two mining concerns which controlled the company, the Central Mines and Rand Mines Group (known as the Corner House Group) and Johannesburg Consolidated Investments. From 1931 when the Trust was created, until 1948, there were only two trustees, namely John Martin and Sir Reginald S. Holland. They were both chairmen or past chairmen and directors of the Central Mining Corporation and were themselves responsible for the creation of the Trust. In addition to these posts, John Martin had been the general manager and managing director of the Argus Company, the President of the Chamber of Mines and a director of the Bank of England[2].

The Press Commission concluded that while Martin and Holland were the trustees, they had virtually complete control over Argus Group newspapers. The deaths of these two powerful men brought about important alterations in the structure of the Argus organization, changes which helped shift the emphasis away from the direct mining control of the Argus Group. This came about not so much because the mining interests decreased their shareholdings (which they did) but because the creation of the Voting Trust and the

[1] Press Commission Report, Annexure IV, p. 119.
[2] Press Commission Report, Annexure IV, p. 123. Also see H. Lindsay Smith, op. cit., Chapter XI, who lists John Martin's other interests and attacks him for abusing his powerful position in the Press.

principles it embodied had established the idea (if not the fact) that interests independent of the mining corporations ought to control the policies of the newspapers.

These changes occurred when the existence of the Voting Trust was threatened. After the deaths of Martin and Holland in 1948 and 1949, the members of the board of Central Mining became concerned about their predecessors' decision to settle the votes conferred by the Argus shares on the trustees. For what the settlement of votes really did was to deprive the corporation itself of direct influence on the affairs of the Argus Company. Hence if the control of the corporation changed hands the new directors would find themselves deprived of any say in the affairs of the company in which the corporation had very large financial interests, whilst the previous controllers of the corporation would still retain their influence in the control of the company. In addition, the corporation was dissatisfied with the proviso that their extensive shareholdings would in such an event be frozen, at least to the extent that they had first to be offered to the Argus voting trustees before they could be disposed of on the open market. The Voting Trust was also threatened by the fact that in 1953 Johannesburg Consolidated Investment Company (JCI) already a substantial shareholder in the Argus Company, increased its shareholding to 33·35 per cent of the issued share capital. Until 1948, JCI had not been aware of the existence of the Voting Trust and thereafter wanted nothing to do with it.

The trustees were not prepared to abandon the Voting Trust and began negotiations with the mining interests. The trustees did their best to make the Argus Company wholly independent of the two mining companies. They tried to persuade the interested parties to set up trusts similar to those governing the Manchester *Guardian* or *The Times*.[1] The trustees did not succeed in either of these objectives but they did improve the position of the Trust. For they succeeded in persuading both JCI and the Corner House Group to reduce their shareholdings in the Argus Company and to allow the trustees to dispose of these shares to sympathetic buyers who would be prepared to vest their voting rights in the Trust. The mining companies were released from the Voting Trust arrangements. This left the two mining groups as the biggest shareholders in the Argus Company but it also left the Voting trustees able to control the votes of a larger number of shares than any other individual or groups, since the shares were deliberately disposed of in small parcels.

[1] For details of the Trusts which control the *Guardian* and *The Times*, see Francis Williams, *Dangerous Estate* (London: Longmans, Green & Co., 1957), p. 252 et seq.

Furthermore, and most importantly, after 1957, when the mining groups were released from the conditions of the Trust, there were changes in the personnel of the Trust. They were drawn exclusively from the Argus Company and no trustee had any interests in any of the mining companies. The deliberateness of this policy was confirmed when W. M. Frames, a trustee-designate, with powerful interests in the Corner House Group, was passed over and the manager of the Johannesburg branch of the Argus Company was appointed instead. From 1957 until 1961, representatives of the Argus Company constituted a majority of the company's board of directors–four out of seven. After 1961, when an extra board member was appointed, four directors were connected exclusively with the newspaper interests, that is the Argus Company, two with the Corner House Group and two with JCI. These three groups between them appointed the directors of the Argus Company and at all times after 1957, an Argus Voting trustee chaired the board.

The most important effect of these changes was that the business expertise and administrative flair of the mining groups was not lost but mining interests were less directly involved in the functioning of Argus Group newspapers.

(b) Effects of Ownership

In 1966, Rosalynde Ainsley repeated Lindsay Smith's claims that the mining interests of the Argus Group's owners prevented the group's newspapers from attacking mining administration and particularly from campaigning against low mining wages and the conditions of non-White mine labour.[1] Yet both confirmed that in other respects Argus Group newspapers had been vigorously critical and demanded social reforms for the non-Whites. But the more important point was that no establishment English-language newspaper had exposed South African mining interests to severe scrutiny. The reasons for this were not to be found simply in the fact that some newspaper proprietors were so closely associated with mining interests. Rather it expressed the more complex dilemma confronting the whole English-language Press. As a White, 'responsible' institution, it had vested interests in maintaining the *status quo*. Its interests in mining were a part of its vested interests in the stability of the country's economy and the White institutions of the society of which it was a part. Yet for the newspapers in the British tradition the journalistic ethic exercised a powerful influence towards more general opposition to established interests.

[1] Rosalynde Ainsley, op. cit., Lindsay Smith, op. cit.

The English Presses' opposition to those interests on whose perpetuation they relied for their own continued existence, stemmed from a particular definition of the Presses' role as that of a critical observer and the voice of interests which could not otherwise be heard. This underlines the importance of the restructuring of the Voting Trust which embodied the recognition that the company ought to be administered by interests independent of mining interests, that the officials of the company and not the corporation ought to be in a position to select their newspapers' editors. It did not go so far as to embody the principle that editors must be independent of the commercial company's interests, but the movement was in that direction.

Perhaps the most important feature of the Argus Group's long association with mining interests was the strength of its business management which gave the group's newspapers profits and financial independence. It benefited too the quality and quantity of its news and feature services. but it also put the stamp of strong management on the appearance of the group's newspapers.

All editors of Argus newspapers in recent times were appointed from within the group itself: they were tried and tested Argus Group men, conscious of management and of circulation and of the advertising problems of newspapers. Thus from the outset there was a measure of uniformity about the men selected to edit Argus Group newspapers. Further, the powerful central organization of the group, and its emphasis on management qualities tended to produce editors with marked management capabilities and stressed the editor in his role as administrator rather than 'personality'. The administrative-editor is a common enough feature of large modern newspapers but the editors of the Argus newspapers were very clearly of this mould, distinguishing them from editors of other newspaper groups in South Africa.

Yet every Argus editor expressed his firm adherence to the principle of editorial independence and the expectation that the newspaper ought to reflect the personality of the editor. The editor of the *Cape Argus* said that he had never discussed his political views with either the management or any member of the board of directors, for he said 'the managers and I do two quite different jobs. I see to the editorial running of the newspaper and the managers perform a quite separate and different management function.'

The editor of the Argus Group's Durban daily, the *Daily News* equally affirmed his independence from management and directorial boards. He said 'I would not take orders from management or boards. Occasionally I am told of the disapproval of certain members of the board for a particular stance I have taken, but never anything stronger than that. I would certainly never refer to the board or to management before adopting a particular stance on any issue.'

Equally, however, they all agreed that a board would not 'select an editor who was not suitable' and that 'eccentrics do not become editors'.

South African Associated Newspapers (SAAN)

(a) Financial Structure

The South African Associated Newspapers Ltd. was formed in 1955 and enlarged in 1959 when the group acquired two further dailies in the Eastern Province. In addition to owning three major daily newspapers (the *Rand Daily Mail, Eastern Province Herald* and the *Evening Post*) and two of the three English-language Sunday papers, SAAN had a minority interest in the Argus-controlled *Pretoria News*.

In the previous chapter, it was noted that prior to 1955 two separate companies operated the *Rand Daily Mail* and the *Sunday Times* and that the *Sunday Express* became a wholly owned subsidiary of the Sunday Times Syndicate in 1946. The history of Rand Daily Mails Ltd. and Sunday Times Syndicate Ltd. was tied closely to the careers of Sir Abe Bailey, R. Ward-Jackson, G. H. Kingswell and A. V. Lindbergh, one of the founders of the CNA. These people were all large shareholders in each of the two newspaper companies and Ward-Jackson, Kingswell and Lindbergh served for many years with the nominees of Sir Abe Bailey as directors of both companies. Ward-Jackson was also the editor of the *Rand Daily Mail* for twenty years. After their deaths their executors or administrators and their descendants directed the affairs of the companies.

By 1953 the largest shareholder in both the *Rand Daily Mail* and the *Sunday Times* was the Bailey estate which held 59·23 per cent of the shares in the *Rand Daily Mail* and 26·17 per cent of the shares in the *Sunday Times*. The Bailey interests in the two companies were administered, after the death of Sir Abe in 1940, by the executors of the Bailey estate. After the formation of SAAN in July 1955, the Bailey executors no longer had control of the *Rand Daily Mail* although they were still the largest shareholders in SAAN, with 49·71 per cent of the shareholding. The constitution of the board of directors was indicative of the power balance within SAAN after 1955. An agreement was reached that of the seven board members, the Ward-Jackson, Kingswell and Lindbergh Groups were each entitled to appoint one director; the Bailey Group was entitled to appoint three directors. The seventh director was to be appointed by the Bailey Group with a majority of the other groups. Further it was agreed that all matters to be decided by the board which materially affected the interests of the company or its shareholders, or the policy of any of its publications, must be decided only at a board meeting at which every director was present, whether personally or through his alternates.

Between 1955 and 1962 some changes in the shareholdings of SAAN took place, although no fundamental changes occurred in the distribution of interests on the board. First the Kingswells sold out their interests to the Bailey and Lindbergh interests and later the Ward-Jackson shareholdings were sold to a private trust. Thus the Bailey interests acquired a majority of the shares in SAAN although the shares were divided between several groups of Bailey interests. Then in 1962 SAAN became a public company and the Bailey interests were left with just over 50 per cent of the shareholdings in SAAN.

It is important at this point to describe more fully the structure of the Bailey Group and its various interests, as it reveals an intricate interlinking with other relevant newspaper interests in the country (See Table 2). The Bailey Group consisted of Bailey's Nominees (Pty) Ltd. and its wholly owned subsidiary, Union and Rhodesian Mining and Finance Co. Ltd. Control of the two companies was in the hands of the executors and administrators of Sir Abe Bailey's estate who were all shareholders and directors of Bailey's Nominees and who in consequence controlled Union and Rhodesian Mining.

The subsidiary company, Union and Rhodesian Mining and Finance Co. Ltd., employed a subsidiary of Syfrets Trust Co. Ltd. as its secretaries, and Syfrets acted as the representative of a section of the Bailey interests on the SAAN board. In addition a fairly substantial amount of the assets of Union and Rhodesian Mining was invested in Anglo-American, the Corner House Group and Johannesburg Consolidated Investments, who were all shareholders in the Argus Company.

(b) Effects of Ownership

The important question to answer is to what extent the owners of SAAN were in a position to influence the policies of their newspapers and what their attitudes to the exercise of that influence were. In an International Press Institute survey, conducted by Colin Seymour-Ure in 1969[1] the editor of the *Sunday Times* was reported

---

[1] Colin Seymour-Ure, 'Policy-Making in the Press' in *Government and Opposition*, Autumn 1969, p. 495.

as saying that the owners of the newspaper had never interfered with the policy of their newspapers. As an example of editorial independence the editor cited an incident in 1968: Clive Corder, the chairman of Syfrets, acting on behalf of the Bailey interests and a number of other shareholders (representing 65 per cent of the SAAN shares) sold their interests in SAAN to the Argus Group. Shortly after the takeover had become public, Corder was criticized severely by the *Sunday Times*, particularly as he had failed to consult the chairman or the managing director of SAAN until after the deal had been negotiated. As a result of the intervention of the Prime Minister, the sale was not completed, and Corder resumed control. But there were no subsequent repercussions on the newspaper's editor.

Seymour-Ure further quoted the editor as saying that:

'In no single instance have my decisions been challenged or questioned, nor has any pressure been placed upon me to follow a course different from that of my own choosing.'

He also pointed out that the *Rand Daily Mail*, another paper in the SAAN group, supported a political party different from that of the *Sunday Times* and generally had policies different from that of his newspaper.

Undoubtedly the SAAN Group newspapers were much less management-ownership controlled than the newspapers of the Argus Group, and editorial independence from proprietorial interference was extensive. But it is also true that editors were selected from within a reasonably limited political spectrum, and if Mervis of the *Sunday Times* found no interference from above it was at least partly because he had chosen to adopt policies which were fundamentally acceptable to the owners of the newspaper. Mr. Mervis was also the most profit-conscious editor in the country and the circulation of his paper provided ample evidence of this to his board. It was hardly surprising that he was 'never interfered with'. This did not prove to be the case for the most recent ex-editor of the *Rand Daily Mail*, Mr L. O. V. Gandar. In 1965, the *Rand Daily Mail* published a series of articles on prison conditions which had serious reprecussions both for Gandar and the newspaper. Shortly after publication of the articles there was a major editorial reshuffle in which Gandar was ostensibly 'promoted' to the position of editor-in-chief, from his previous position as editor of the newspaper.

The events leading to and subsequent to the editorial reshuffle are illuminating in the context of this chapter.[1] The *Rand Daily Mail* had

[1] There is no documentary evidence to substantiate this explanation of Gandar's demotion and ultimate departure from the newspaper, but extensive

63

supported the Progressive Party since its inception in 1959. There were certain members of the board who were sympathetic to this viewpoint and they ensured Gandar's freedom to continue his support for the party. By 1965, when the articles on prison conditions appeared, there was already dissatisfaction amongst some members of the board concerning the policy of the paper, particularly as it was claimed that the newspaper was losing readers, although this was in fact not true; the paper had lost a percentage of white readers but had increased its non-White readership. When the prison condition articles appeared, there was an immediate reaction amongst the board members, some of whom wished to remove Gandar right away.

In late August, Gandar was approached by a director of the company, who asked him to take immediate and indefinite long leave. Gandar was told that this was a board decision. In fact there had not been a formal board meeting, and the decision had been taken unconstitutionally by one group of directors. In response to this threat, support for Gandar was canvassed throughout Johannesburg and an important group of senior journalists threatened to resign if Gandar was removed.

It is important to note, in the events leading to Gandar's effective removal that before he had assumed the editorship of the *Rand Daily Mail*, Gandar emphatically had established the principle of editorial independence. He had demanded that the principle be spelled out in the correspondence prior to his acceptance of the post, so that he would not be exposed to proprietorial interference as he believed his predecessor had been.

Thus the very fact that the board had contracted not to interfere with the policy of the paper was probably responsible for the fiasco which resulted in the attempt to dismiss Gandar. For if the board could not force Gandar to change the paper's policy it could in the last resort dismiss him. Gandar was not dismissed for several reasons. First, the board was divided and those members of the board who had not been a party to the original directive (asking Gandar to go on long leave), disliked the manner in which Gandar had been dealt with. They were also incensed by the high handedness of an influential SAAN newspaperman who had rallied the support of the other members of the board in his bid to oust Gandar. The newspaperman in question was driven to employ such dubious tactics by his belated

interviews with members of the editorial staff involved in the reshuffle and some of the proprietors of the company, has led to the conclusion that the events occurred as here described. Some of those interviewed disagreed with this interpretation.

discovery that one of his 'own men' on the board was Gandar's staunchest supporter. As events turned out Gandar and his powerful opponent were both defeated: Gandar in the sense that he lost overall control of the paper, his detractor in the sense that he did not succeed in removing Gandar. And considering his eventual belief that Gandar, in the increasing ardency of his anti-nationalism had become un-South African, his failure was the more remarkable. Second, the support for Gandar from his colleagues and from outside the newspaper was overwhelming and caused the board to re-think its attitudes to Gandar. Finally, once it became clear that the Government would lay charges against Gandar, the board felt compelled to give him their support.

The Gandar affair did produce some changes in the running of the newspaper, though they were less fundamental than might have been expected. Gandar was ousted, but at the same time Gandar's news editor, and his own appointee, Raymond Louw, replaced him as editor. The most significant result was a minute circulated to all editors in the group, requesting that if a story was likely to incur heavy costs for the newspaper (as indeed the Gandar trials did), the management must first be consulted. Despite this serious precedent of managerial control, the degree of editorial freedom in the SAAN newspapers and the lack of proprietorial interference, remained a notable feature of the group.

One SAAN editor disagreed with his colleagues in the group on their independence from the SAAN board. John Sutherland, the editor of the *Evening Post*, felt that no editor could dictate policy if he did not own the newspaper, and cited as an example his newspaper's sometime support of the Progressive Party. He maintained that although the paper was regarded by the Progressives as a 'friendly' newspaper, 'my relationship to the board of the *Post* does not allow me to be very friendly to the Progressives. The reason for this, from their point of view, is that the paper will fare better commercially if I do not become too friendly towards them.' The editor further felt that the attitude of the circulation manager of the newspaper affected policy-making a great deal, as demands were constantly being made on him to improve circulation sometimes at the expense of personal editiorial judgment.

Sutherland's claims merely served to confirm the distinctions between Argus and SAAN Group newspapers. Organizationally, the SAAN Group did not have the same coherence: local boards and individual editors tended to be much freer in determining their relationships to each other. The 'natural' antagonism between the management and editorial sides of a newspaper's production was sharper in SAAN newspapers than in those of the Argus Group and this led to a greater diversity and individuality within the SAAN Group. Further, the fact that a board, comprised of sometimes opposing interests (rather than an easily identifiable and self-perpetuating group of trustees), was the ultimate source of sanction for group policy, permitted SAAN editors a more personal impact on the policies of their newspapers.

Nasionale Pers Beperk (NPB)

(a) Financial Structure

The financial structure of NPB companies was in stark contrast to those of the English-language newspapers. When in 1915 *Die Burger* (the first of NPBs newspapers) was started, thousands of pamphlets were distributed in an attempt to raise the necessary capital, and great difficulty was encountered in finding subscribers for the new company. By 1953, the issued capital of NPB was £400,000 dividend into £1 shares and the shares were registered in the names of 3,239 shareholders. The largest shareholders were the Santam-Sanlam Group, a consortium of all-Afrikaner enterprises in the insurance field which came into being after *Die Burger* was created, with the intention of accumulating Afrikaner capital. The Santam-Sanlan Group held 21·67 per cent of the shares, while 10·93 per cent of the shares were held by 2,690 shareholders, each holding fewer than 100 shares.

This wide spread of shares most clearly reflected the economic position of the Afrikaners who had not accumulated any capital as the financiers backing the English Press had done. Equally, the conditions regulating the transfer of shares, even when held in very small numbers, reflected the political rather than profit commitment of the directors of the companies. The directors of NPB were from the start, accorded the right to refuse to transfer or register any share. By this term in the company's Articles of Association, the directors were able to ensure the continuation of the policies of NPB. Shareholders, who elected the directors, were allowed a maximum of fifty votes at a meeting no matter how many shares they held. To ensure that no one unsympathetic to the paper's policy could vote, all sales and transfers of shares were investigated and the background of the buyer thoroughly examined. According to the editor of *Die Burger* a prospective shareholder would certainly be asked how he voted and there were indeed instances when share transfers were refused, as in the case of Professor D. Oosthuizen of Rhodes University, Grahamstown, who was bequeathed a 100 foundation shares in *Die Burger* by his mother. Professor Oosthuizen employed a lawyer to fight the company's decision and a long battle ensued. But he was eventually forced to sell his inherited shares at an agreed price to a suitable buyer selected by the company.

NPB controlled three daily newspapers, *Die Burger, Die Volksblad* and *Die Oosterlig* and one Sunday newspaper, *Die Beeld*. It is important that despite the indisputable political associations and affiliations of the NPB Group, its board of directors included the smallest number of party politicians of any Afrikaans newspaper or newspaper group. By June 1956, only one cabinet minister, C. R. Swart, leader of the National Party in the Orange Free State, served on the board of NPB, with only one other political 'representative', Senator C. A. van Niekerk, President of the Senate. The other members of the board were drawn from the Santam-Sanlam Group and from NPB itself. The seventh director was the attorney for both NPB and the Santam-Sanlam Group.

This was a change from earlier years as from 1925 until 1948 the majority of members on the board of NPB were National Party MPs. Dr Malan became a member of the board in 1935 and remained a member until June 1949, a little more than a year after he had become Prime Minister. Dr W. A. Hofmeyr, who was one of the founders of NPB and of Santam-Sanlam, was for many years a director on the board and a Nationalist Party Senator. He was in addition one of the founders of the National Party in the Cape and for many years acted as secretary of the party.

After 1948 there were always National Party MPs on the board of NPB but the majority of the directors were not actively engaged in the party political life of the country.

(b) Effects of Ownership

There is evidence in the style particularly of *Die Burger* and in the attutudes of the newspaper to the National Party, that the low count of party-political men on the board of NPB had some effect on the running of NPB newspapers. NPB created the most successful financial formula for its newspapers of any of the Afrikaans newspaper companies. One of the most influential Nationalists in the country in the 1960s was the editor of *Die Burger*, Piet Cillie, who by 1969 had been with *Die Burger* for thirty five years. He claimed that he 'picked up the policy of the paper through his skin'. The contacts between the owners, as represented by the board of NPB, and the editors were multiple. According to Cillie, the board held to the tradition of imposing no directives and of not approaching him individually. But if there was a need to convey a corporate board attitude to the editor, it was done through the managing director. Cillie described the relationship in this way:

'I live with many of these people. Every day the managing director comes in for a few hours. The chairman and vice-chairman of the board are both ex-editors of the newspaper and there is a great deal of consultation: they are very useful as sounding boards. Also I go to them as seniors, particularly if I ever have any doubts–though admittedly that is very rare.'

The other daily newspapers in the group–*Die Volksblad* and *Die Oosterlig* took their cues from *Die Burger*. They received *Die Burger's* leaders daily and the editor of *Die Burger* conveyed messages from the board to the other editors.

Die Burger (and NPB) was almost as aware of commercial constraints as it was of expressing its political views and in this respect was for a long time unique amongst Afrikaans newspapers in combining the two successfully. *Die Burger's* editor claimed that economic necessity forced *Die Burger* to enter the Transvaal and start *Die Beeld,* since there was an expanding market in the Transvaal which could not be left untouched. Earlier in its history NPB had wished to open a Sunday paper on the Rand but had desisted for political reasons. The political opposition still existed when *Die Beeld* was initiated but by 1965, NPB felt that it was economically essential to pursue the project to its conclusion. *Die Beeld's* editor–an ex-assistant editor of *Die Burger*–said that the need for the Cape to get its political views expressed in the Transvaal was the prime motivation for NPBs initiative on the Rand, although he in no way contradicted the 'economic necessity' argument.

Within Nasionale Pers, as in the Argus Group, there was no implicit antagonism between the management and editorial staff; on the contrary there was a constant exchange of views at all levels, of both a formal and an informal nature. But unlike the Argus Group, the editor was a key figure in determining the general and particular policy of the paper, though within the limits of ideological and party-political commitments. A further distinction must be made between the group's major papers, *Die Burger* and *Die Beeld,* and the lesser papers, *Die Volksblad* and *Die Oosterlig.* For while it was probably true that the editors of *Die Burger* and *Die Beeld* had greater freedom in determining the policies of their newspapers than any English-language newspaper editors, the editors of the minor newspapers of the group were strictly supervised from Keerom Straat, the Nationale Pers headquarters in Cape Town.

The dominance of the editor, rather than the board or management, in the Nasionale Pers newspapers was consistent with the function that the Cape Press was expected to fulfil within the political machine, reflecting the political rather than profit motivations of its promoters. At the same time the management and the board of NPB frequently included senior men drawn from the editorial side of the newspaper, who were actively involved in the policy-making processes of their newspapers. Management also had an important function to fulfil in making NPB newspapers economically viable; although at all times they were sympathetic to editorial purposes and in no way threatened the editor's ability to dictate the policy of the paper.

Whilst Nasionale Pers newspapers dispensed with the 'tradition' of appointing politicians as editors, they did not eliminate the belief that editors ought to have powers at least commensurate with those of the most powerful politicians. This was particularly important, for the editors of Afrikaans newspapers generally derived their influence from their relationship to the party structure rather than from the role of editor. The editorship of a newspaper gave the Afrikaans editor his position in the party structure but the power of the Afrikaans editor was more directly derived from his relationship to the party and the Government than from his editorial role.

Afrikaanse Pers Beperk (APB)

(a) *Financial Organization*

Afrikaanse Pers (1962) Beperk was formed in 1962 from an amalgamation of Afrikaanse Pers and Dagbreekpers Beperk. The new company (referred to henceforth as APB) controlled the afternoon daily newspaper *Die Vaderland* and the Sunday paper *Dagbreek en Sondagnuus.*

The original Afrikaanse Pers (which was incorporated in 1931) laid down that the control of the company was to be in the hands of a Founders' Board. Two of the three members of the board were General Hertzog and Senator Brebner who became the majority shareholders in the company. In 1935 Hertzog and Brebner created a trust, the Afrikaanse Persfonds, on which they settled a substantial percentage of shares in *Die Vaderland,* enabling the trust to appoint two-thirds of the directors of the company. The objects of the Persfonds was to 'establish and maintain an independent National newspaper in the Afrikaans language . . . in the interests and service of the Afrikaans-speaking National Afrikanerdom (*sic*)'[1]. In terms of the trust of Afrikaanse Persfonds, General Hertzog had the sole control

[1] Press Commission of Inquiry, Annexure IV, p. 28.

of Afrikaanse Pers and its newspaper, *Die Vaderland* and after his death this control passed to Havenga.

Dagbreekpers Beperk was formed in 1947 and its Articles of Association set out the policy to be followed by any newspaper owned or controlled by the company:

> 'It shall be one of the purposes or objects of the Company that any newspaper of which the Company may be the proprietor or publisher ... shall not be party political; ... that on the balance of its editorial policy, it shall be impartial on the aspirations of any political party or organisation for a republic, and on the subject of the severance of the British connection by the Union, that it shall not oppose the interests of any major industry in the Union and shall not in principle be anti-Semitic, and that it shall be its aim and object to strive for and achieve closer co-operation of the two White races in the Union on the principle of South Africa first.'[1]

At its inception and in keeping with its Articles of Association, the Afrikaans interests had equal representation with the English interests on the board of Dagbreekpers. This was guaranteed by the appointment of two classes of directors, one half to be appointed by the holders of 'A' shares, and the other half by the holders of 'B' shares, with all decisions requiring a majority of votes of each class of directors. The 'A' shares represented the Afrikaans interests and a very high percentage of the shares were held in small units. The 'B' shares were held initially by Strathmore Exploration Ltd., a company with three shareholders and with extensive mining interests.

The merging of *Dagbreek* and Afrikaanse Pers began as early as 1947 when Dagbreekpers bought out Afrikaanse Pers' six-month-old Sunday paper, *Sondagnuus*. The need for more funds led to many changes in the group. In 1953 further financial assistance was required and the Strathmore Group, which until then had been the main source of finance, even sponsoring and supporting the 'Afrikaans' interests in the newspaper, were not prepared to increase their investment further. Apart from financial considerations, Jack Scott, the chairman of Strathmore, was embarrassed by the political views the newspaper had expressed during the 1953 election and he offered Marius Jooste (who helped to run *Dagbreek* and represented the 'A' share interests on the board) the option of purchasing the entire shareholding of the Strathmore companies in Dagbreekpers Bpk. and Dagbreek Trust (Pty) Ltd.

Jooste approached Strijdom, the Minister of Lands and the leader

---

[1] Press Commission Report, Annexure IV, p. 216–17.

70

of the National Party in the Transvaal at the time, who agreed to raise the capital. Strijdom and other prominent Transvaal National Party members succeeded in placing all the shares. They achieved this, according to the findings of the Press Commission Report, mainly through their contacts with supporters of the party in the Transvaal and through the National Party itself.[1] The Dagbreek Trust was created to ensure that control of the newspaper's policies was kept in the hands of approved trustees. This was achieved by giving Dagbreek Trust a controlling interest in Dagbreek Trust Ltd. By June 1955, the National Party of the Transvaal held a substantial number of shares in Dagbreek Trust Ltd., and the first members of the Trust included the Prime Minister and four members of his government, Strijdom, Verwoerd, Ben Schoeman and J. de Klerk, together with M. V. Jooste and the editor of *Dagbreek*, W. van Heerden. Provisions were made to ensure the continued existence of the Trust, and included stringent regulations governing the transfer of shares.

There were no further changes until 1962 when Afrikaanse Pers, *Dagbreek's* old competitor, was threatened financially largely as a result of another attempt at producing a Sunday newspaper, *Sondagblad*. Marius Jooste, by then the managing director of Dagbreekpers, and one of those who had broken from Afrikaanse Pers in 1946, acted amidst rumours of takeover bids by the Argus Group and Nasionale Pers, and succeeded in forming the new company, Afrikaanse Pers (1962) Beperk. The merger marked the final assimilation of the old Havenga wing of the party into the Transvaal wing of the National Party.

After 1962 Dagbreek Trust continued to be the controlling body in the merged structure. The trustees in that year included the then Prime Minister, Verwoerd, three cabinet ministers, one National Party Senator, and the Administrator of the Transvaal, F. H. Odendaal.

(b) Effects of ownership

The intimacy of APBs association with the National Party, both in terms of its shareholdings and its directors, need be demonstrated no further. Yet the editor of *Die Vaderland*, A. M. van Schoor, insisted that he was not 'the mouthpiece of politicians. I have my own views on public affairs and I propound them. There is freedom of thought in the National Party.' At the same time, not sensing any contradiction, van Schoor admitted that he was an 'old-style' Afrikaans editor and that he never tried to oppose the party–unlike

[1] Press Commission Report, Annexure IV, p. 213.

the editor of *Dagbreek*, who he saw as a much more 'independent' editor.

The editor of *Die Vaderland* had a formal meeting with his board once a month but met them informally much more frequently. The chairman of the board in 1970 was B. Schoeman, a cabinet minister and the leader of the Transvaal National Party. Like the editor of *Die Burger,* van Schoor claimed that his understanding of Nationalist policy was 'so deep' that there was no question of a fundamental disagreement about objectives with his board.

Unlike *Die Burger's* editor, van Schoor deplored the commercialization of journalism which had become a 'business dictated by the Frankenstein of circulation'. He insisted that nothing beneficial was derived from the battle for circulation and that as editor he did not concern himself with such matters.

The distinctive traditions of the two major newspapers within APB were not destroyed by the financial re-structuring which made them members of the same group. The dominating political figures of Hertzog and Havenga, for whom the newspaper provided personal mouthpieces, deprived editors of *Die Vaderland* of the opportunity to assert themselves as key-men in newspaper or party politics. *Dagbreek* on the other hand, with its independent tradition and non-alignment in party political terms, relied on the person of the editor to create the paper's political prestige. Willem van Heerden, the paper's first editor and a close associate of Verwoerd, created a unique role for *Dagbreek,* in which the paper possessed a considerable influence politically, while remaining outside the party machine. Once *Dagbreek* 'joined the fold' and was backed by party funds, it did not lose its independence, for the men who had created *Dagbreek* (particularly van Heerden and Marius Jooste) returned to APB on their own terms. They themselves had initiated their re-entry to the party machine and they saw to it that the influential possibilities of the paper's editor would not be compromised in exchange for group membership. At the same time the benefits to *Dagbreek* of Nationalist backing were to permit the paper a more politically partisan attitude than the earlier ownership-structure had allowed and to create an even more influential role for itself as an institution within the party.

Voortrekkerpers Group (VPB)

In September 1935, leaders and supporters of the Cape National Party met at Stellenbosch and formed a committee to collect funds to establish an Afrikaans-medium daily paper in the Transvaal, which would support the National Party. Through the columns of *Die Burger* and *Die Volksblad,* Malan and the committee appealed to

National Party supporters and sympathizers to invest in shares in the proposed newspaper company. Under this scheme individuals and branches and organizations of the National Party bought shares in units of £100 and as a further incentive in appealing to their nationalism, the names of new shareholders were listed by the newspapers. The major portion of the shares in the company were taken up by Cape Nationalists who held 52·54 per cent of the shares, followed by the Transvaal with 29·17 per cent and the Orange Free State with 14·87 per cent.

The first board of directors of the new holding company (Voortrekkerpers Bpk.) consisted of nine members, six of whom, including the chairman, were drawn from the Cape. Four of the Cape directors were MPs, one a Provincial councillor and two were connected with NPB. The Transvaal and OFS were represented by MPs. The first chairman of the board was Senator W. A. Hofmeyr, who was also chairman of the NPB board and of Sanlam.

The shares of VPB were held so widely and in such small numbers, that it was impossible for any small group of shareholders to control the company. The largest shareholder, Nasionale Pers, held only 3·5 per cent of the issued share capital. The provision in the Articles of Association that the directors, if they deemed it in the interest of the company, could in their absolute discretion refuse to transfer or register any share in the company, guarded the editorial policy of the company's newspaper *Die Transvaler*.

In June 1956 some of the more eminent directors of the company were the Prime Minister, Strijdom, who was also chairman of Dagbreek Trust Ltd., T. E. Donges, a cabinet minister, Adv. F. C. Erasmus, a cabinet minister, Adv. C. R. Swart who was a director of Nasionale Pers as well as a cabinet minister and Verwoerd, a trustee of Dagbreek Trust, a cabinet minister and the paper's first editor. After Strijdom's death, Verwoerd, as Prime Minister, became chairman and he in turn was followed by J. B. Vorster. Every Nationalist Prime Minister after 1948 was a director of the company and the three Prime Ministers from the Transvaal chaired the board, although in 1968 Vorster resigned the chairmanship of both VPB and APB mainly it seems to disentagle himself from the inter-provincial antagonisms and the 'verligte-verkrampte' conflict in the National Party.

(b) Effects of Ownership

Unlike his counterpart on *Die Vaderland*, the editor of *Die Transvaler*, Carl Noffke, declared himself very concerned with the circulation of his newspaper. He suggested that Afrikaans newspapers were increasingly conscious of economics, in line with the growing economic awareness of the Afrikaner. This was undoubtedly true but the very appointment of Noffke illustrated the failure of VPB to modernize itself sufficiently to compete wholeheartedly in the market for circulation. VPB never appointed a professional journalist to the editorship of the newspaper and its circulation bore witness to the failure of *Die Transvaler* to achieve popularity as a newspaper. The influence of the newspaper's board in making political appointments to the editorship of the paper proved a commercial failure. While Noffke had had some journalistic experience in working for the South African radio networks in Paris, his appointment could not be justified on journalistic grounds alone.

Despite an increased awareness of commercial demands Noffke expressed a dilemma of the Afrikaans Press when he said 'we could devote more attention to news and not to comment. At the same time we want to retain the authority of the newspaper: *Die Transvaler* has always been the paper containing the most information about the happenings in the National Party'.

Noffke, who claimed a small amount of editorial independence, stated that *Die Transvaler* was the official organ of the National Party in the Transvaal, 'although it is not controlled by the National Party. Its independence lies in the fact that the board of directors and management can decide on the newspaper's role. And in the same way as the board is free to criticize the National Party should they so choose, so it is free to interfere with the policy of the newspaper'. But, of course, the board of *Die Transvaler* consisted predominantly of very high-ranking National Party and Government members which seemed to make nonsense of the editor's claims.

Die Burger, both because of its traditions and because of the decline in the influence of the Cape in national politics, was forced to assert the voice of Cape nationalism and in so doing to assert itself as a force in national politics. *Die Transvaler* on the other hand, as the spokesman of the ascendant and most powerful group in the party, was forced into the role of maintaining the existing power-balance in inter-provincial Nationalist politics. With every Prime Minister after Malan coming from the Transvaal and being its chairman, *Die Transvaler* had little opportunity to establish itself as a separate institution within the Government and the party.

Despite the fact that finance for *Die Transvaler* originated primarily from the Cape, *Die Transvaler* under Verwoerd established itself unmistakably as a Transvaal institution. It is significant that during the one time when *Die Transvaler* was more than a party mouthpiece–when its functions included the initiation as well as the communication of policy–it represented a minority force in the party. At that time the Cape Nationalists dominated the party and the Transvaal had only a single Nationalist member of Parliament.

Thus in its early years, *Die Transvaler's* role was dictated by political circumstance as much as by the person of its editor. In later years, the numerous high-ranking politicians of the National Party on the paper's board and its position as the official organ of the Transvaal Party prevented the emergence of genuinely powerful and independent editors in *Die Burger* mould, although *Die Transvaler* like every other Afrikaans newspaper, was affected by the emergence of the 'verligte-verkrampte' crisis in the National Party.

Cape Times Ltd.

(a) Financial Structure

No shareholder in the Cape Times Ltd. held such a number of shares that he could control the company nor strictly speaking was there any coherent group of shareholders owning a sufficient number of shares which would have enabled them to control the Cape Times Ltd. However, Syfrets Trust Co. Ltd. from the nature of its business and its historical relationship with the *Cape Times* was in effect the dominant force in the *Cape Times*.

Three years after the formation of the Cape Times Ltd. in 1901, E. R. Syfret became chairman of the company and in 1919 when Syfrets Trust Co. was formed he became its first chairman. On his death, the new chairman of Syfret's Trust succeeded Syfret as chairman of the Cape Times Ltd. Thereafter the Syfret's chairman was traditionally also the chairman of the Cape Times, except for a brief period after 1956 when he was a board member only.

In addition to the holding in the *Cape Times* of the Syfret's Trust Co. Ltd. two of Syfrets' directors personally held shares in the *Cape Times*. Also in the ordinary course of their business, over the years Syfrets purchased and held shares on behalf of their clients who through the issue of proxies added to the voting rights of Syfrets.[1] The second largest shareholder in the *Cape Times,* The Cape Times Employees Endowment Trust (which held 17·05 per cent of the issued share capital of the company) traditionally gave the chairman of the *Cape Times* a proxy for the shares they held and as the chairman was usually chairman of Syfrets Trust, the voting power of the Trust was quite substantial.

Despite the obvious influence the Syfrets group could bring to bear

---

[1] Press Commission Report, Annexure IV, p. 201, et seq.

on the *Cape Times* at no time did Syfrets Trust represent a majority of the directors on the board of the *Cape Times*. It did, however, play an important role in the management and control of the affairs of the *Cape Times*.

(b) *Effects of Ownership*

In 1968 Clive Corder was the chairman of Syfrets and the *Cape Times* and the most important shareholder in Syfrets Trust. He claimed that as a matter of policy the board did not interfere with the editorial side of the newspaper, 'providing the broad lines laid down by the board are adhered to, or in other words that the traditions of the newspaper are upheld'. He said that the area within which Syfrets did try to exercise their influence or control was in the financial policy of the *Cape Times,* for a newspaper had to be run on business lines and make a profit or it would go to the wall.

The editor of the *Cape Times* since 1947, Victor Norton, largely confirmed the chairman's view that the board did not interfere with the running of the newspaper and that in the terms of his contract he was free to edit the *Cape Times* 'in the traditions of the newspaper'. Within the *Cape Times* there was effectively a fairly even distribution of power between owners and editors, for the concept of editorial independence was itself a deeply ingrained part of the paper's tradition, as was its consciousness of profits. However there were occasions when the two traditions have conflicted. For example, whilst Anthony Delius was the paper's political correspondent[1] pressure was exerted on the editor to silence Delius on the grounds that Delius' political perceptions might threaten the paper's circulation. The editor, although profit conscious, thought the principal of editorial independence of greater importance and refused to give in to this pressure.

The fact that the editor was able to stand up against pressure from the board and yet survive reveals both the strength of the tradition of editorial independence, and the type of circumstances in which the board believed it had a right to intervene. Equally it must be assumed that there were instances when the owners rather than the editor succeeded in modifying the content of the paper.

The Independent Press

The ownership structures of the three newspapers which were not group affiliated, the *Natal Mercury*, the *Natal Witness* and the *Daily Dispatch*, were quite different from those of any other newspaper companies. The *Natal Mercury* and the *Natal Witness* were owned by

[1] See Chapter 6.

single families, and the *Daily Dispatch* was owned in part by a charitable trust and in part by the editorial and managerial staff of the newspaper.

The *Natal Mercury* was dominated by members of the Robinson family, who started the newspaper, and who always either managed or edited (or both managed and edited) the newspaper. There was never any question about who controlled the policies of the newspaper for it was always the members of the Robinson family who were involved in the paper at any particular time. In 1968 J. Robinson edited the *Natal Mercury* and under his editorship the *Natal Mercury* for a period of time supported the National Party, the first and only English-language newspaper to do so.

The major portion of the shares in the East London *Daily Dispatch* were held by a charitable trust and the remaining 30·39 per cent of the shares in the controlling company were held by employees of the company, including in 1968, the editor Donald Woods. He believed that the financial structure of the newspaper greatly strengthened the hand of journalism and that having an interest in the newspaper's profits was an incentive to produce a better newspaper and in no way affected the content of the newspaper. If anything, the financial independence of the paper enabled the group to produce one of the most outspoken newspapers in the country. While there was some evidence that this was true the editor also stated that the first duty of a newspaper was to make a profit, for if it failed in this priority, it failed in all else. This combination of direct editorial involvement in profit seeking and the claims of a journalistic ethic led the *Daily Dispatch* to seek a wider African readership and to increase its coverage of non-White affairs.

Conclusion

The ownership of South African newspapers closely reflected the economic and political structure of the society. The English-language newspapers were generally financed with 'big business' English capital and closely co-operated with each other to protect their financial interests, ensuring that no competitors could survive. On the other hand the Afrikaans newspaper groups were owned by many small shareholders, drawn exclusively from the Afrikaans sector of the population, and were relatively much poorer than their English-language competitors. All newspaper proprietors belonged to the White group, including the proprietors of the growing non-White Press.

A distinguishing characteristic of the newspaper industry in South Africa was that two very different kinds of business were operated.

The largest sector of the Press, the English-language Press, was powerfully profit motivated, whilst the Afrikaans sector of the Press was run primarily to disseminate a political view, and was prepared to make few concessions to profit.

Critics of the English Presses' domination by mining interests have tended to ignore the internal organization of newspapers as a factor operating in favour of public service journalism and against the exclusive representation of mining interests. They have also tended to ignore the practicalities of newspaper production. Journalists rather than proprietors produce newspapers, and important decisions of policy are made daily by newspaper editors who in turn rely upon the journalists they employ to observe events. Newspapers in the mould of the English Press invariably acquired an existence independent of their promoters, especially when the concept of editorial independence was so highly valued.

In the Afrikaans newspaper too, the editor had a central role but his influence was determined primarily by his position within the structure of National Party politics. There was little if any conflict between the ownership and editorial sides of Afrikaans newspapers and in the case of *Die Burger* the tendency was to recruit editorial employees to the directorial boards.

Finally and most importantly it must be said that the internal restraints on the content of the Press deriving from its ownership, were, after 1948, of lesser importance than pressures from Government sources. Prior to 1948, in the days of John Martin and Reginald Holland, the profit ethic and the mining interests were almost certainly a more serious influence on the content of newspapers and the Presses' performance. For prior to 1948, a United Party Government, representing broadly the English interests and the mining interests, was in power, and it was those interests which the English Press supported. In the Nationalist Government the English Press and its promoters saw a Government which was hostile to the interests it had for so long respresented. In consequence the English-language Press became more rather than less watchful and demanded a greater accountability from the Government for an increasingly diverse range of interests.

4

Who Reads the Newspapers?

The answer to the question of who reads what newspapers contains within it an explanation of governmental attitudes to the Press: for government's reactions are a response to its beliefs about the impact of newspapers on their readers. The Government could prevent the reading of a particular newspaper by banning it, but it could not control the readership of existing and freely available newspapers. This had a peculiar significance in the South African context. For it meant that the Press was one of the few racially non-exclusive institutions in the society in that all racial and linguistic groups had access to it.[1] Newspapers were only directly accessible to the literate but many more people than actually see a newspaper acquire information about its contents.[2]

As was argued in the introduction to this study, accessibility was not in itself a measure of the Presses' relevance as a multi-racial institution in a rigidly racially structured society. The pertinence of the Press as a racially inclusive institution was dependent on the existence of two types of mass communication structures and the differences in the contents and readership of their newspapers.

This chapter is not concerned to answer questions about the effects of newspaper content on their audiences, and no attempt is made to discuss directly the connections between a newspaper's political attitudes and a reader's choice of newspaper. Nor is there any analysis of readership interest, that is, which parts of a newspaper are read by whom. Rather, an attempt is made to provide a substantiated explanation of governmental attitudes to the Press through a detailed analysis of the audiences themselves, answering questions about how many individuals of each race and language group read Government or Opposition newspapers, what trends in readership could be observed and what factors influenced newspaper readership.

[1] In the sense that all the mass media are owned and controlled by Whites, the newspapers are racially exclusive institutions, but in the sense that all racial groups have access to the Press as readers, they are non-exclusive.

[2] See, for example, E. Katz, 'The Two-Step Flow of Communication' in Wilbur Schramm (ed.) *Mass Communications* (Urbana: University of Illinois Press, 2nd Ed., 1960), p. 346 et seq.

Before discussing the information contained in two readership surveys in any detail, it is of value to stress a few general points about the South African Press and its readers. First, the English-language newspapers always maintained a numerical and circulation dominance over their Afrikaans-language competitors and evening newspapers had larger circulations than morning newspapers. There were, in 1968, thirteen English-language dailies compared to five Afrikaans-language dailies. The circulation figures for January–June 1968 show that whilst 2,151,000 people read an English-language daily, only 808,000 South Africans saw an Afrikaans daily. The average number of copies sold per day were 742,000 and 189,000 respectively.

The second important point is that only the English-language Press ever attracted readers from all racial and linguistic groups. The Afrikaans Press, as befitted its origins and general character had an almost exclusively White and predominantly Afrikaans-speaking

Table 3

Profile of White Daily Newspaper Readership by Province: 1968

(expressed as a % of newspapers' readers)

	Cape	Natal	Transvaal	OFS
ENGLISH DAILIES	%	%	%	%
Cape Argus	98·8	0·4	0·7	0·1
Cape Times	98·0	0·9	0·9	0·2
Daily News	1·9	95·9	2·1	0·1
E.L. Daily Despatch	96·8	1·0	2·1	0·1
Eastern Province Herald	98·1	0·5	1·2	0·2
Evening Post	96·3	1·0	2·5	0·2
Friend	3·4	0·5	5·7	90·4
Natal Mercury	1·9	97·1	1·0	—
Natal Witness	4·3	92·8	1·7	1·2
Pretoria News	0·8	0·4	98·6	0·2
Rand Daily Mail	1·3	1·6	93·9	3·2
Star	2·0	1·3	93·2	3·5
AFRIKAANS DAILIES				
Die Burger	95·9	0·9	2·5	0·7
Oosterlig	98·6	—	1·1	0·3
Transvaler	1·7	3·0	91·4	3·9
Vaderland	1·7	1·6	93·8	2·9
Volksblad	11·4	0·3	8·5	79·8

readership. Third, urban centres always tend to have a greater exposure to the mass media and the English-speaking group were urban dwellers and thus more prodigious newspaper readers than the Afrikaners.[1] The urban trek of the Afrikaners did not really get under way until the late 1940s and it was only by 1951 that a greater number of Afrikaners lived in the towns and cities than in the rural areas, and exceeded the number of English-speakers living in urban areas.

There is one factor of overriding importance in determining newspaper readership, and that is race. In a society so rigidly divided along racial lines, 'total readership' frequently is not a very meaningful term. Hence in discussing other determining factors, of age, sex, size of community, language and provincial distribution, the most useful approach is in most instances to treat each racial group separately.

Lastly, there is the 'provincial factor'. All daily newspapers in South Africa relied primarily on local rather than national readership. Some newspapers, including all four Johannesburg dailies, sold a small number of newspapers in all provinces, and the Orange Free State (OFS) Afrikaans newspaper, Die Volksblad, had a percentage of its readers in both the Cape and the Transvaal (Table 3). But with the exception of Die Volksblad, no daily newspaper drew less than 90 per cent of its readers from its own province.

In the following analyses, the distribution of the population by race and by province should be kept in mind and where particularly relevant, attention has been drawn to the variations. The Transvaal had

Table 4

Total Adult Population Distribution
by Province: 1962 and 1967

(expressed in '000s and to the nearest thousand)

Province		Cape		OFS		Transvaal		Total	
1962	1967	1962	1967	1962	1967	1962	1967	1962	1967
RACIAL GROUP	'000	'000	'000	'000	'000	'000	'000	'000	'000	'000
White	685	753	237	273	179	205	967	1,142	2,068	2,373
Coloured	728	860	25	28	15	18	62	76	830	982
Indian	11	11	213	251	—	—	38	45	262	307
African	1,673	1,885	1,264	1,422	628	708	2,848	3,266	6,413	7,281
Total	3,097	3,509	1,739	1,974	822	931	3,915	4,529	9,573	10,943

[1] See Daniel Lerner, 'Communication Systems and Social Systems' in Wilbur Schramm, op. cit., pp. 136–40.

Table 5

Daily Newspaper Readership Totals
by Province: 1962 and 1967

(expressed as a percentage of total adult population of each racial group in
each province)

Province	Cape		Natal		OFS		Transvaal		Total	
	1962	1967	1962	1967	1962	1967	1962	1967	1962	1967
RACIAL GROUP	%	%	%	%	%	%	%	%	%	%
White	74·6	75·0	81·1	83·1	68·8	60·4	74·3	70·4	74·8	72·5
Coloured	27·8	30·0	61·7	59·5	—	—	42·0	41·4	29·7	31·8
African	7·6	6·7	4·6	3·4	4·8	4·4	8·1	13·3	7·0	8·8
Indian	—	—	54·6	50·4	—	—	—	—	55·7	52·7

the largest adult population followed by the Cape, Natal and the
OFS (Table 4). The Africans were the largest group of the population
and constituted the largest percentage of the total provincial population in every province. The Whites were the second largest group of
the total population followed by the Coloureds and the smallest
group, the Indians. The Coloured and Indian population were concentrated in the Cape and Natal respectively. There were more
Coloureds in the Cape and nearly as many Indians in Natal as there
were Whites in those provinces. The largest number of Whites lived
in the Transvaal – nearly as many as lived in the other three provinces
taken together.

Natal and the Cape had the highest percentage of Whites reading
newspapers, as befits their early newspaper traditions and Natal,
with its predominantly English-speaking population had the greatest
percentage of White readers (Table 5). This situation was reversed in
the OFS which is an Afrikaans-speaking province with the lowest
percentage of its white population reading daily newspapers. The
highest percentage of African readership was in the Transvaal, where
there was the greatest concentration of urban Africans, whilst the
lowest African readership of daily newspapers occurred in Natal.

The Surveys: (a) Readership of Daily Newspapers

The first comprehensive survey on the reading patterns of all adult
South Africans (those over sixteen years of age) was carried out by
Market Research Africa (MRA). This was commission by the Newspaper Press Union (NPU), which represents the newspaper proprietors, and was published in 1963. The period of fieldwork for the

first survey was June–December 1962; a second survey, completed in 1968, was carried out between September 1967 and February 1968. This chapter will analyse extensively the results of the two surveys in relation to the daily and weekly Press.[1] As the surveys were commis-

Table 6
Reading Claims of Daily Newspapers: 1967

Newspapers	Cape Argus	Cape Times	Daily News	D. Fields Advertiser	Daily Dispatch	E. P. Herald	Evening Post	Friend	Natal Mercury
RACIAL GROUP									
WHITE									
No. of readers '000	204	187	166	19	57	85	69	40	166
No. of readers per copy	2·0	2·9	2·2	2·9	2·5	3·1	3·1	4·5	2·6
COLOUREDS									
No. of readers '000	169	133	18	14	\7	27	32	7	9
No. of readers per copy	1·6	2·1	0·2	2·1	0·3	1·0	1·4	0·8	0·1
INDIAN									
No. of readers '000	5	4	107	1	1	2	3	—	81
No. of readers per copy	—	0·1	1·4	0·2	—	0·1	0·1	—	1·2
AFRICAN									
No. of readers '000	36	29	36	15	44	15	29	15	15
No. of readers per copy	0·3	0·4	0·5	2·3	1·9	0·5	1·3	1·7	0·2
TOTAL									
No. of readers '000	414	353	327	49	109	129	133	62	271
No. of readers per copy	3·9	0·4	4·3	7·5	4·7	4·7	5·9	7·0	4·1

[1] South African newspapers do not normally disclose circulation figures but in recent years the *Financial Mail* has begun to publish some details of circulation.

sioned by the NPU and financed in part by NPU advertisers, the primary interest of the research was to collect material useful to advertisers: hence the focus on readership rather than circulation. Circulation figures are only of importance to newspaper proprietors who are concerned with the number of people who actually buy their newspapers. But for advertisers, students of the Press and an understanding of Government reactions to the Press, it is more important to know how many people actually see a newspaper and are exposed to its attitudes and influences.

At the same time it must be noted that circulation figures and readership do not necessarily have a direct relationship with each other. In South Africa publications reached racial groups other than those intended to make up their primary readership. Within the White group there was a one-way readership process with Afrikaans speakers reading English-language publications to a far greater extent than English speakers read Afrikaans publications.

In addition Afrikaans-language newspapers tended to have greater numbers of readers per copy than the English-language newspapers. This means that the differences between the circulation of English and Afrikaans-language newspapers were frequently greater than indicated by readership figures. To take one example, the *Rand Daily Mail*, although it sold three times as many copies as its morning competitor, *Die Transvaler,* had only a little more than twice as many readers.

Readership as defined by MRA was established on whether an informant had looked at a copy of the publication concerned 'yesterday', for dailies and 'during the past seven days' for Sunday papers. The standard categories of breakdown used by MRA were racial group, sex, age, size of community and home language, as earlier studies had suggested these to be the main factors controlling readership.

The surveys do not mention education as a factor affecting readership, but it is almost certainly of prime importance. There was in South Africa an extremely high correlation of those racial groups with the most advanced educational facilities and achievements with the highest readership percentages. Within the White group there were also marked differences in educational achievement between the English-and Afrikaans-speakers; in 1970 the percentage of English-speaking matriculantts was twice as high as that of Afrikaans-speaking matriculants. This was reflected in the greater reading of newspapers by English South Africans.

Only three adults in eleven saw a daily newspaper in 1968. Of these 72·5 per cent of the adult White population, 52·7 per cent of the

Indian group, 31·8 per cent of the Coloured population and only 8·8 per cent of the African population saw a daily newspaper. Predictably, illiteracy was highest amongst African adults – well over half the adult population was illiterate – followed by the Coloureds and finally the Indians, of whom only 19·0 per cent were said to be lliterate. White illiteracy was not measured by the survey.

Although there was a slight overall increase in readership of daily newspapers between 1962 and 1968, the results are somewhat misleading in that a 1·8 per cent increase in African readership, equalling 193,000 readers, hid the more important trends in reading habits. For the increase was restricted to African and Coloured readers while proportionate numbers of White and Indian readers declined by 2·3 per cent and 3 per cent respectively.

One of the most significant findings of the surveys was in fact that both the Afrikaans and English-language dailies were falling behind – the population growth and were failing to attract new White readers. While the actual White readership of dailies increased by nearly 300,000, the percentage of readers dropped from 74·8 per cent to 72·5 per cent of the potential White adult readership. And the Afrikaans Press suffered even more than the English Press, despite the fact that nearly two-thirds of the White population were Afrikaans-speaking. In 1962 34·0 per cent (703,000) of the White population saw an Afrikaans daily whilst in 1968 only 31·5 per cent (747,000) read an Afrikaans newspaper. The decline in the English Presses' White readership was much smaller: 53·7 per cent in 1962 compared to 53·3 per cent in 1968 (1,265,000 compared to 1,547,000 readers).

Within the White group the importance of the English-speakers' early newspaper traditions emerges. In 1967 only 15·2 per cent of the English-speaking population did not see a daily newspaper at all, compared to 36·3 per cent of the Afrikaans-speaking adult population. Furthermore, only 5·3 per cent of the English-speakers read an Afrikaans newspaper while 31·4 per cent of Afrikaans-speakers read an English daily. But then only 50·2 per cent of Afrikaans-speakers read an Afrikaans daily newspaper compared to 84·1 per cent of English speakers who saw an English-language newspaper.

In comparing these figures with those in 1962 it emerged that the greatest decline in daily newspaper readership had occurred amongst the Afrikaans-speaking readers of the Afrikaans-language newspapers. Whilst there was a 2·7 per cent decline in Afrikaans speakers reading Afrikaans newspapers, the English Press only lost 0·4 per cent of its Afrikaans-speaking readers. The effect of these variations meant that by 1968 only 18·8 per cent more Afrikaners saw an

Afrikaans-language Nationalist supporting daily, then saw an opposition English-language daily.

As the greater part of the White population was Afrikaans-speaking it was vital for the maintenance and growth of White readership, for most dailies to increase their percentage of Afrikaans readers. With the exception of one newspaper, the *Star,* every daily paper which maintained or increased its percentage of White readership also maintained or increased its Afrikaans-speaking readership. There were seven English-language dailies and two Afrikaans-language dailies which managed to do this. Of the remaining eight dailies which shared an overall decline in their White readerships, six failed to maintain or increase their Afrikaans-speaking readerships and the remaining two only just maintained their Afrikaans-speaking readerships.

All four Johannesburg dailies lost a percentage of their White Afrikaans-speaking readers and in the case of the *Rand Daily Mail* this was accompanied by a loss in the absolute number of Afrikaans-speaking readers. It is possible that the *Rand Daily Mail's* political attitudes affected its White readership profiles. But another factor must also be suggested: the *Rand Daily Mail* circulated quite heavily in Pretoria where the *Pretoria News* undoubtedly deprived the *Rand Daily Mail* of some of its readership. In addition, the Pretoria newspaper situation was in a state of flux as a new Afrikaans daily, *Hoofstad Nuus* was started there in 1967. Neither *Die Transvaler* nor *Die Vaderland* succeeded in maintaining their percentages of readers from the Afrikaans-speaking group, and in the case of *Die Transvaler* this was accompanied by a relative and absolute loss of its already very small English-speaking readership. And both Afrikaans dailies lost porportionately more Afrikaans-speaking readers than the *Star.*

Despite the fact that both a greater percentage and a larger absolute number of English-speaking South Africans read English-language newspapers, by 1968 Afrikaans-speakers constituted more than 30 per cent of the White readership of eight English-language dailies, compared to six in 1962. And two English-language newspapers had a majority of Afrikaans-speaking White readers. These two newspapers, the *Pretoria News* and the Bloemfontein *Friend*, both Argus-owned and situated respectively in the Administrative and Judicial capitals of South Africa, were located in predominantly Afrikaans-speaking towns. But whereas the *Pretoria News* increased its percentage of Afrikaans to English readers by 8 per cent (out-selling both *Die Vaderland* and *Die Transvaler* in Pretoria) and increased its total White readership, the *Friend* lost both a relative and absolute number of its Afrikaans-speaking readers. The *Friend's* loss of readership was a reflection of the overall decrease in the adult White readership of newspapers in the province as a whole. All newspapers circulating in the OFS lost a percentage of their potential readership, including *Die Volksblad,* which was the only newspaper circulating in the Province which managed to increase its absolute number of Afrikaans-speaking readers, although it too lost a percentage of Afrikaans-speaking readers.

The *Natal Witness* was the one newspaper to increase its percentage of Afrikaans-speaking readers more than the *Pretoria News,* with 22·6 per cent of the paper's readers being Afrikaans-speaking in 1962, increasing to 33·0 per cent in 1968. This is explained by the influx of Afrikaans-speaking people into Natal and particularly in and around the Pietermaritzburg area where the *Natal Witness* was published. The other two Natal newspapers, the *Natal Mercury* and the *Daily News,* still had the smallest percentage of Afrikaans to English readers of any dailies in the country, though no single Afrikaans newspaper had as high a percentage of English-speaking readers to Afrikaans-speaking readers.

Die Burger, with the highest percentage of English to Afrikaans-speaking readers of the Afrikaans daily newspapers, lost English readers between 1962 and 1968, and by 1968 only 7·7 per cent of its readers were English-speaking. *Die Vaderland* which increased its English-speaking readership, still only had 6.9 per cent of its readers as English-speaking.

Amongst non-Whites too a marked preference for English-language newspapers is revealed. Even the Coloured group, of whom 89 per cent were Afrikaans-speaking, displayed only a minor interest in Afrikaans newspapers. In the Cape, where the largest number of Coloureds was concentrated, the percentage of the adult Coloured population who read English-language newspapers was low but on the other hand Coloured readers constituted a very high percentage of both the *Cape Times'* and *Cape Argus'* total readership. In 1968 they accounted for 32·2 per cent of the readership of the *Cape Times* and 40·5 per cent of the *Cape Argus.* In Natal where most of the Indian community live, Indian readers constituted a substantial percentage of the readership of English-language dailies, though not as substantial as the Cape Coloured percentages. This was the case only because there are far fewer Indians in Natal than Coloureds in the Cape, for a greater percentage of the Indian group read daily newspapers than any other non-White group.

Despite the fact that as yet such a small percentage of the African population read a daily newspaper, some English-language newspapers drew a very high percentage of their total readership from the African population. The *Daily Dispatch*, which circulated in an area where there is a relatively small white population headed the list with a 40·3 per cent African readership. After a survey done for the paper in 1967 showed that the *Daily Dispatch* had virtually saturation cover of the White population in East London, the management of the paper decided deliberately to seek non-White readers in an effort to increase their total readership. The *Rand Daily Mail*, 29·5 per cent of whose readers were African (62.7 per cent White), also started trying to win new African readers. It employed an African editorial staff and began producing a 'Township Edition'. After the *Rand Daily Mail* came the *Evening Post* and *Star* with 21 per cent of their readers being African. While the *Evening Post* had an additional 24 per cent Coloured readership, the *Star's* White readers constituted 71·5 per cent of the paper's total readership.

By 1968, less than 50 per cent of the *Cape Argus'* total readership were White. This was due to a substantial increase in the number of Coloureds and Africans reading the newspaper, rather than the result of a decline in White readership. For in fact the paper increased its White readers but there are more Coloureds than Whites in the Cape and the Coloured population is growing considerably faster than the White population. Although the increase in the numbers of Africans reading the newspaper was extremely small when taken as a percentage of the total African population, the actual African readership of the *Cape Argus* more than doubled between 1962 and 1968. The only other newspaper with a smaller White readership than non-White readership, was the smallest of the Argus Group's newspapers, the *Diamond Fields Advertiser* in Kimberley. Once again increases in Coloured and African readership were partly responsible, but also the paper lost both a percentage and an absolute number of its small White readership.

A considerably smaller proportion of the readers of Afrikaans newspapers were non-White. *Die Burger* had the largest non-White readership, with the Coloureds constituting 12·0 per cent of its readers and no African or Indian readers. The percentages of *Die Transvaler's* and *Die Vaderland's* readers who were African were 2·5 per cent and 4·9 per cent respectively, with an even smaller Coloured readership and no Indian readers at all. The importance of multi-racial readership to the English-language Press was such that while six English-language dailies increased or maintained their White readership, nine achieved an overall growth in readership percentages as a result of non-White readership. The Afrikaans Press on the other hand had to rely exclusively on the growth of White readers, with the result that only one Afrikaans-language daily, *Die Oosterlig*, the smallest and least important of the Afrikaans dailies, succeeded in increasing its percentage readership of the total population.

In all racial groups men outnumbered women readers both numerically and in proportion to their numbers. In the White and Coloured groups there were more women than men in the total population whilst for the African and Indian groups, men outnumbered women in the population. Sex was least important as a factor affecting readership amongst the Coloureds; for both the Indian and African population groups, sex determined readership to a large extent. Of Indian men 64·4 per cent read a daily newspaper while only 40·4 per cent of Indian women read a daily paper. And amongst the African group, 13·6 per cent of the men saw a daily compared to 4·8 per cent of African women.

Only two newspapers, the *Daily Dispatch* and *Die Oosterlig* had more White women readers than male readers. The *Daily Dispatch* revealed several other unusual features. It has already been noted that a noticeably high percentage of the paper's readers were Africans. In addition, of that number, 41 per cent were women, a remarkably high percentage, especially compared for example to the *Rand Daily Mail* of whose total African readers 85·1 per cent were men. Several factors have to be taken into account: the actual readership of the *Daily Dispatch* was very substantially less than that of the *Rand Daily Mail*; second, there are proportionately more African women than men in the Cape (and Natal) whilst in the Transvaal there are more African men than women. A third feature is the sexual imbalance in the African population, resulting from a migratory labour policy which brought African men and not their wives and families to the cities. In 1962 28·7 per cent more African women than men lived in rural areas, and the *Daily Dispatch* had a sizeable rural distribution.

Finally there is the fact that a greater percentage of the female population (for all races) appeared to read afternoon rather than morning newspapers. As there was no afternoon newspaper in the East London area, the *Daily Dispatch* effectively got both morning and afternoon readers.

The MRA surveys divided the daily newspaper readership into four groups: 16–24 (Group A), 25–34 (Group B), 35–49 (Group C) and 50+ (Group D). There was little consistency between the 1962 and 1968 overall White readership figures according to age, but the comparative figures do reveal an increase in daily newspaper readership in Group A–the youngest group of adult readers–while there was a decline in percentage readership for all other age groups. The increase in Group A, the second smallest sector of the White adult population, appears to be due entirely to an increase in the youngest group's readership of English-language newspapers. In other words the English-language newspapers managed to attract new young readers while the Afrikaans newspapers failed to do so, although the Afrikaans population was growing faster than the English population. The East London and Port Elizabeth English-language newspapers and the *Rand Daily Mail* were the only English-language newspapers to show a decline in their youngest White readership, while the only Afrikaans daily to increase its young White readership was the OFS paper, *Die Volksblad.*

The readership of both English and Afrikaans-language newspapers shared a decline in Groups B and C while the readership by Group D of English-language newspapers increased slightly. As Group D was the largest sector of the White population the maintenance of traditional readers was of greater importance within the White group than in any other racial group. White readership profiles according to age also reveal that a greater percentage of Groups A, B and C than of Group D saw an Afrikaans-language daily, whereas there were no very marked differences between the percentages of any age group reading the English-language newspapers.

For all three non-White sectors of the population, the oldest and smallest group had the smallest percentage of readers. African readership of dailies increased in all age groups between 1962 and 1968. This was largely due to an increase in the readership of the Argus controlled 'African' newspaper, the *World* which became a daily between 1962 and 1968. More Africans continued to see English-language dailies than the English-language *World*. The increase of readership was at its greatest in the group of greatest percentage readership, namely Group B. The greatest absolute numbers of readers also came from Group B, despite the fact that the largest sector of the adult African population was Group A.

The distribution of the Coloured population according to age was quite different from that of the White group but similar to that of the African group. The largest group was the youngest, with a gradual decline in the population as it grew older, since the population was growing more rapidly and dying younger than the White group. Thus, while there was a percentage growth in readership in Groups B, C and D, and a decline in Group A, Group A had the largest absolute number of readers. Growth of Coloured readership was restricted to the English-language Press. *Die Burger,* the only Afrikaans newspaper with a sizeable Coloured readership, revealed a decrease in readership in all age groups. It is likely that the less sympathetic attitudes of *Die Burger* to the Coloureds accounts for the loss of Coloured readership in the older groups and the failure to attract new young readers. As will be discussed in a later chapter. *Die Burger* once provided a sympathetic voice within the Nationalist group for the Coloured people but was defeated in 1961 in its attempt to get a 'better deal' for the Coloureds.

The Indian population distribution by age was much the same as the Coloured population. But while Coloured readership in all but the youngest group grew, Indian readership grew only in the youngest group, with a decline in all other age groups. The factor which probably had most to do with the decline in readership in Groups B, C and D amongst the Indians is the Group Areas Act. The implementation of the Act removed the Indian population from urban centres although they still lived in the urban area. Of all the non-White groups, the Natal Indians were the most integrated into the industrial and commercial life of the province and removal from the urban centres might well account for the loss of interest, amongst the older groups, in English daily newspapers. But the fact that the youngest group was increasingly reading a daily newspaper makes it likely that Indian daily Press readership will grow in the future.

More revealing than age as a factor affecting readership, was the size of community in which people lived. The surveys took into account four types of community: *cities* were defined as urban centres with 20,000 or more Whites; *towns* as centres with 2,000 to 19,999 Whites; *villages* as centres with under 2,000 Whites; and *rural areas* as consisting largely of the farming community. The contrast between rural South Africa and the large cities was very great. More of the total South African population lived in rural areas than in any other type of community. On the other hand the rural areas grew least, in both absolute and relative terms, with the exception of the village, whose population seriously declined between 1962 and 1968. Populations in two of the four types of areas grew quite considerably with the largest growth being recorded in the towns. Thus where percentage readership in the towns fell this was frequently accompanied by a marked increase in absolute readership while in the villages where percentage readership rose–as it did for the Indian and African groups–there was an absolute decrease in readers.

The general decline in White readership was consequent upon a serious decline in daily newspaper readership in all but the city, where readership of daily newspapers rose. The percentage increase of the White city readers was the smallest of all racial groups although the

Whites were still the biggest readers of daily papers in the city. Both the Coloured and African groups increased their city readership quite considerably, while Indian city readership declined.

Seven English-language newspapers drew more than 80 per cent of their White readers from the city, a further four, more than 70 per cent and the remaining two, the *Daily Dispatch* and the *Natal Witness* had 58·1 per cent and 62·3 per cent of their White readers living in the city. The Afrikaans-language Press, on the other hand, had a markedly different profile, reflecting the rural origins of the Afrikaner and the fact that in many respects the Afrikaans Press failed to urbanize and sophisticate the content of their newspapers. For *Die Vaderland*, the Afrikaans daily with the highest percentage of its readers in the city, less than 70 per cent of its readers resided in a city whilst *Die Burger* drew only 37·5 per cent of its readers from the city. Most significantly the Afrikaans Press lost a substantial percentage of city readership: in 1962, 39·2 per cent of the White population residing in a city read an Afrikaans daily, whilst in 1968 only 28·4 per cent did. Only one Afrikaans newspaper, *Die Oosterlig*, succeeded in increasing its very small percentage of white city readership.

The historical dominance of the English-language Press in the cities perhaps makes it less remarkable that the Afrikaans Press was unable to make much headway in winning new city readership. But in the fast-growing towns, populated by newcomers from the rural and village areas, the Afrikaans Press should have had a considerable advantage. However, it emerges that between 1962 and 1968 the Afrikaans Press lost a significant percentage of its town readers as did the English Press. But where the English Press lost 2·1 per cent the Afrikaans dailies lost 4·9 per cent of their town readership. The most notable failures of the Afrikaans Press were in the Cape and the Transvaal, the two dominant provinces. In the Cape, *Die Burger* lost a percentage of its town readership, whilst the *Cape Argus* increased its percentage. *Die Burger* still retained the largest town readership of any daily newspaper and increased its absolute town readership, but the fact that the *Cape Argus* increased its percentage of town (and city) readership lessens *Die Burger's* readership achievement in the town. In the Transvaal the *Star* substantially increased its percentage of White town readers, giving it very nearly as many as *Die Transvaler* and *Die Vaderland* which both lost a percentage of their town readers. The only Afrikaans-language newspaper to increase its percentage of White readers living in the town, was *Die Volksblad*, which lost readers in all other communities.

A greater percentage of the White population outside of the city saw an Afrikaans daily than saw an English daily but the differences were relatively small, and between 1962 and 1968 they became even smaller in the town and the village. It was in the rural areas, populated almost exclusively by Afrikaners that the Afrikaans-language dailies dominated. At the same time only 34·1 per cent of the second smallest (and declining) White population group read an Afrikaans daily compared to 20·1 per cent who read an English-language daily. And in the five years under observation, the rural and village readerships of both Afrikaans and English-language newspapers declined substantially.

Although the English-language newspapers suffered the sharpest decline in rural readership this was far less significant for the English Press than for the Afrikaans Press, whose rural readers comprised a higher percentage of total readership than any of the English newspapers. And the fact that the Afrikaans newspapers depended almost entirely on White readership increases the seriousness of these changes.

All English-language newspapers which were read by Coloureds increased their Coloured readership in the city and the *Cape Argus,* with an increase of 6·7 per cent of the Coloured city readership, increased its absolute Coloured readership by 51 per cent. *Die Burger* lost Coloured readers in the city but increased its Coloured readership in the town, although both the *Cape Argus* and the *Cape Times* had a bigger Coloured town readership.

The *Rand Daily Mail* increased its share of the African city readership by 1·3 per cent, between 1962 and 1968 and increased its actual number of African city readers by nearly 50 per cent. The *Star* lost African readership in all sizes of communities except for its small rural African readership. And the *Star* with the East London *Daily Dispatch* had the largest African rural readership. In Natal, all English-language dailies lost a percentage of Indian readers in the city, where the majority of Indians live.

As is evident size of community is an important factor affecting newspaper readership in South Africa. For all racial groups the greatest number of newspaper readers were concentrated in the city and readership declined as the community got smaller. Only three newspapers which failed to increase their White readership in the city were able either to maintain or increase their percentage of readers. In every size of community three papers, the *Diamond Fields Advertiser,* the East London *Daily Dispatch* and the *Rand Daily Mail* failed to increase or maintain their percentage of White readers, but succeeded in increasing or maintaining their Coloured, Indian or African readers. Of the nine dailies which succeeded in increasing their White city readership, seven showed an overall increase or maintenance of readership percentages of the total adult population. The two exceptions to the rule, that the paper which succeeds in the city, succeeds, were the *Natal Mercury* and somewhat surprisingly the *Star*. The *Natal Mercury* failed to maintain its share of readers for three reasons: it lost readers in all other communities than the city, it lost a percentage of its Indian readers; and it also failed to attract new readers from the very large African population in Natal. The *Star* which increased its White readership more than any other newspaper in the country, and increased its city and town readership very considerably, failed to maintain both its absolute and relative numbers of African readers. This factor accounted for the overall percentage decline in readership of the *Star*.

In a sense the Afrikaans newspapers were more vulnerable than English-language newspapers to size of community as a single factor affecting readership. Because most English-language newspapers had a sizeable number of readers drawn from more than one racial group, fluctuations in racial readership could have a considerable effect on readership. Afrikaans newspapers on the other hand relied to a greater extent on extra-city readership, and almost totally on a single race for readership increases. The only Afrikaans newspaper to increase its city and overall readership, was *Die Oosterlig*. Because of the Afrikaans Presses' greater dependence on rural and village readership, the papers were more vulnerable to the desertion of rural and village areas by the White group particularly, and what appeared to be a general decrease in the numbers of people who read newspapers in the rural areas. The problem for the Afrikaans dailies in the future is that those rural dwellers who move to the city or town where the greatest number of potential readers are concentrated, might be converted to 'city ways'. In other words, they or their children are, according to the trends shown in the surveys, likely to read English rather than Afrikaans-language newspapers.

The Surveys: (b) The Sunday Press

Between 1962, when the first survey was completed, and 1968, there were major changes in the Sunday newspaper field, and the effects of these changes were still being felt. The merger of Afrikaanse Pers and Dagbreek Pers in 1962 resulted in the demise of *Die Vaderland's* short-lived Sunday paper venture, *Sondagblad,* leaving *Dagbreek* as the only major Nationalist Sunday paper, until 1965. The coming of *Die Beeld* in that year brought about major changes, not only in the balance of provincial politics, but in the whole Sunday newspaper industry. From the outset *Die Beeld* was conceived of as a national (rather than provincial) Sunday newspaper and was published simultaneously in the Transvaal, Cape and OFS, with its headquarters in the Transvaal. The national approach of *Die Beeld* speeded up the attempts by other Sunday newspapers to sell throughout the country.

The *Sunday Times* led the *Sunday Express* in air-freighting copies of their papers to the Cape and Natal, followed shortly afterwards by the setting up of provincial printing presses in the Cape and later in Natal. In response to *Die Beeld's* successful invasion of the Transvaal, *Dagbreek* moved into the Cape area, breaking a long-standing agreement between South African newspapers not to encroach on each others circulation areas. And for the first time in modern South African newspaper history, a truly competitive situation existed in the Sunday field.

The most immediate consequence of this development was a sharp decline in the readership of weekend editions of the daily Press in the Cape, and *Die Volksblad* in the OFS. Durban's Argus-owned *Sunday Tribune* also lost White readers in competition with the national Transvaal-based, Sunday newspapers. But the total readership of all four Sunday newspapers which existed in 1962 increased by 1968, whilst within two years of its creation *Die Beeld* had acquired a readership equal to that of *Dagbreek's*.

These fluctuations in the Sunday Press make it difficult to observe trends, although comparative readership profiles already revealed some interesting new features of weekly Press readership.

A much greater percentage of the adult population saw weekly newspapers than daily newspapers. This was true for all racial groups although as might be expected the inter-racial ratios did not vary very much. The most significant differences between daily and Sunday reading habits are to be found within the White group, where the gap between the numbers of English and Afrikaans-speaking readers narrows quite considerably. Whereas 27·5 per cent of the White population did not see a daily only 11·0 per cent did not see a Sunday newspaper.[1] The greater readership amongst the White group was primarily due to the greater numbers of Afrikaans-speakers reading weekly newspapers, for 24·5 per cent more Afrikaners saw a weekly than saw a daily newspaper.[1] Perhaps the most interesting feature of the post-*Beeld* newspaper profiles, was the greater polarization of White Sunday paper readers according to the language group to

---

[1] These percentages include the readers of week-end editions of dailies as well as a few newspapers not discussed in the tables.

which they belonged. Both the *Sunday Times* and the *Sunday Express* lost a percentage of their Afrikaans-speaking readers, resulting in the *Sunday Express'* showing an overall loss of White readership, whilst *Dagbreek* increased its White Afrikaans-speaking readership by more than 200,000. Both the *Sunday Times* and the *Sunday Express* revealed a marked increase in their English-speaking readers and in the case of the *Sunday Times,* there was a growth of 171,000.

Thus whilst in the daily Press the biggest decline in readership was in the percentage of Afrikaners reading Afrikaans-language newspapers, in the Sunday Press there was a decline in the percentage of Afrikaans-speakers reading English-language newspapers,[1] and in the case of the *Sunday Tribune* the paper failed to maintain its percentage of English-speaking readers. These variations were reflected in the percentages of individual newspapers' own readerships according to the language group of their readers. Thus whilst in 1962, 38·1 per cent of the *Sunday Times'* White readers were Afrikaans-speaking, only 34·3 per cent were in 1968. But as was true of the daily Press, every English-language weekly had a substantially higher proportion of readers from the alternate language group than the Afrikaans Press had. By 1968, *Die Beeld* had a small percentage more English-speaking readers than *Dagbreek* and more than any daily newspaper, but even then only 7·2 per cent of *Die Beeld's* readers were English-speaking.

The most important feature then of the greater readership of weeklies by Afrikaners was that they tended to read Afrikaans rather than English-language weeklies, although more Afrikaners saw English-language weeklies than saw English-language dailies.

The differences in provincial reading habits of the Whites in evidence in the daily readership profiles, are markedly less important in the weekly profiles. Natal maintained its very high White readership with 91·4 per cent of the adult population reading a weekly. But the OFS, the province with the lowest percentage of daily (and Sunday) newspaper readers, had an 87·1 per cent Sunday newspaper readership. The greater inter-provincial distribution of the major Sunday papers increased the importance of the province as a factor determining

---

[1] If the readership of weekend editions and other minor newspapers are included, the polarization effect is further confirmed. For whilst in 1962, 20·3 per cent of English-speakers saw an Afrikaans-language weekly, in 1968, only 14·0 per cent did so. In 1962 43·3 per cent of Afrikaans-speakers saw an English-language weekly, whilst in 1968 only 37·3 per cent saw an English newspaper. But where Afrikaans-speaking readers of Afrikaans weeklies increased, English-speaking readers of English-language newspapers declined.

readership. All four Johannesburg-based weeklies drew the greatest percentage of their readers from the Transvaal. *Die Beeld's* provincial readership profile reflects the paper's origins as a Cape-backed as well as a national newspaper. *Die Beeld* had a greater White readership in the Cape and in the OFS than any other newspaper. The success of *Die Beeld* in the OFS was probably due to the fact that Nasionale Pers already had a daily newspaper there, *Die Volksblad*, as well as to the fact that *Die Beeld* actually published in the province. *Dagbreek* still dominated *Die Beeld* in the Transvaal (and in Natal) as was to be expected, and succeeded in increasing its percentage readership in all other provinces. The *Sunday Times,* which in 1968 was read by 45·8 per cent of the White population (and 16·0 per cent of the total population), was read by a substantial percentage of the White population in all provinces, although the paper lost a large percentage of readers in the OFS and a small percentage in the Transvaal. The paper compensated for this loss of readership by nearly doubling its absolute White readership in the Cape, the second largest province.

Size of community remains an important factor in determining White readership of Sunday newspapers though the differences between readership percentages of one size of community and another are very much less marked. On closer examination it emerges that there was greater consistency in the daily and weekly readership profiles of English-language newspapers by size of community than there was of the Afrikaans-language newspapers. To take the most extreme example, 38·5 per cent of the White town population saw an Afrikaans daily whilst 71·0 per cent saw an Afrikaans-language Sunday newspaper. Whereas 34·9 per cent of the white town population saw an English daily compared with 48·1 per cent who read an English Sunday newspaper. This is consistent with the extra-city concentration of Afrikaans speakers who read weekly rather than daily newspapers.

As a percentage of its own White readership, *Die Beeld* had the smallest city concentration of readers of any of the Sunday newspapers. But *Die Beeld* captured a larger percentage of readers from all non-city communities than any of the older Sunday newspapers, with more than 40 per cent of the White communities living in towns, villages and the rural areas, reading the paper.

As in the case of the daily Press, the weekly Press picture changed when introducing multi-racial readership figures. For whilst only one English-language Sunday paper, the *Sunday Times,* managed to increase its percentage of White readers, all three major English-language Sundays increased their overall percentages of readers in the population as a whole. In other respects non-White readership patterns of the Sunday Press did not vary greatly from those of the daily Press, except that as was true of the White sector, more non-Whites read weekly than daily newspapers.

All Sunday newspapers increased their non-White readerships; notably, the *Sunday Times* increased its Coloured readership from 10·1 per cent in 1962 to 15·1 per cent of the total Coloured population in 1968. *Dagbreek* also increased its small Coloured readership although once again *Die Beeld* had acquired a larger Coloured readership than *Dagbreek* by 1968. The *Sunday Tribune* managed to retain a larger percentage of Indian readers than any of the competing Transvaal Sundays, with 51·6 per cent of the Indian population reading the paper. All newspapers increased their African readerships and most particularly the *Sunday Times*.

The most important features about the reading habits of the South African population can now be summarized. Newspaper readership profiles reflect the racial and linguistic divisions in the society. The extent of readership of the daily and weekly Press is a reflection of the hierarchical racial structure with the highest percentage of readers in the White group followed by the Indians, Coloureds and Africans. Within the White group, the daily newspaper reading traditions of the primarily urban English speakers are reflected in their high readership percentages. The rural origin of the Afrikaner is indicated by the lesser interest shown in daily newspapers, and in the appeal of Afrikaans-language newspapers in the rural areas.

Both the English and the Afrikaans-language daily Press failed to maintain their percentages of White readers, with the greatest decline in the Afrikaans-speaking readership of Afrikaans-language dailies. The most notable failure of the Afrikaans daily Press was its inability to attract a greater percentage of city and town readers. In other words the Afrikaans Press failed to keep pace with the overall growth in the numbers of Afrikaans speakers living in the cities and towns and the Afrikaans-language dailies lost a greater percentage of their Afrikaans readers than did the English-language Press between 1962 and 1968. This revealed that once in the city there was a tendency for the Afrikaner to read a more sophisticated English-language daily newspaper rather than an Afrikaans daily.

Furthermore the Afrikaans-language newspapers relied almost exclusively on White Afrikaners for their readership. Of those Afrikaners who read a daily, only 18·8 per cent more saw an Afrikaans rather than an English-language daily. Thus whilst 1,265,000 of the White population saw an English-language opposition daily, only 747,000 saw a Government supporting Afrikaans-language daily.

In the Sunday Press field important changes were taking place with a substantially increasing readership of Afrikaans Sunday papers by Afrikaners at the expense of their readership of English-language Sunday newspapers. Even the *Sunday Times*, which had a larger number of Afrikaans-speaking readers than any one of the Afrikaans-language dailies, lost a percentage of its Afrikaans-speaking readers. Still, more Afrikaans-speakers read English-language weeklies than English-language dailies whilst the numbers of English-speakers who saw Afrikaans weeklies was not significantly greater than the numbers who saw Afrikaans dailies.

For all other racial groups there was a very marked tendency to read English rather than Afrikaans-language dailies and weeklies. Although the percentage of Africans who read newspapers was small, the fact that Africans are the largest group in the population means that non-White readers sometimes constituted a high percentage of the total readership of individual newspapers. By 1968 the White readers of the third largest daily in South Africa, the *Cape Argus,* constituted less than 50 per cent of the paper's readers. The non-White readership percentages of English-language dailies is likely to become very much more important in the future than it has been in the past. With the advent of television, newspapers will be faced with serious competition as channels of advertising display. The fact that newspapers rely so heavily on advertising for their viability, will force the English-language Press to win advertising by finding a substantial number of new readers. The obvious readership growth area is the African. It seems certain that for these reasons (even if no others) the English-language Press will show an increasing interest in enlarging their African readerships and in competing seriously with the newly emergent Press directed specifically to the African market.

It is possible too that the Afrikaans-language Press will make a concerted effort to win more Afrikaans-speaking readers by emulating the Sunday Press experiment. It seems inevitable that Nasionale Pers will start a new Afrikaans daily in the Transvaal, which would further increase the importance of the Afrikaans Press in the structure of Nationalist politics.

The importance of the English Presses' appeal in the first instance to the Afrikaner and in the second instance the African, has already had serious repercussions for the Press, as the following chapter will show. If more Africans read the English Press it seems likely that they would make increasing demands on it, to increase attention to the African and his interests. The problem for the Press is that while Government cannot control newspaper readership, it can restrict the Presses' content. Bearing the readership profiles in mind (and the probable prognostications for the future), the following chapter on Government pressures on the Press, can it is hoped be better understood.

5

Suppression of Opposition: Restraints on the Press

The style and content of a newspaper is a product and compromise of frequently competing forces. Perhaps the single most important factor influencing the political content of newspapers in South Africa was that of governmental restraints. That this was so is significant, for it is indicative of an attitude which was essentially opposed to the existence of an independently critical Press.

To a greater or lesser degree governments everywhere have attempted to impose some restrictions on the contents of newspapers. In the liberal–democratic theory of the Press it is believed that there is a 'natural' conflict between government with its demands for secrecy and the Press with its dependence on exposure.[1] This means that the degree of the Presses' freedom to act as watchdog or as opposition force within the society is determined by the political values of the society itself. In other words, the extent to which opposition or criticism is expected or tolerated will finally determine how far the Press may go in its criticism of government or the society. Though as the Press is itself in a position to influence political values (if it so chooses) it can help extend the boundaries of what is permissable.

In South Africa, Government's attitudes to the Press and particularly the opposition Press, resulted in the emergence of a complex variety of direct and indirect pressures which had the intention of regulating the political content of newspapers. Between 1948 and 1968, these pressures have most notably included the setting up of a Press Commission of Inquiry, the creation of a Press Code of Conduct and pressures based on a very extensive body of laws. Indirectly

[1] See, for example, W. E. Hocking, *Freedom of the Press* (Chicago: The University of Chicago Press, 1957); Frede Castberg, *Freedom of Speech in the West* (London: George Allen & Unwin Ltd., 1960); Wickham Steed, *The Press* (Harmondsworth: Penguin Books Ltd., 1938); Francis Williams, *The Right to Know* (London: Longman Green & Co., 1969) and Z. Chafee, *Government and Mass Communication* (Chicago: The University of Chicago Press, 1947).

Government also applied pressure on the independent Press through a highly discriminatory information-policy, which denied one section of the Press (in this case the major section) access to political or official information.

In the Nationalist Government's 'campaign' against the independent Press, the Government had two primary objectives: first, it sought to safeguard its political principles; and second, to ensure its own continuation in office. Government came to see the apartheid ideology not merely as the policy of a political party which chanced to be in office, but as a fundamental 'truth' against which only the blasphemous spoke. The importance of this for the Press was the growing tendency to identify all opposition to apartheid with subversion and criticism of its defenders with treason.

Thus in seeking to secure itself in office and to eliminate all serious opposition to its apartheid ideology, the Nationalist Government abrogated to itself very extensive powers. There can be little argument that in twenty years the Government had provided itself with the machinery to limit the freedom of its institutional or individual opponents. This chapter will look at how the Government used its very extensive powers and with what consequences for the Press.

The Press Commission

The setting up of the Press Commission just two years after coming to power, revealed the Nationalists' concern with the Press, particularly the English-language Press. Their unease was reflected both in the Commission's terms of reference and during the Parliamentary debates of 1950, following the original motion early in the year.

The motion as proposed by Dr A. J. van Rhijn[1] read:

> 'That whereas this House is of the opinion that a free Press is essential to a free democratic society, and whereas it is convinced that a self-disciplined freedom ultimately constitutes the best safeguard for the maintenance of the freedom of the Press, and that all activities and tendencies to undermine and abuse such freedom which exist or are taking root in this country should therefore be combatted, it accordingly requests the government to consider the advisability of appointing a Commission....'

Thus from the outset two important facts emerged: first, that a free Press was acclaimed as desirable, despite the self-disciplinary rider; and second, that the Commission started from the assumption that this freedom was being abused.

[1] Hansard, Vol. 70, Col. 414, January 1, 1950.

The Commission was to inquire and recommend on three main issues, and was to be in three corresponding parts. The first part was to deal with control of the Press–to provide details of the Presses' ownership, its news agencies, publishers and distributors and to inquire into the existence of monopolistic tendencies and their influence on the Press. Part two was to deal with the activities of stringers and correspondents for newspapers and news agencies abroad and part three with the South African newspapers themselves, dealing with their degree of responsibility, accuracy and their sense of patriotism.

The three parts of the Commission reflected firstly Nationalist concern with the greater financial success and resources of the English-language Press compared with their own Afrikaans newspapers, and their attachment to big business and the mining industry. The second part reflected Nationalist disquiet about South Africa's (and the Afrikaners') image abroad, for which they held the English-language Press responsible, while part three paralleled Nationalist fears about the internal influence of the English Press and the effects of newspaper content on both the Afrikaner and the African.

The terms of the Commission's references made it clear from the start that there was no question of the Commission taking a dispassionate or non-partisan look at the South African Press, as indeed its methods of investigation and its eventual findings confirmed.

The Commission, which was appointed in January 1951 and met for the first time later that month, consisted of seven members, of whom only the chairman, Mr Justice J. W. van Zyl, a judge of the Cape Supreme Court, and Professor L. I. Coertzee, a Nationalist M P were still Commissioners when the final report appeared in 1964. And when the fourteen years were up, the Commission had only dealt with the first two parts of its inquiry, the third part, on the South African Press, being abandoned.

The Commission began by sending a questionnaire to editors of all South African newspapers, containing seventy questions of great complexity, each question elaborately subdivided. The Commission also impounded copies of all cables, including service messages, filed over a number of years by correspondents whom it wished to interrogate. Before the Commission began hearing witnesses, every journalist was required to fill in a form giving details of his birthplace, education, experience and knowledge of the two official languages. Questionnaires were also sent to SAPA, the CNA, NPU, printing unions and other interested parties.

The Commission set about collecting and sifting tens of thousands of Press clippings sent outside South Africa and classifying them from 'good' to 'very bad'. It acquired from the State Information Service 35,000 foreign Press cuttings on South Africa. For six months the Postmaster-General supplied copies of all Press messages handled by his department. All Press cables from May 1950 to July 1955 were classified and read and the major urban newspapers from 1946 to 1954 were studied in detail. Foreign correspondents were required to submit files of any manuscripts, documents or articles sent through the post. Newspaper proprietors were required to submit answers to a questionnaire giving details on finance and circulation.

The Commission, held *in camera*, started taking oral evidence in 1955 and many months were spent in questioning prominent South African journalists. English-speaking journalists were taxed about their ability to read, speak and understand Afrikaans, examined on their answers to the questionnaires and called on to explain why they had written or published certain news reports or leading articles.

For many years the Commission's work was obscured from the view of both the Press and the public. Responsibility for its control was switched from one Government department to another, and every year brought promises from the responsible Minister about the costs and the expected completion date. As early as June 1953, it was forecast that it would have completed its work by mid-1954. In June 1957, a spokesman for the Department of External Affairs (under which the Commission fell for a while) said that the report was expected to be in the hands of the printers by December of that year. Later forecasts proved similarly incorrect.[1]

Numerous disconcerting reports from English-language journalists about methods used by the Commission resulted in the International Press Institute Executive Board–consisting of leading editors from fifteen countries–appointing a special investigator to conduct an inquiry into the Commission in 1956. During the investigation evidence was taken from South African editors and reporters, stringers representing foreign publications in South Africa and foreign correspondents. All witnesses said they had been confronted with a selection of 'damaging' cables and cuttings and a carefully prepared case had been made out against them. There was no means of knowing in advance which cables and cuttings the witness would be questioned about and he was often required to defend stories he had filed years previously and scarcely remembered. One witness arrived before the Commission with a complete file of cuttings designed to refresh his memory about almost any document with which he might

[1] See IPI Report, July 1964.

be confronted. But as soon as the Commission realized his intention, the brief case and its contents were impounded.[1]

As most of the evidence gathered during 1956 came from English-speaking witnesses, the IPI, of which only English language news-papers were members, sent a short questionnaire to the editors of all Afrikaans newspapers in August 1957, in an attempt to gauge their views on the Commission and to know how they had fared as wit-nesses. *Die Transvaler* immediately published the IPI letter, exposing the existence of the Survey, and issued a patriotic appeal to Afrikaner editors not to co-operate with the Institute. Nor did they. No single Afrikaans editor completed the questionnaire and in their letters of reply to the Institute they pointed out that the Commission was a domestic affair and that previous activities of the Institute had been closely observed by Afrikaans newspapers. *Die Transvaler* forwarded the correspondence it had held with the IPI to the Commission.

What emerged from the IPI inquiry was confirmation that the Commissioners were hostile to English-language journalists, whilst the response of the Afrikaans Press in expressing their solidarity with the Commission, the Government and with South Africa, confirmed the political nature of the Inquiry.

The first report of the Commission, dealing with organizational, technical and financial aspects of the South African Press was pub-lished in April 1962. It achieved very little of what it had set out to do. In the first place eleven years had elapsed since the Commission had started its investigations, a fact emphasized by the Report itself, and the financial structures, shareholdings and inter-newspaper ties had, in some cases, changed considerably during the decade. Its con-clusions after such extensive and intensive research were remarkable only to the extent that they stated the obvious–the Commission saw the South African Press dominated by three groups (Argus, SAAN and Nasionale Pers) and found monopolistic practices in the CNA.

The South African Press Association (SAPA) particularly came in for a great deal of criticism. The Commission's complaints centred around the inadequacy of the Afrikaans Presses' representation on SAPA. The Report claimed the the English-language newspapers together controlled 87·4 per cent of the votes–and a minimum of 75 per cent were necessary to pass a motion. Moreover, singly or in combinations, elements of the English Press could muster the 25 per cent-plus needed to block any change. The 1962 Report recommended

[1] IPI files (Zurich) on the investigation of the Commission.

THE PRESS AS OPPOSITION

that unless the Afrikaans Press were given more representation on SAPA, the Association's licence should be revoked.[1]

In the second report, published in May 1964, the Commission concentrated on the activities of 'stringers', resident and visiting full-time staff members of foreign newspapers and the news dispatched to foreign news agencies from South Africa. Further, the Report concentrated almost exclusively on news of a political or racial nature, taking the periods May 1950–July 1955 and adding to it the period February to April 1960, the period when Sharpeville, Macmillan's visit and the attempted assassination of Verwoerd caused news to flood out of South Africa as seldom before.

Its 1964 conclusions were not much more revealing than those in 1962. The Commission found that news sent abroad condemned the South African Government's policies, that it was sent by anti-Nationalist journalists and that it rarely quoted Government justifications for its actions. The Commission's standards of judgment were central to the Report and its conclusions. It categorized reporting as 'good', 'faulty', 'bad' and 'very bad'.[2] In an attempt to justify its highly emotive categories, the Commission 'quantified' the information and produced conclusions such as: 9·4 per cent of material sent to the British Press was 'good', 14·6 per cent faulty, and 75 per cent was bad or very bad, while precisely 75·95 per cent of the 1,665,214 words cabled to the British Press in the period under review was such that it gave a distorted picture of the South African racial and political scene.

In addition the Commission found that the reports failed to tell of the successful manner in which all race and language groups in South Africa had adjusted themselves, 'so as to live to a remarkable extent, in peace and harmony with one another', The reporting deliberately concealed the 'barbarity or semi-civilized nature of the Native. The cannibalistic and barbaric acts of violence that are from time to time perpetuated by the Natives are not reported or if reported, are represented as having resulted from the frustration occasioned by the

[1] See *News/Check*, Vol. 2, No. 23, May 27, 1964, for a summary of the 1962 findings.

[2] The Commission defined its categories as follows: *Good* when reporting and comment is fair and factual and the selection is reasonably representative of all points of view. *Faulty* when the reporting is in some respects not sufficiently fair, factual and the selection not sufficiently representative nor the comment sufficiently justifiable. *Bad* when reporting is unfair and tendentious, the selection tendentious and partisan for one or more groups or interests, comment over-partisan. *Very bad* when the reporting is either blindly partisan or unscrupulously tendentious, the selection is so prejudiced and or unscrupulous as to distort the South African political and racial scene.

106

supposedly unjust, harsh and oppressive treatment meted out to the Natives by the Whites'.

These breathtakingly distorted views about the non-Whites again confirmed the political bias of the Commissioners who were, as a part of their mandate, required to look into the objectivity of the Press in its reporting. Thus neither the Commission's findings nor its recommendations came as any surprise.

The main recommendation to emerge from the Commission was for the setting up of a statutory Press Council, for, the Commission said the Newspaper Press Union's Board of Reference did not satisfy the fundamental requirements of a body designed to discipline or encourage the self-control of the Press. The Press Council, as envisaged by the Commission would be able to impose unlimited fines on newspaper owners, and in addition, the Council would be given powers of reprimand and of ordering publication of its judgments. It was recommended that there should be no appeal from the Press Council's decisions and that contempt of the Press Council should be an offence triable by the courts.

Even more serious was the recommendation that all journalists should be required to register with the Press Council every year on payment of a fee. Authority to despatch cables should only be granted to journalists who were registered with the Council, and the Post Office should be required to file all Press cables handed in, and make them available to the Press Council. Copies of all news reports filed to the foreign Press other than by cable should be filed with the Press Council's registrar.

The reaction of the South African Press was predictably along linguistic lines—the English Press was uniformly critical of the Commission and its findings, whilst the Afrikaans Press gave prominence to the Commissions criticisms of English-language journalists, many of whom were 'named' in the Report. It joined with the politicians in their criticism and threats of legislation to follow the Commission's findings.

For example, the *Rand Daily Mail* said in an editorial on May 12, 1974, that it was difficult for 'any sensible person to treat it seriously, but unfortunately it will have to be taken in deadly earnest because it can—and almost certainly will—be used as the excuse for legislation which will amount to Government control of the Press.[1] While *Die Vaderland* in its leading article of May 12, 1964, said that 'The accused have been identified: full-time representatives of international news agencies, publications, writers from abroad—people without any

[1] IPI Survey, *Government Pressures on the Press* (Zurich: International Press Institute, 1955), p. 108.

responsibility towards South Africa. But there were also people with a duty of responsibility towards the land of their birth or of their citizenship; members of the editorial staffs of English-language newspapers.'

Despite the misgivings of editors about legislation likely to follow from the second and final report of the Commission, no laws directly related to the Commission's findings were promulgated. Nor was any statutory Press Council introduced, nor SAPAs licence invoked, possibly because the Afrikaans Press found it a financially beneficial arrangement for themselves.

The importance of the Commission was not in any way diminished by the fact that no legislation emerged from it. For fourteen years it hung over the Press, constituting an ever-present threat: in itself it acted as a kind of censorship, making every English-language journalist more cautious of what he wrote. Quite apart from laws and regulations governing the day-to-day activities of journalists, they felt themselves '. . . exposed to the ill-will of the Government, which accuses them of maliciously distorting the facts and running down the country in the eyes of foreigners'.[1] And Government Ministers were themselves quite willing to use the threat of the Commission to silence opposition. Throughout the fourteen years, Ministers made constant reference to the sanctions that would be imposed once the Commission's findings were made public.

The Press Board and the Press Code of Conduct

The continued sitting of the Commission was only one feature influencing the political climate within which the newspapers had to work throughout the 1950s. In 1954 (before the Press Commission had even begun to hear evidence) the Government set up a Commission of Inquiry in Regard to Undesirable Publications, which reported in 1957. It was thought that the Commission would deal only with pornographic and obscene material, but in fact recommendations for drastic censorship in regard to political publications were made.

In the first place the Commission recommended that an authoritative body other than the courts should be set up to make decisions about which publications were undesirable. Books and magazines would fall under the exclusive jurisdiction of the Publications Board, but 'when the question arises whether newspapers . . . are undesirable, any authority charged with the enforcement of the relevant legislation should be able to consult the Publications Board . . .'.[2] In other words

[1] IPI Survey, *Government Pressures on the Press* (Zurich: International Press Institute, 1955), p. 108.

[2] *Report of the Commission of Inquiry in Regard to Undesirable Publications*, p.156, Col. 2.

the Publications Board would function as the official authority on all definitions of 'undesirable' and would save the ordinary courts from any confusion about legal definitions of 'undesirable' literature. Hence, according to the Commission's findings, the law would be enforced in a uniform and consistent manner. Effectively, however, this would have meant a Government-appointed Publications Board imposing its judgments on the courts which under an appended draft Censorship Bill, were empowered to ban publications.[1]

Furthermore the Board would have access to all material prior to publication of newspapers or magazines which were designated as 'controlled' and be able to forbid distribution of particular editions of such publications.

Had all the recommendations of the Inquiry been accepted, a blanket pre-publication censorship of the political content of newspapers would have been introduced into South Africa. Instead, the Government used the extensive and intimidating recommendations of the Commission as a weapon with which it eventually persuaded members of the Newspaper Press Union (NPU), the Presses' proprietors, to set up their own Press Board.

Thus in 1960 the Deputy Minister of the Interior, Mr P. W. Botha, introduced an Undesirable Publications Bill in Parliament, providing for pre-publication censorship. After the first reading it was referred to a select committee. An enormous public outcry, which included both English and Afrikaans journalists, and the need to give the NPU more time to consider setting up a Press Board, resulted in the Bill being dropped. But in 1961, the Minister re-introduced the Bill, leaving out the pernicious pre-publication clause. On being referred again to a select committee, the clause was re-introduced and the Bill came before Parliament in the 1962 session, though it was not considered until 1963 when it was finally enacted as the Publications and Entertainments Act.

As it turned out the South African Press was excluded from the provisions of the Act. But through the Act the Government achieved what it had set out to do: it forced the Press to introduce a self-disciplinary Code, in exchange for which members of the NPU–that is virtually all South African newspapers–were excluded from the Act's provisions.

The five-year threat of the impending Act 'persuaded' the NPU to agree to the setting up of an internal Code of Conduct. The NPU had resisted pressure to set up such a Code for many years but in

[1] See 'Fighting Talk' (Johannesburg: Fighting Talk Committee, Nov. 1957), pp. 8–10 for a good analysis of the Commission's findings.

January 1962 the text of a draft Code of Conduct for the Press, and of a proposed constitution for a Board of Reference to give effect to the Code, was issued by the NPU. Mr M. V. Jooste, President of NPU (and chairman of Dagbreek Pers) at the time stated that 'Any suggestion that outside interference or pressure has in any way influenced the formulation and contents of the proposed code is quite erroneous'. But the implementation of the Code at the very time when the Undesirable Publications Bill was finally put before Parliament could not be regarded as a coincidence.

Besides, several newspaper managements believed that political pressures had prompted the creation of the Code. This view was shared by the South African Society of Journalists which at this time represented only English language journalists, Afrikaans-language journalists having been forced to resign some years earlier by their managements. When the Code was adopted at a meeting of the NPU in March 1962, twenty-five managements voted in favour of the Code including the entire Nationalist Press, the Argus Group and the *Cape Times*. Seven newspaper managements voted against it including SAAN and the Bailey Group (*Drum* and *Post*). The SAAN Board of Directors expressed their dissatisfaction with the setting up of the Code but decided, in the company's interests, to abide by the Code and accept the authority of the Board of Reference. The Code itself was broadly similar to Press codes existing in other countries but it contained a clause 3(d) which both the SASJ and the dissenting managements believed would restrict the political content of newspapers. The clause read, 'While the Press retains its traditional right of criticism, comment should take cognisance of the complex racial problems of South Africa, the general good and the safety of the country and its peoples'.

The SASJ made several attempts to prevent the proprietor's Union from negotiating with the Government to set up the Board and accept the Code. Initially, in response to a request by the Secretary of the House of Assembly, the SASJ submitted a memorandum to the Parliamentary Select Committees of 1961 and 1962 considering the Undesirable Publications Bill, opposing many clauses of the Bill and suggesting changes. But the SASJ was excluded both by the NPU and the Government in the bargaining which resulted in the Press Code.

In 1961, the SASJ approached the NPU in an effort to have its views taken into consideration in the event of the NPU bartering exemption from the Bill for a Press Code. The NPU replied to the SASJ that the 'time was not ripe for liaison and that, if liaison should be established, it should be on an *ad hoc* basis, and not be of a permanent nature'. Subsequently the SASJ learnt that a deputation from the NPU had been received by the Prime Minister to discuss 'voluntary' Press control, and having been rejected by the NPU, the SASJ requested direct talks with the Prime Minister. But in a reply from the Prime Minister's office, the SASJ was told that as the Prime Minister was holding discussions with the NPU, it would not be fitting for him to meet with representatives of the SASJ. Prior to its adoption of the Press Code, the NPU did permit representatives of the SASJ to speak at a meeting of the NPU members, but by then the decision to co-operate with the Government had already been taken. As a final sanction against a Code which the SASJ claimed allowed the NPU to do the Government's job for it, and in response to Government pressure, the SASJ refused to subscribe to the Constitution or to accept the jurisdiction of the Press Board.

An argument put forward by protagonists of the Code notably the Press Board's chairman, ex-Judge President Heinie de Villiers, was that such codes existed in other countries, including Britain. But in putting forward such an argument, the NPU failed to take account of the differences in the political systems within which such a code would operate. Since its inception in 1953, Britain's Press Council, which like South Africa's Press Board was a voluntary body, had investigated complaints mostly from the public concerning newspaper ethics, such as questions of unnecessary identification of innocent persons with those accused of grave crimes, misleading advertising, callous indifference to private tragedy, etc. However, the British Press Council consistently refused to lay down or even draft a formal code of ethics but restricted itself to decisions on particular cases.

In the fifteen cases brought before the South African Board up to 1968, seven of the complaints were brought by MPs or Members of Provincial Councils, five by Government departments or Afrikaner organizations and two from 'opposition' organizations. One of these was the South African Institute of Race Relations, an organization concerned with the collection and communication of information about the non-Whites. The other 'opposition' organization was the Black Sash, a women's organization created in 1956 to oppose the Nationalist's manipulation of the Constitution. The Afrikaans Press which had acquiesced in the setting up of a self-disciplinary Code were surprised to find that they too were subject to the sanctions of the Press Board, and of the fifteen cases heard five were complaints against the Afrikaans Press.

Yet the SASJ's fears that the Board would be used primarily to

111

sanction the political content of newspapers, as opposed to maintaining ethical standards, proved to be only partially true, though for unexpected reasons. The Government had hoped that despite the voluntary, rather than statutory nature of the Board, the fact that the Board was set up by the NPU, would ensure that newspapers toed the line. They worked on the assumption that proprietors had total control over the editorial policies and staff of their newspapers, and would be able to impose discipline from above. This did not prove to be the case and in several instances editors severely criticized the Board and its findings, undermining its effectiveness and credibility. One example was the case of J. H. Steyl, MPC, versus the *Sunday Times*. Mr Steyl, Secretary of the National Party in the Transvaal complained that a *Sunday Times* political report was incorrect. The Board upheld Steyl's complaint. In the same issue in which the Board's findings were published (*Sunday Times,* February 9, 1964) the editor severely rapped the Board for what he submitted were fallacies in its findings. He suggested that if the minutes of the Board's meetings were made public, confidence in the Board would 'be shocked so seriously that I doubt whether anyone will consider it worthwhile in future to submit a case to it again'.

Because of the Board's failure to fulfil the role which Government had intended for it, namely to introduce an effective system for the Press to discipline itself, the Press Code also failed to protect the 'freedom' of the South African Press from further Government encroachment as was originally intended, at least by the NPU.

Yet in setting up the Board in response to Government pressure, in creating the machinery which could so easily be converted to a more effective statutory body and in allowing the inclusion of clause 3(d), the NPU did not emerge as a defender of the independent Presses' freedom. That was left to the journalists and some editors of the English-language newspapers. Government dissatisfaction with the Press Board was confirmed when the 1964 Report of the Press Commission, recommended that a statutory Press Council with extensive powers to enforce its will should replace the existing Board.

Pressure Based on the Laws

In a 1955 survey on *Government Pressures on the Press,* the International Press Institute concluded that the most widespread tendency towards control of the Press derived from the needs of 'national security'.[1] The Institute accepted that the Press had to accept some

---

[1] IPI Survey, *Government Pressures on the Press* (Zurich: International Press Institute, 1955), p. 117.

limitations on its freedom in order to maintain a balance between the security of the State, the rights of the public and its own independence. But there has existed a natural conflict between Press and Government in determining what those limitations should be and the tendency was for Governments to increase their unaccountability by hiding under the umbrella of the interests of State security and the secrecy that it allegedly required.

In South Africa a massive complex of overlapping laws grew up between 1948 and 1968 to preclude an ever widening area of subjects from being available for public scrutiny. South Africa was named in the IPI Report as one of the countries in which the 'balance' between security of the State and Press freedom had not been maintained. The Press suffered a serious loss in its freedom as a result of a body of laws which became an instrument for maintaining a political party in power rather than an impartial arbiter between competing interests. Blackwell and Bamford[1] suggest that three methods of balancing the claims of a free Press against governmental demands have predominated in South Africa. The first was by direct State interposition, that is censorship; the second method was that of internal self-control by the Press and the third was the reliance upon courts of law to impose sanctions. For the most part, they claim, the emphasis has been on the third method, which envisaged 'freedom and not license' and was most favourable to a free Press. Technically the third method continued to be the most commonly used, but the State increasingly interposed, not so much by way of direct censorship, but by adding drastically to those situations in which publication was prohibited.[2] Furthermore, by excluding the courts in many instances, the Government ensured that it and it alone could decide when a breach of 'security' or a threat to the 'national interest' had taken place, and what penalties should be imposed.

But even when the courts were not excluded, when they were called upon to adjudicate upon any given law (and even assuming an independent judiciary which has been the case hitherto)[3] they were themselves confined by the content of the law. No matter how discriminatory the laws themselves may have been, the courts were bound to interpret them according to their formulation. Perhaps the most unnerving feature of Nationalist law to newspaper editors was

---

[1] Leslie Blackwell and Brian R. Bamford, *Newspaper Law of South Africa* (Capetown and Johannesburg: Juta & Co., 1963).
[2] Ibid., p. v.
[3] See, for example, H. R. Hahlo and E. Kahn: *The Union of South Africa: The Development of its Laws and Constitutions* (London: Stevens & Sons Ltd., 1960).

that much of post-1948 legislation was so loosely drafted as to make it increasingly difficult to know when an offence was being committed.

The increased use of the method of State interposition, the loose drafting of legislation which was invoked only rarely, in combination with the Press Commission and the Press Board had the overall effect of transferring the emphasis to the second method, that of internal self-control. The question of whether pressures on the Press were deliberately aimed at achieving this end can best be answered through a detailed analysis of the laws which have had a bearing on the political functioning of the Press.

The Suppression of Communism Act, 1950

At the same time as the setting up of the Press Commission was being debated in Parliament, the Suppression of Communism Act was placed on the Statute book, greatly extending the Government's existing powers for controlling the Press. Under Section 6 of the Act of 1950, the Governor General (after 1961 the State President) was enabled to ban any publication aimed at furthering the principles or promoting the spread of communism and *inter alia* it became an offence under the Act to convey information, the publication of which was calculated to further the achievement of any of the objects of communism. In addition the State President was empowered to ban any organization which he deemed to be 'unlawful' and in terms of the Act this would preclude the publication of any of that organization's expressed views. There was no appeal to the courts against a banning order unless it could be proved that the President had acted in bad faith.

The fact that there was no recourse to the law courts was a matter of particular concern to newspapers, for it marked the beginning of direct State censorship as opposed to relying on the courts to impose sanctions. In addition the law was so loosely drafted that it could at times be quite impossible for an editor to know whether or not he was breaking the law, as the definitions of 'communism' were so vague and wide as to permit of any number of arbitrary interpretations; especially as the President himself had the discretion to decide what was 'communist'. In other words a member of the executive could apply his own definitions of communism to the factual situation and his determination could not be challenged in the courts.

Immediately after the Act had been passed, the Cape Town, Johannesburg and Durban offices of the left-wing weekly newspaper, the *Guardian* were raided by the Criminal Investigation Department of the Police, and this was followed by a banning order in 1952. The paper soon re-appeared under a new name, *Advance,* but like its predecessor was banned under the Act in 1954. Yet again it re-appeared, this time as *New Age* but finally it too was banned in 1962, though not before its editor had herself been restricted under the Suppression of Communism Act. For in 1962 an amendment to the Act was passed, preventing a newspaper from registering under more than one name by providing that registration of any newspaper would lapse unless it was published once a month. As most of the left-wing newspapers were short of capital they could not publish as regularly as the Establishment Press. And the stringent registration fee of R20,000 (£10,500) which would be forfeited if the paper were banned, made the continued re-emergence of extreme left-wing newspapers impossible. Although in practice the fee was seldom required, the decision as to whether it should be paid rested with the Minister of the Interior.

Further amendments to the Act prohibited newspapers from publishing any statements, regardless of subject matter, by a banned person–whether alive or dead–without the express permission of the Minister of Justice. By 1968 there were approximately 600 banned people whose views ranged from committed communist through African nationalist to 'liberal'. These regulations probably produced the most serious inroads into the free functioning of the Press in South Africa. In terms of the day-to-day running of the newspaper, it meant that editors were compelled to keep a constantly updated list of banned persons and make daily reference to it. For the range of banned persons was wide and might as likely include a London-based leader of the anti-apartheid movement as a local African house-wife.[1] The prohibition was effectively wide enough to include news-paper reports of evidence given and statements made in courts of law [2] Although the Minister of Justice clarified this point, he did so in such a way that newspapers were still unable to be certain about what they were permitted to print within the law. The Minister said that publication of political statements inside the courts was permissible 'providing that the evidence or statement is relevant to one of the issues in the trial and the occasion is not abused for the airing of political views'. This meant that newspapers had to make the difficult

[1] The Unlawful Organizations Act (No. 34 of 1963) repeated many of the provisions of the Suppression of Communism Act. The State President was empowered to declare any body, organization, group or association of persons, institution, society or movement as an unlawful organization. The policies or utterances of any listed persons were not permitted to be published. Thus, to take an extreme example, it would be impossible for a South African newspaper to publish anything that Stalin ever wrote or said.

[2] See Kelsey W. Stuart, op. cit., p. 72.

legal decision as to what was relevant and what was simply the defendant airing 'irrelevant' political views.

One further prohibition contained in the Suppression of Communism Act, was the Minister of Justice's power not only to prevent 'listed' persons from communicating with other banned people but to forbid their receiving any particular visitors. Under this section a journalist attempting to interview a person prohibited from receiving visitors would be committing an offence, as in the strict interpretation of the law he would be inciting the commission of a crime. This prohibition affected newspapers from abroad as well. If any of them published a statement by a banned person, the South African distributors cut out the offending words.

The intention and effect of this Act and its amendments was to eliminate an entire segment of political opinion from the public arena. In other words, the public could not without the consent of the Minister, know the views of the extreme and radical opposition. Through the Minister's general consent to the publication of court proceedings, the English Press did on occasion take advantage of the 'loophole' to publicize banned views as it did for example during the so-called 'Rivonia' trial in 1964, in which banned African National Congress members were accused of sabotage. The fact remained, however, that 'extreme' views had to wait upon events for their expression in the South African Press. But the real problem for the South African Press lay in defining extremism. Working in a political system within which a definition of extremism was always being enlarged, the Press was in a constant state of uncertainty about what it was or was not permitted to say.

The Public Safety and Criminal Law Amendment Acts, 1953

Despite the far-reaching powers of the Suppression of Communism Act, it was only the first in a series of increasingly repressive laws which affected the functioning of the Press. The 1952 'Defiance Campaign' sparked off a new and more concerted Nationalist attack on the English-language Press, conducted through Afrikaans newspapers and Parliamentary debates.[1]

During the campaign nearly 10,000 non-Whites and a few Whites were jailed for defying six selected discriminatory laws. Initially, the English-language Press paid little attention to the campaign but as it gathered momentum, so the English Press increased its coverage of events, punctuated with searching editorials about what defects in the Nationalist Government's handling of the South African situa-

[1] See George Clay and Stan Uys, 'The Press: Strijdom's last Barrier' in *Africa South*, October–December 1957, p. 21.

tion had led to the protest. At no time, however, did they actually support the campaign.

Leading Nationalists were quick to protest at the English Presses' coverage of the events and the then Minister of Labour, Mr B. Schoeman, accused English Press editors of supporting the campaign. Threats were made of Government action against newspapers publishing 'irresponsible' reports and towards the end of 1952 warnings of a Criminal Law Amendment Bill were publicized.

Rioting in the Cape Province clinched the matter: the January 1953 Parliamentary session witnessed the passing of both the Public Safety Act and the Criminal Law Amendment Act. Disturbed by the events of the previous year and with a general election coming up, the country's official Opposition party voted with the Government for the passing of the two laws. It was left to the English-language Press to oppose the passage of two further pieces of legislation which threatened seriously to curtail its and the country's freedom.

Faced with the problem of large groups of non-Whites who were prepared to flout the laws and take the consequences, the Criminal Law Amendment Act increased penalties for contravention of the country's laws when *inter alia*, they were infringed by way of protest, or in support of a campaign against or for the repeal or modification of any law–or by the use of language or any other action calculated to cause the commission of such an offence.

The terms of this law made it extremely difficult for editors to speak freely or criticize any existing laws or the enactment of any future laws, for there was no way of knowing whether criticism might not result in the law being broken in protest. Thus, for example, it became possible for a newspaper to print an editorial on the pass laws, which if it resulted in any individual destroying his pass, could render the newspaperman liable to a sentence ranging from five years imprisonment to a whipping of ten strokes. Strictly interpreted, newspapers reporting an inflammatory speech, or making an appeal for funds to support a campaign or organization which at some future time actively flouted the law, could themselves be breaking the law. As newspapers had no means of foretelling whether a said speech or campaign would result in others breaking the law (assuming it were indeed possible to identify a simple cause and effect relationship between events) they were, in a very real sense, always at risk.

The advice given to journalists in the *Newspaperman's Guide to the Law*[1] (written by the legal adviser to SAAN) on how to deal with the provisions of the Criminal Law Amendment Act, revealed the most

[1] Kelsey Stuart, op. cit., p. 76.

likely effect of the Act on the working of the Press. Mr Stuart suggested that the safest course was 'to examine all campaigns against laws very carefully before in any manner becoming associated with them. In reporting such campaigns the "dead pan" approach is the wisest unless it is absolutely certain that illegal acts form no part of them.' In other words, Mr Stuart advised a cautious tone rather than caution on the side of total silence. But the effect of the 'dead pan' approach could, and to some extent did, succeed in muting criticism. As Brookes and Macaulay have said, 'Direct censorship of political opinion becomes an unnecessary and clumsy weapon with which to silence criticism, when by indirect means such as these such an atmosphere of caution and fear is infused that the voice of public protest, although not silenced, ceases to have that clarion note of warning . . .'.[1]

Under the provisions of the Public Safety Act, a law passed at the same time as the Criminal Laws Amendment Act, the Government was empowered to declare a state of emergency in the event of unrest and to suspend any legislation considered inconsistent with its regulations. In March 1960, following the Sharpeville crisis, where a number of Africans protesting against the pass laws were shot by the police, a state of emergency was declared in the country, with repercussions for the Press.

The emergency regulations entitled the Government to prohibit the printing, publication or dissemination of material considered to be subversive and it became an offence to publish or disclose the name identity of any person detained or arrested under the emergency regulations.

To start with two left-wing weeklies (*New Age* and *Torch*) were banned. In May 1960, John Sutherland, the editor of the Port Elizabeth newspaper, the *Evening Post,* was charged with contravening the emergency regulations. The charge arose from publication in the *Evening Post* of a report describing the unfavourable impressions about South Africa of two Canadian visitors. They had found South Africa 'a country afraid to talk'. Fred Carneson, director of the banned *New Age* was also charged with publishing subversive literature in contravention of the emergency regulations. In addition, 13,000 copies of the Liberal Cape Town fortnightly, *Contact,* were impounded and the newspaper's editor, Patrick Duncan, subsequently charged with contravening the emergency regulations.

A few day after the withdrawal of the emergency regulations–the

---

[1] E. H. Brookes and J. B. Macaulay, *Civil Liberty in South Africa* (Cape Town: Oxford University Press, 1958) p. 78.

emergency was lifted on August 31, 1960–a summons was served on Mr Sutherland and publishers of the *Evening Post*. In November, the chief magistrate of Port Elizabeth dismissed the charges on the grounds that the accused could not be prosecuted under the emergency regulations because the regulations had lapsed before the summonses were issued. A similar ruling was given by the regional magistrate in Cape Town a few days later in the case of Mr Carneson. But another Cape Town magistrate did not accept this argument and Mr Duncan was sentenced to a fine of R900 (£500) or 350 days imprisonment on being found guilty of publishing two subsverive statements.

The matter was not allowed to rest there. The Attorney General of the Eastern Cape took the editor of the *Evening Post's* case to appeal, and by a majority decision of two to one, a full bench of the Eastern Cape Division of the Supreme Court confirmed the magistrate's decision. A further appeal made to the Appellate Division of the Court, the ultimate court of appeal in South Africa succeeded: it was stated that, unless a contrary intention appeared in a repealing law, legal proceedings could be instituted or continued under the original law, as that original law had not been repealed[1]–only the emergency was terminated. The case was remitted to the chief magistrate in Port Elizabeth for further hearing. On June 23, 1961, this magistrate found the editor and the Eastern Province Newspapers guilty, but only on a technical offence.

Despite the untypical nature of the emergency period, the Government's handling of the Press during that time illustrated several important and consistent features in the relationship between the Government and the Press. First, the emergency regulations which permitted Government by decree, gave the Government undisputed and absolute control over the Press. In banning *New Age* and *Torch* and in confiscating copies of *Contact,* the Government immediately silenced the radical opposition Press. Yet equally the Government had the power under normal circumstances to ban these newspapers, a power which it chose to exercise in banning the *New Age's* predecessors in 1952 and 1954. The fact was, however, that Government waited for the powers given it under the emergency to ban the fringe Press again and even then it did so only temporarily. The re-emergence of the radical weekly from *Guardian* to *New Age* was arguably the result of a loophole in the Suppression of Communism Act, but at all times Government had the competency to close the loophole.

[1] Muriel Horrel, *A Survey of Race Relations* (Johannesburg: South African Institute of Race Relations, 1961), p. 57.

One explanation of this must be that despite the authoritarian content of much legislation, a measure of legal and judicial process persisted, and that almost all the laws inhibiting the Press were formulated to deal with specific crises, to enable Government to crush opposition. In dealing with the *Evening Post,* Government's behaviour and intentions were somewhat different. In the first place the *Evening Post* was a major daily and a part of the Establishment White Press. The extraordinary persistence of the Government in charging the *Evening Post* was partly the result of a vendetta against the particular newspaper, especially as its editor was at that time a most outspoken critic of Government as well as an occasionally vocal supporter of non-White nationalist aspirations. The paper's transgression was in this instance so trivial as to make the vendetta-theory seem indisputable. But the primary aim of the Government was to intimidate the rest of the Press into exercising self-censorship. As a South African journalist wrote in an IPI *Report* in May 1960,

> 'Newspaper readers are being kept ignorant of many of the most important events of the present emergency, not because of any openly declared censorship on the Press, but because circumstances have forced newspapermen in South Africa to exercise a censorship on themselves ... Some newspapers have suppressed all photographs of the victims of the Sharpeville shooting.'

Yet as the legal machinations of the *Evening Post* case showed, the Government, in choosing to employ the courts to impose sanctions on the Press, did not quite achieve its intended ends of forcing the Press to censor itself.

The Riotous Assembly Act, 1956, and the General Law Amendment Act, 1962

The Riotous Assembly Act of 1956 defined still further sets of situations in which publication was prohibited. Under the Act, the Government could ban a publication which it considered to be calculated to engender hostility between one racial group and another. Thus, if a newspaper referred to the grievances of the African *vis-à-vis* the Whites or of Coloured *vis-à-vis* the Indians, its editor ran the risk of being jailed and heavily fined.[1]

Under the Act the onus of proving that information was not of such a nature that the probable result of its publication would be to

[1] See article by Horace Flather (then editor of the *Star*) entitled 'Restrictions on Information', IPI *Report*, January 1953.

engender feelings of hostility between the races rested with the appellant. As with the Criminal Laws Amendment Act, the implications of the Riotous Assemblies Act were enormous. Any campaign conducted by a newspaper, perhaps describing social inequities or the different standards at which the White and the non-Whites of South Africa lived, or the unequal facilities available to the different groups could be interpreted as inciting feelings of hostility between racial groups. Constitutional demands for social reform of any kind could be an offence under the Act. Yet again, they might not; but the uncertainty about what would constitute an offence could not fail to induce a certain caution in the approach of editors.

The Native Administration Act (No. 38 of 1927) also made provision for penalizing the promotion of hostility between Africans and Whites. It differed from the Riotous Assembly Act in that 'intent' had to be proved. In 1950, the *Sunday Express* was charged under the Act for a cartoon which had appeared in the paper depicting a White assaulting Africans, with the Prime Minister bowing to two other Africans from the Protectorates. The Supreme Court in allowing an appeal against the convictions found that 'even strong criticism . . . of a Government and its policy is permissible in a country where freedom of speech prevails . . . even when such a policy is attacked in relation to Native Administration'.

The Riotous Assembly Act, like the Suppression of Communism Act also provided for the banning of persons but permitted appeal to the courts. Whilst the banning of persons could take several forms, it was the prohibition of persons from 'attending gatherings' which was of particular relevance to the Press. For the General Law Amendment Act of 1962 provided that any person who

'without the consent of the Minister or except for the purposes of any proceedings in any court of law, records or reproduces by mechanical or other means or prints, publishes or disseminates any speech, utterance, writing or statement . . . made or produced or purporting to have been made or produced anywhere at any time by any person prohibited . . . from attending any gathering'

committed an offence. Thus the statements of any person banned in such a way could no longer be published, whether made before or after the creation of the law and no matter what the subject matter. Although the 1962 Act did create some new offences, in general it confirmed the trend of previous Acts. It underlined too the Government's reluctance explicitly to censor the political content of newspapers, when it could effectively do so through the silencing of individuals who expressed unpopular beliefs.

121

Official Secrets and Defence

In 1965 a further important Act, the Official Secrets Amendment Act was passed through Parliament adding to the already massively restrictive Press legislation. In keeping with the security laws of several Western democracies, the Official Secrets Act of 1956 made it an offence to publish information relating to official secrets, defence and atomic energy. But the 1965 amendment extended the bounds of the original Act's scope by making it an offence not only to publish, but even to possess any document of information which related to 'munitions of war *or any military or police matter'*[1] The inclusion of 'police matter' in the Act aroused particular concern amongst journalists. The *Rand Daily Mail,* for example, commented on April 23, 1965, that 'It is easy enough to see how convenient it might be for the Minister to plead the "interests of the State" when using his powers to prevent the South African public and the outside world from knowing what his Security Branch is doing'. Newspapers would be left to guess how much they might report without fear of penalty, for police matter was defined as any matter relating to the preservation of internal security of the State or the maintenance of law and order by the South African police.[2]

The inclusion of 'police matter' was intended seriously to curtail the activities of journalists, who by the very nature of their work acquire information and documents of value as news which might at some time 'be directly or indirectly useful to an enemy'. The scope of the Act's new provisions were so wide, as to make a contravention of the Act by journalists a daily probability. Thus newspapers had to rely on the benevolent whims of the administration to ensure that they were not charged with contravening the Act. Yet by 1968, there had been no convictions under the amended Act.

The Official Secrets Act in conjunction with the Defence Amendment Act of 1967 created a virtual blanket prohibition on all matters connected with South Africa's defence without the express permission of the Minister of Defence. The extensiveness of the Defence Act's provisions led most newspapers to refer all matters connected with defence, no matter how tenuously, to the authorities prior to publication. An example, quoted by Benjamin Pogrund in the *Rand Daily Mail*[3] revealed just how seriously editors were affected by the Act. He related how a golfer in Port Elizabeth observed a jet trainer

[1] Italics added to the principal Act.
[2] *A Survey of Race Relations, 1965*, p. 30.
[3] *Rand Daily Mail*, November 23, 1968. Article entitled 'Newspapers and the Law'.

flying overhead after taking off from a nearby airfield. As he watched, a pair of trousers, followed by a tie fluttered down from the aeroplane. The Press found it necessary to refer the report to the Department of Defence for permission to publish.

Prisons and the Police

(a) The Prisons Act, 1959

The Prisons Act of 1959 affected the rights of newspapers to publish pictures or stories relating to prisoners, prisons or any prison administration. It became an offence under the Act to sketch or photograph any prison or prisoners, or without the written authority of the Commissioner of Prisons, 'to publish any false information concerning the behaviour or experience in prison of any prisoner, or ex-prisoner or concerning the administration of any prison, knowing the same to be false, or without taking reasonable steps to verify such information, the onus of proving that reasonable steps were taken to verify such information being upon the accused'.

The promulgation of the 1959 Prisons Act was a direct Government reaction to a number of articles critical of prison conditions, which had been appearing in the Press. Mr C. R. Swart, the then Minister of Justice, informed Parliament that the need for such a law resulted from sensational newspaper and magazine stories which were considered harmful. In particular, he cited the instance of a photograph appearing in the magazine *Drum*, which revealed non-White prisoners being forced to dance around Johannesburg's Central Prison courtyard in the nude, to prove that they were not hiding anything (such as drugs of knives) on their persons.[1] Mr Swart also complained of newspapers publishing stories about prisoners condemned to death. 'We just want to restrict those who publish false stories', he said.[2] What concerned the Press however was that the prohibition of 'true' and not 'false' stories about prison conditions was the obvious intention and effect of the Act.

The terms of the Prisons Act inevitably restrained editors from finding too frequent fault with the prison system. But in 1965, after a fairly long silence on the subject, the *Rand Daily Mail* acted. On June 30 and July 1 and 2, the *Rand Daily Mail* published a series of highly critical articles based on the experience of an ex-political prisoner, Harold Strachan (as told to a senior reporter Benjamin Pogrund) revealing the conditions under which prisoners had to live.

On July 2, the editor, Mr L. O. V. Gandar stated 'We went to

[1] See Anthony Sampson, *Drum* (London: Collins, 1956).
[2] Hansard, March 5, 1959, Cols. 1948–49.

considerable lengths to check and cross-check the accuracy of the material we obtained and having satisfied ourselves completely on that score, we felt strongly that it was in the public interest for this information about prison conditions to be published.' The following day he demanded an official investigation into prison conditions, and threatened that unless swift action followed, the newspaper would publish further evidence.

Government reaction was swift. On July 2–the day the third Strachan article was to be published–police raided the *Rand Daily Mail* offices, seizing the typescript of the articles and notes dealing with prison conditions. Mr Pogrund was questioned by the police and an attempt was made to persuade Mr Gandar not to publish the third article. On three further occasions the newspaper's offices were raided and other documents and tape recordings seized.

Mr Strachan was served with a five-year banning order, prohibiting him from attending public gatherings, and hence prohibiting any further statements by him from being published.

Undeterred by the experiences of the *Rand Daily Mail* the *Sunday Times* published a statement by the head warder at the Cinderella Prison in Boksburg, Mr J. A. Theron, on July 25, in which he confirmed that certain types of torture took place in prison. And on July 30, the *Rand Daily Mail*–true to its threat–published further sworn statements by Mr Theron, Warder G. J. van Schalkwyk, Mr Isaac Setshedi and Mr Filasberto Taimo–all men with experience of prison.

On publication of his statement, Mr Theron was suspended from duty, and his home was searched. He was instructed not to leave home or communicate with other prisoners or warders. Mr van Schalkwyk, Mr Setshedi and Mr Taimo were arrested, as was Warder G. C. Prins from Cinderella Prison who had made a statement to the *Sunday Times* but had not yet signed the affidavit.

In August, the Department of the Interior withdrew the passports of Mr Gandar and Mr Pogrund. Also in August, Mr van Schalkwyk was charged and pleaded guilty to making false statements about the treatment of prisoners, and was sentenced to three years imprisonment, reduced to eighteen months on appeal. Mr Taimo pleaded not guilty to a charge of contravening the Prisons Act. He was found guilty and sentenced to six months imprisonment. Warder Prins was found guilty of being in possession of dagga (cannabis) and having financial dealings with prisoners, neither charge being exactly relevant to the issue of 'false statements'. He was sentenced to R100 (£55) or ninety days imprisonment.

Mr Theron was fined R60 (£33) by a prisons disciplinary court for contravening prison regulations – receiving a present from a relative of a prisoner, carrying a letter for a prisoner, promising to obtain parole for a prisoner in return for a reward, and allowing a prisoner to have a visit which he was not entitled to. On October 4, he appeared in the Regional Court on twelve charges, including making a false statement under oath. In 1967 he was found guilty and was sentenced to four years imprisonment reduced to twenty four months on appeal.

Setshedi was found guilty of making a false statement under oath but on appeal in 1968, his conviction was set aside, the judges finding that the State had failed to prove its case.

Two years after the appearance of the first prison condition articles, summonses were served under Section 44(f) of the Prison Act, on the managing director of SAAN, the editor-in-chief (Mr Gandar) of the *Rand Daily Mail,* the reporter Mr Pogrund, the editor of the *Sunday Times,* and the legal adviser to the newspaper publishers. The charge against them was of publishing false information about prisons without taking reasonable steps to verify the information. The *Sunday Times* subsequently published an apology and the charges against it were withdrawn. It was also agreed that Mr Gandar would represent SAAN, which left him and Mr Pogrund to face the charges when the hearing began in November.

The prison condition articles and their consequences are of great importance in understanding how the Government exercised control of the English-language Press. The body of laws relating to the Press are quite as important as intimidatory weapons as in fulfilling their more strictly punitive role. In practise over the twenty years of this study, the laws were infrequently invoked and the 'threat' in general far exceeded the actual sanctions imposed. But for the laws to serve their purpose, they had to have an evidential existence at least part of the time. It is not suggested that the Government was not genuinely outraged by the criticism implied in the prison exposures: it interpreted the articles as a political attack on itself. But in its response to the articles, the Government was 'teaching' the English-language Press a lesson as well as demonstrating that the threats were not idle. Further, in bringing to court all the Presses' informants, the Government's intentions were to undermine the credibility of the opposition Press by casting serious doubts on the quality of people who co-operated with the English Press.

In July 1969, Mr Gandar and Mr Pogrund were found guilty on both charges. Mr Gandar was fined R100 (£55) (or three months) on each of the two counts; SAAN was fined R150 (£85) on each count and Mr Pogrund received a three months suspended sentence without the option of a fine on each count. The penalties imposed on the company were by any standard not severe. But the costs of the case, which exceeded R250,000 (£135,000)[1] undoubtedly acted as an additional deterrent to any editor considering a similar exposé in the future.

Of equal concern to newspaper editors were the findings of the Judge President of the Transvaal, Mr Justice Cillie, who failed to clarify the law so as to give newspapers a guide for future action. Mr Cillie stated that Mr Gandar and Mr Pogrund had failed to prove that they took reasonable steps to verify information that was published, despite the fact that the paper had taken the precaution of getting sworn affidavits from its informants prior to publication. Yet he admitted that equally there was no evidence that they knew the information was false, and even accepted that some of the allegations made by the paper were true.

The judge agreed with a defence submission that it was not the purpose of Section 44(f) of the Act to inhibit a newspaper from a normal function of exposing public abuses. He said he did not think it was always necessary to ask the authorities, in this case the Department of Prisons, for comments on information received. But if this were not done it did deprive readers of hearing the other side of the story.

The findings in the Gandar case left the Press, if anything, more uncertain about how in future to expose abuses when they occurred. Although the judge confirmed that it was not always necessary to consult the authorities prior to publication, he implied that it was advisable. In other words, in order to be sure of avoiding prosecution, newspapers must seek official sanction for criticizing officialdom.

(b) Criminal Procedure Act, 1955

The Prisons Act to some extent covered Press criticism of the police and prison administration, but it was the Criminal Procedure Act which provided the machinery for the subpoena of witnesses to answer questions before a magistrate, which caused most concern to working journalists. If the police believed that an individual possessed any information which might help them in an investigation, they had the right under Section 83, to force him to disclose that information. Section 83 did not of course apply exclusively to journalists but they more than any other group in the society, were most frequently threatened by it. Journalists are, by the nature of their work dependent on good contacts to provide them with information and need in return to promise confidentiality if they are to retain their contacts. Equivalent laws exist in many countries including Britain and journal-

---

[1] *A Survey of Race Relations, 1969*, p. 58.

ists everywhere have sought to be exempted from the penalties of such laws, though with varying success. The extent to which the 'source' law hampers working journalists is dependent firstly on how often it is invoked or threats to invoke it are made, and what the penalties are for refusing to disclose the required information.

In South Africa, seven English-language journalists had been committed to prison under the Act by 1968, and two others subpoenaed but not committed. In 1964 the Act was amended to extend the period of imprisonment from eight days (at a time) to one year, sentence to be repeated annually if the journalist were still to refuse to disclose the information. Once again, the law was not invoked that frequently and nor were journalists detained for any great length of time. But journalists were constantly questioned by the police and threatened with its invocation and the extension of the initial sentence to a year's imprisonment undoubtedly intimidated many journalists. Benjamin Pogrund has concluded[1] that

> 'Where a newspaper these days is faced by a report on which a reporter may be questioned by the police for his sources, it has become almost axiomatic that the report be dropped forthwith ... There are still newspapers which weigh up the hazards of publication against public interests; but they are isolated.'

Thus the law in this area was used to a considerable extent as a political weapon, particularly by the standards of Western democracies.

But finally it must be said that if the police were seriously seeking information, rather than simply wishing to intimidate newspapers into silence, or punish individual journalists, the Act was a clumsy weapon when 180-day detention could be imposed without trial under the Criminal Procedure Amendment Act of 1965. By this method Government could – and did – detain journalists for the purpose of eliciting information.

The Press and the Police

The Newspaper Press Union, in an attempt to further clarify the relationship between the Press and the police, concluded a new agreement with the Commissioner of Police in 1967. The original agreement accorded certain privileges, including access to senior officers in the force – to holders of Press Identity Cards, which were themselves issued by the Commissioner. The Press on its side agreed, through the NPU, not to hinder the police in the course of their work.

[1] Article entitled 'Newspapers and the Law', *Rand Daily Mail*, November 23, 1968.

The new agreement incorporated most of the previous agreement but added a clause making editors obliged to communicate to the police, prior to publication, information concerning crime or 'state security' which the Press might have obtained from sources other than the police. It was also agreed that if the information concerned crimes of 'extraordinary seriousness or State security' the police might ask the editor not to publish the information. A second addition to the agreement promised that whenever a member of the police force was quoted but not identified in a report, the newspapers should on request provide the name of the informant to the police.[1]

By 1968 the effects of the agreements had not yet been fully tested or felt. But potentially it could be yet another serious obstacle to the Press in its reporting of police matters. The pre-publication censorship clause could produce a situation where the police by their definition of 'state security' or 'serious crime' could effectively control newspaper content. The demand that police informants be identified must inevitably result in even fewer officials giving information to the Press.

Under the Nationalist Government there was a steady build up of repressive legislation aimed at controlling the extra-Parliamentary opposition. In most cases the terms of the laws far exceeded their application and the laws themselves were rarely invoked, though the State defined a growing number of circumstances in which it was permitted to interpose directly, and in which publication was prohibited.

Evidence that the Press had to some extent withstood Nationalist intimidation was to be found in the fact that legislation governing the political content of newspapers continued unabated after 1948. It must be asked why Nationalists did not use their extensive powers to ban Establishment newspapers outright or at least to enforce existing legislation more stringently and more frequently. A more complete answer to this question must wait until the conclusion of this study. But some tentative conclusions will be posed here. Part of the answer must be that the English Press itself succeeded in conveying to the Nationalists some of the ethics of independent journalism, a value which the Afrikaans Press at least came to recognize as worthwhile. On the other side there was amongst Nationalists a deeply felt concern about their image abroad, despite their refusal to give up any fundamental apartheid principles to win approval from outside South Africa. The sensitivity of the Afrikaner to world opinion was evidenced in the Press Commission's terms of reference, in the increased activity abroad of the State Information Office after 1948 and the

[1] Kelsey Stuart, op. cit. p. 92 and 93.

setting up of a Ministry of Information in 1961, with the express purpose of improving South Africa's image abroad. It was felt by many Nationalists that the existence of the English-language Press gave credence to South Africa's claims to be a democratic country. Thus, for example, Dawie, *Die Burger's* political columnist, said in 1966 (May 7, 1966) that visitors from abroad had been particularly impressed by the free and critical Press in South Africa. Another such example is a statement by Mr Vorster, when Minister of Justice: he suggested that in the interests of the democracy, the English Presses 'unpatriotic actions are part of the burden we have to bear'. (Reported in the *Rand Daily Mail,* March 16, 1966.)

Thus the Nationalists were faced with a dilemma: how should they silence an opposition Press which exposed the South African population to 'liberalistic' ideas, and through its international connections contributed to the unpopularity of the Afrikaner outside of South Africa, without arousing further disapprobation from a hostile 'world opinion'. Their answer up until 1968 was: by forcing the Press to censor itself, to exercise internal self-control. This explains the vast complex of overlapping, loosely-defined, and seldom invoked laws: their primary function was intimidation. The rationale appeared to be that complex, frequently promulgated vaguely worded legislation would slip past the critical eye of international opinion more easily than would the actual enforcement of that legislation–a rationale which the Gandar case, for example may seem to justify.

The Nationalist Government had some success. But the English-language Press, with its long tradition of independent journalism, makes it seem unlikely that the Government will succeed in future in totally silencing its opposition Press. That is, not until it is prepared explicitly to ban a White, Establishment institution, as it did the anti-Establishment left-wing papers through the 1950s and early 1960s. But even here the contradiction in Nationalist threats and actions was expressed for as a final edition of *Spark* commented on March 28, 1963, in all the years of its existence, from *Guardian* to *Spark,* it had never been convicted of any offence against any law on account of its content. Its closure was due rather to the registration regulations and the fact that the Government had banned all the leading personnel of the paper and others who might have taken their place.

It may be that the Government is generally satisfied with the degree to which it has curtailed the Press, since it can always use these methods to silence the Press on any new issue which may prove embarrassing. Whether the Press can remain intimidated, given its traditions, without the Government banning newspapers, remains a moot question.

6

The Press and Government

The relationship between Press, Government and the political system is highly complex and interaction occurs on various levels simultaneously. For the Press as a whole, the Parliamentary journalists are most immediately in a position to assess how the relationship between Press and Government operates. Effectively the network is sufficiently extensive to incorporate all journalists who are dependent on Government sources for their information, as well as the editors and proprietors of newspapers.

Good contacts and 'sources' are an essential requirement for effective journalism but so then is some measure of independence from those 'sources'. In South Africa the English-language Press had a great deal of independence from Government, in the sense that it opposed the Government on almost all issues and consequently had very little in the way of Government 'sources'. The Afrikaans Press on the other hand had all the 'sources' and little of the independence. For both groups of newspapers the extensive deprivation of one or the other of the primary assets of good political journalism, resulted in the English Press being largely ill-informed on the inner workings of Government and the Afrikaans Press being unable to publish much of the information it had in its possession.

The English Press adapted itself to Government secrecy by relying very extensively on the Afrikaans Press as a source of information (and learning to read between the lines) and by championing social campaigns and thus forcing issues into the political realm. In this way the English Press acquired additional information on Government policy by eliciting policy statements on relevant issues. But with few exceptions it had to rely on the public statements and activities of politicians, inside and outside Parliament, for its understanding of Government. It benefited little, if at all, from the private confidences of Government members.

The Afrikaans Press mitigated its lack of independence from Government by sometimes manipulating to its advantage provincial differences and rivalries. Individual newspapers trumpeted the cause of their province, to assert its dominance and consequently them-

130

selves within the Government. When in 'opposition' loyalty to the provincial party on occasion might have superseded loyalty to the Government. In this way disagreements and disputes within the party and Government became known. The expression of conflicts within the party through the Afrikaans Press was rare before the creation of the Republic. But after 1961, disagreements began to seep into the news more frequently and by 1966, *Die Beeld's* campaign against the 'verkrampte movement' at the time of the 'verligte-verkrampte' (literally 'enlightened' and 'hard-liner') split forced a breach within Government and party–and the Afrikaans Press too for that matter–which shocked and surprised most Nationalists and particularly Nationalist politicians themselves.

The secrecy of Government affected the entire Press: the English Press in the sense that it was minimally assisted in its efforts to acquire information and the Afrikaans Press in that it seldom used its knowledge of Government activity without the express permission of Government.

The Press Gallery and Lobby Correspondents

Only two English-language newspapers maintained both a lobby and a gallery correspondent in Parliament while all the Afrikaans newspapers (or newspaper groups) employed separate lobby and gallery correspondents. The failure of the English Press to separate the two functions was significant, for the roles of the lobby and gallery are quite different. In Britain, for example, the gallery correspondent merely reports what is said on the floor of the House, summarizing and interpreting the debates. The lobby correspondents on the other hand are interested in activities off the floor of the House, in ferreting out events behind the debates and in keeping in touch with the policies and future policies of Government and Opposition.

The failure of the bulk of the English-language Press to use two men to perform two essentially different (and full time) jobs was partly a result of the refusal of the Speaker to extend the privilege to greater numbers of representatives (apparently because space was limited), and partly because of the futility of putting more men into Parliament when there was virtually no communication betwen Nationalist M Ps and English-language correspondents. The opposite was true for the Afrikaans newspapers. The lobby correspondents of the Afrikaans Press were an important link in the chain of communication between Government and editors, particularly as the administrative and legislative capitals were more than 1,000 miles apart.

While English lobby correspondents had great difficulty in learning about Government the relationship with Government for both

English and Afrikaans Press varied from correspondent to correspondent. Some English Press correspondents won favour from time to time, and Ministers and Government members at least agreed to speak to them, while on at least one occasion, an Afrikaans Press lobbyman was entirely ignored. As an example, Karl Prosser, who in 1962 was the first representative of the English Press to become chairman of the Press Gallery Association (PGA) has claimed that he had fairly easy access to departmental heads, probably because of his position as chairman. On the other hand, when *Die Beeld* was created in 1965, the then Prime Minister, Dr Verwoerd, refused to speak to the paper's correspondent or to its editor, and most MPs took their cue from the Prime Minister. *Die Beeld's* editor, Schalk Pienaar, a highly respected ex-assistant editor of *Die Burger* and the creator of the column 'Dawie', was ignored by MPs when he first appeared in the lobby as editor of *Die Beeld*. Mr Vosloo, the paper's lobby (and political) correspondent, who had previously worked for Dr Verwoerd's paper, *Dagbreek*, was never again granted an interview by Dr Verwoerd. Once the 'verligte-verkrampte' split had become an accepted fact, MPs again associated with *Beeld* journalists, though it was not until the death of Dr Verwoerd that *Die Beeld's* journalists were fully accepted.

The issuing of lobby and gallery tickets was a privilege bestowed by the Speaker of the House who could withdraw it at his discretion. As a matter of principle the PGA was consulted before a new ticket was issued and could express disapproval of the prospective correspondent; but the final say rested with the Speaker. Unlike the PGA which never exercised its prerogative, the Speaker used his discretionary powers on several occasions both to suspend and to withdraw lobby and gallery tickets from Press representatives. Although it is customary for Parliamentary Press facilities to be a 'privilege' bestowed by the Speaker, as indeed it is in Britain (which provided the model for South Africa's Press–Parliamentary structure), the nature of politics and the political divisions in the South African Parliament permitted abuse of the system. Correspondents, whose personal political attitudes were offensive to the National Party Government–and ultimately its formal representative, the Speaker, could be and were temporarily or permanently excluded from Parliament.

Events leading to the permanent banishment in 1964 of the *Cape Times'* political correspondent, Anthony Delius, was a case in point. Mr Delius, a staunch and consistent opponent of the Government, who was gallery and lobby correspondent from 1958 until 1964, was first suspended in 1962. The reason for his suspension was an article criticizing the arrangements made in Parliament regarding the removal of historical Parliamentary portraits. This article infringed the ruling against reporting anything heard or seen in the House, other than formal speeches. The harsh one-year suspension of Mr Delius was quite clearly out of all proportion to his offence. It was an equivalent peccadillo, which in 1964 brought about the permanent withdrawal of Mr Delius' tickets. He had reported that Dr Vorster, the brother of the then Minister of Justice, had sat in the visitors' gallery and listened to the Minister addressing the Assembly. This, strictly interpreted, was a breach of Parliamentary rules and the Speaker informed Mr Delius, that as he had been warned several times before for similar offences against the dignity of Parliament, his ticket was to be permanently withdrawn. Mr Delius had indeed been 'warned' and threatened. The messages he received seldom came formally from the Speaker; more usually, warnings were sent via the Afrikaans Press correspondents until a message, purporting to be from the Prime Minister himself, told Mr Delius that 'you have now filled up your book'. Before the final message was delivered, Mr Delius was warned that the *Cape Times* would lose its contract for printing the papers of the House. The paper responded by forming a separate company to handle its printing contracts.

There could be no doubt that Mr Delius was removed from Parliament because of his political attitudes rather than as a result of his relatively minor transgressions of Parliamentary rules. Perhaps the most revealing feature of the Delius affair was the innumerable 'chances' the Government gave Mr Delius to make himself an acceptable member, in its terms, of the Parliamentary Press corps. It is noteworthy too, that despite his wide powers the Speaker required a breach of the rules, on the part of Mr Delius, in order to exclude him.

The chain of events revealed the consistency of the Nationalists' methods in dealing with the English Press. It was suggested in the previous chapter, that the primary purpose of Press legislation, of the Press Code and even of the Press Commission was intimidation in that they were intended to induce the Press to censor itself. In dealing with an individual newspaperman, the 'threats' of the Government were more specific and more immediate, but the intention was the same: to persuade Mr Delius (or his sponsor-newspaper) to indulge in self-censorship. Having failed in this purpose, the Speaker acted directly, but within an existing framework of rules.

The consequences for Mr Delius personally were severe enough: his removal from Parliament effectively put an end to his career as a political journalist and shortly after his expulsion he left South

Africa. But more importantly Mr Delius' fate was a salutary caution to other political journalists who consistently criticized Government or Government members. After Mr Delius' first expulsion in 1962 the SASJ had written to the Speaker requesting that he should clarify what represented an offence against the dignity of Parliament. The Secretary of the House of Assembly, replying on behalf of the Speaker, said:

> '... it is not possible for him (the Speaker) to lay down standards which the Press should observe in relation to Parliament ... It is entirely in Mr Speaker's discretion whether or not an article which is published offends against the dignity of Parliament or is an attempt to ridicule Parliament in any way ...'[1]

The Speaker's refusal to clarify what constituted a punishable offence against Parliament's dignity ensured that he alone could define an offence and decide when to implement the rules in order to exclude politically unacceptable newspapermen.

By 1968 there were forty members of the gallery and lobby and fifteen lobby ticket holders. The possession of a lobby ticket entitled a correspondent to enter the lobbies of both the House of Assembly and the Senate. The lobby is situated immediately outside the chamber of the House, and Government and Opposition MPs congregate in the lobby on their way into or out of the chamber. The concept embodied in the lobby was that correspondents should mingle with MPs from both sides of the House though, as will be shown, the practice was different from the theory.

The Press Gallery Association, of which both lobby and gallery correspondents were members, helped to create a camaraderie between the representatives of the English and Afrikaans Press, though when under stress the division between English and Afrikaans journalists reappeared. In 1964, for example, when Mr Delius was expelled from Parliament, representatives of the English Press asked that the PGA chairman approach the Speaker and discuss Mr Delius' expulsion. But the representatives of the Afrikaans Press, who constituted a majority, refused to agree on the grounds that the PGA could not dictate to the Speaker.

Despite the inevitable stresses amongst the correspondents representing the two language groups, more contact and communication took place between members of the PGA than occurred at any other level between the Afrikaans and English Press. They spent most of their days working together and often eat together in the PGAs

[1] As reported in *The South African Journalist*, June–July 1962, p. 2.

dining-room and many of them went to Pretoria during the recess. Also, the PGA formally provided its members with an added channel of communication by occasionally entertaining ministers to lunch and through the annual PGA party which the Prime Minister was invited to attend. Dr Verwoerd only once attended, when the PGA chairman was a Nationalist, while the less doctrinaire Mr Vorster, attended a PGA party under an English Press chairman.

While it is to be expected that the political views of a particular newspaper and its correspondent must have some effect on the lobby man's contacts, a competent lobby man should have good 'sources' on both sides of the House. Yet in the South African lobby, both groups of journalists claimed to have contacts mainly–and usually exclusively–on one or the other side of the House. The PGA chairman in 1970 said that 'Afrikaans correspondents have a distinct advantage in terms of Government, but we (the English representatives) have all the advantage with the Opposition'. This is a view reiterated by Nationalist members of the Government who commented that as the English papers had all the advantage with Opposition MPs, it was quite in order for the Afrikaans papers to have all the advantage with Government MPs.

The advantages enjoyed by the Afrikaans Press lobby with Government MPs, extended beyond simple confidences between correspondents and MPs. At the beginning of each Parliamentary session, successive Nationalist Prime Ministers met with Afrikaans editors, and after 1966, with Afrikaans lobby correspondents, to discuss policy for the forthcoming year. Under Dr Malan, Mr Strijdom and Dr Verwoerd, joint meetings with all the Afrikaans editors were held in the legislative capital. Mr Vorster, as Prime Minister, varied the system slightly, holding joint meetings as well as private meetings with individual editors. In addition, Mr Vorster broadened the base of the meetings by including the Afrikaans Presses' Parliamentary correspondents. The purpose of the meetings was twofold. They were informatory, in the sense of policy attitudes being passed on to the media but also initiatory, to provide editors with the opportunity of making their impact on certain areas of policy. Of particular importance was the creation of campaign strategies for the forthcoming months. The degree to which editors' voices were heard in policy decisions depended on individual Prime Ministers. Dr Malan and Mr Vorster took most note of the attitudes of Afrikaans editors. Dr Verwoerd, although an ex-newspaperman himself, was 'authoritarian' in his approach to editors and issued instructions to the Press, rather than discussing the role of Nationalist newspapers in presenting new policies. In spite of, or perhaps because of his approach, Dr Verwoerd was on several occasions opposed, particularly by the editor of *Die Burger* who, in the course of the conflict on direct representation for the Coloureds, caused a stir by openly refusing to accept a Prime Ministerial directive at a pre-Parliamentary meeting.

In addition to the pre-Parliamentary briefing by the Prime Minister and the constant contact between Ministers and the Afrikaans Press lobby correspondents, the Afrikaans Press alone were invited to attend Prime Ministerial Press conferences. Very occasionally cabinet ministers gave Press conferences when they wished a specific issue to be discussed, particularly when wide publicity in the English Press was required. The Press conference in the American or even British style was unknown in South Africa but on the few occasions when a Prime Minister gave a Press conference (and only Mr Vorster and Dr Verwoerd ever did so), the English Press was only once invited to attend. On that occasion, the subject of Mr Vorster's Press conference was sport.

As Minister of Justice Mr Vorster had more frequent contact with the lobby than other ministers and as Prime Minister he continued to be more open with the Press than his predecessors. But his approach to the Parliamentary reporters was by no means 'open' in any other than a relative sense. Mr Vorster's one other Press conference was given exclusively to the Afrikaans correspondents and concerned the Herstigte Nasionale Party which was formed in 1969 to represent the 'verkampte' wing of the National Party. Mr Vorster justified the exclusiveness of the gathering by insisting that the issue was a 'party matter' which made it unnecessary to release the information to the English Press. This excuse for not giving important statements to the English-language Press was frequently invoked by Nationalist Ministers and Prime Ministers over the years, though as often as not the subject-matter was of interest or importance to the entire country. Thus, for example, in 1960 an announcement that the draft constitution of the Republic was to be published was given by the Prime Minister to a National Party meeting from which the English-language newspapers were excluded. In this particular instance the story was 'leaked' to some English papers and they managed to carry the story, though they registered their annoyance at being excluded from the announcement (*Rand Daily Mail,* December 2, 1960). A week earlier, Dr Verwoerd had done the same thing with two important policy statements: (*a*) a declaration that the National Party would make no concessions of principle in the cause of White unity and (*b*) his refusal to consider any direct Parliamentary representation for the Coloureds. Both statements were given exclusively to Nationalist newspapers.

This justification for affording preferential treatment to the Afrikaans Press sprang from the National Party's claim to be the sole and true representative of the 'Volk' in the political realm.[1] In so far as the Government felt itself to be accountable to anyone it was to the 'Volk'. Thus when Nationalist politicians suggested that issues (such as those cited above) were exclusively party matters, they really believed this to be true. For the 'Volk' who were represented by the National Party, were being kept informed through the party Press.

But there was also a self-consciousness about the preferential treatment given to the Afrikaans Press which confirms that the exclusion of the English Press was a matter of deliberate policy rather than an ingenuous omission.

Afrikaans correspondents themselves were mildly critical of this explicit bias, though not to the extent that they would tolerate a complaint by their representative body, the PGA. On one occasion the chairman did make an official complaint that the English Press was not issued with statements received by the Afrikaans Press. Members of the Afrikaans Press admonished the chairman, saying he had no right to speak on behalf of the Press in the way he had done.

Paradoxically it was the Afrikaans Press lobbyman whose position most closely resembled that of his counterpart in the British lobby. A good Afrikaans lobbyman would know within a day of the party caucus or even cabinet meeting the issues which had been discussed and usually the positions adopted by the persons involved. Although a British lobbyman might not promise to have the information within the day, he would certainly claim to be able to produce the gist of most caucus and cabinet meetings within a week. The problem for a good lobbyman in Britain would be how most effectively to perform a balancing trick: what information should be made public and should be pursued while at the same time ensuring that his sources were not embarrassed. At some point he could not fail to offend his sources but the mutual needs of lobbyman for information and politician for publicity would ensure the continuance of the information network. In South Africa there was the added dimension for the Afrikaans lobbyman of his own stringent loyalty to the party, though essentially the techniques he employed were much the same as those of his British counterpart.

Prior to the rift which produced the Herstigte Nasionale Party, the need to preserve a united front in Government and party made the Afrikaans lobbyman's task in a sense more frustrating, since he was

[1] See, for example, Sheila Patterson, *The Last Trek* (London: Routledge & Kegan Paul Ltd., 1957), p. 104 et seq.

required not to divulge a considerable amount of information. For the English journalists the problem was the search for that information. When they managed to obtain original information, they occasionally 'scooped' the Afrikaans papers, who were holding stories until the Government found them acceptable.

The reliance of the English Press on Opposition MPs for information produced some informed results. United Party MPs, some of whom were very close to their Nationalist counterparts in their thinking, on occasion learnt information from Government MPs which they then passed on to the English Press. When this occurred the English Press lobbymen were only able to use the information as a lever for acquiring confirmatory evidence from many other sources, including other Opposition MPs, the occasional Government MP, public servants and civil service departments. But even in terms of the civil service, the English Press newspapermen were at a disadvantage as most civil servants were Nationalist appointees. It has been claimed that 71 per cent of all White South African officials were Afrikaans speaking, whilst the percentage of Afrikaans-speakers in the upper echelons of the civil service was considerably higher.[1]

Outside Parliament English-language journalists, whether members of the political staff of their newspapers or not, were frequently and seriously hampered by Government departments and official attitudes. The numerous examples which could be cited of non-co-operation and even harassment of the English Press, did not all arise from a deliberate and coherent Government policy. None the less Government attitudes to the opposition Press seriously affected the ability of newspapers to produce accurate, efficient and full reports of departmental policy.

The policy of non-co-operation varied in its implementation from the withdrawal of existing facilities to a refusal to provide official statements to the English-language Press. As early as 1950, the *Rand Daily Mail* was given a foretaste of what to expect if they chose to disobey a Government request. In November of that year the Prime Minister underwent an operation in Pretoria: the Press was informed but was requested by the Prime Minister not to publish anything about it until after the operation had taken place. The *Rand Daily Mail* chose to ignore the request on the grounds that the health of the Prime Minister was a matter of public concern and that it had heard of the impending operation from independent sources. The director

---

[1] Heribert Adam in 'The South African Power-Elite: A Survey of Ideological Commitment' in *South Africa, Sociological Perspectives,* ed. H. Adam (London: Oxford University Press, 1971). See also Leo Marquard, *The Peoples and Policies of South Africa* (London: Oxford University Press, 1962).

of the State Information Office (which was handling the matter) personally contacted the paper's editor in an attempt to persuade him to accede to the Prime Minister's request but without success. According to the Press Commission Report,[1] which discussed the incident, Dr Malan was very indignant and on his recovery, instructed the State Information Office, the Prime Minister's Office and the Department of External Affairs to sever all relationships with the *Rand Daily Mail*.

The retribution for a seemingly trivial disobedience was undoubtedly severe. But even more important was the explanation given by the Press Commission which revealed an aspect of Government thinking about the Press. The Report first made it clear that journalists were not in a more privileged position than other members of the society and that 'In most spheres of life the severing of relationships is one of the best and most appropriate retaliations for this kind of behaviour'. Second, the Report denied that an editor was entitled 'to demand news or information from any man in public or private life because of the obligation his newspaper owes to its readers'. Rather the editor owed a duty to society 'to behave himself and to conduct his newspaper in such a way that he does not cause people to be reluctant or to refuse to supply him with news . . . in which the readers of his newspaper have an interest'. The Commission concluded that it was not Dr Malan, but the newspaper's editor, who had deprived the *Rand Daily Mail's* readers of a source of news.

A later example of governmental attitudes to the Press was an attempt made in 1959 to introduce a general 'rule' that Government Departments should only give information to the Press through their ministers. It was further requested that correspondents should seek information by way of formal questions asked in Parliament by M Ps. The Prime Minister, Dr Verwoerd, said that although the policy was not official, in that he himself had not issued a directive, individual ministers were free to make their own arrangements regarding communications to the Press.[2]

Fortunately for the Press neither of these policies was implemented. But the fact that such a *modus operandi* for lobby correspondents could have been suggested, was a further indication to the Press of the uncertainty of their position. Whilst the principle that individual journalists were free to confront individual politicians and civil servants remained, the possibility of acquiring information other than official statements, persisted.

[1] The Press Commission of Inquiry, Part 2, pp. 852–53.
[2] See *Rand Daily Mail*, November 4, 1959.

According to Stanley Uys, a political journalist of twenty years' standing (and the lobby correspondent of the *Sunday Times*), it became increasingly difficult after 1948 for English Press journalists to do their job. He stressed the difficulty of acquiring information on which to base assessments of the inner workings of Government. He said that 'some cabinet ministers will not talk to us at all, and most ministers are extremely reticent with English-language journalists: they do not like to be seen talking to the English Press. They hardly ever give us any assistance in making judgments. We tend to base our assessments on the public actions and utterances of politicians'.

There have been times when Nationalist M Ps have 'leaked' information to the English Press. A case in point occurred in the ejection of Japie Basson from the National Party in 1959. There were a series of caucus meetings during which Mr Basson's conflict with the National Party was becoming evident, and at which he raised his points of disagreement with the party and with Dr Verwoerd in particular. The English Press were the first to carry the news of Mr Basson's disagreement with the party and of his resignation. After the story had appeared in the English Press, the Prime Minister called in several M Ps including Mr Basson himself to trace the source of the 'leak' though without success. But for a considerable time after the Basson incident, the reluctance of Nationalist M Ps to be seen talking to English-language journalists increased further and they would only talk to English lobbymen in the presence of other M Ps or at least within earshot of fellow Nationalists. Another result of the Basson incident was that the cabinet adopted the practice of not informing M Ps of events in cabinet to ensure that even the most minor matters within Government should not appear in the English Press unless by the Government's choosing.

English journalists had not only to do a great deal more research than Afrikaans journalists before printing any kind of interpretive story, but also, because their articles were inevitably critical of Government, had to be more wary of the consequences of what they wrote. The *Sunday Times'* correspondent commented that 'One has seriously to consider the consequences of anything one publishes at all, as M Ps are very quick to issue denials even when stories are perfectly accurate'. No paper likes to carry stories which are instantly denied, with the result that stories which seemed impossible to substantiate after publication were frequently excluded. Those that were published had to be backed by substantive evidence.

Another form of pressure frequently applied to English journalists was the method of attacking individual newspapers and newsmen in Parliament itself. Those journalists who were attacked most fre-

quently agreed that while at first it was intimidating, and then weary-
ing, they developed an immunity to the attacks made on them
personally. They saw the attacks as an extension of the steady campaign to discredit the English-language Press, and felt that the
Nationalists had partly succeeded in undermining the credibility of
the English Press.

The International Press Institute confirmed in one of its surveys in
1955 that '... divorce between Government and Opposition has got
so much worse lately that reporters on opposition papers hardly have
any normal contact with ministers or with the administration'. The
survey went further and reported that some editors complained
that there had been instances when the authorities had deliberately
misled a reporter, '... in order to be able to give him the lie afterwards and accuse his paper of printing tendentious news. A case in
point was the "news" that South Africa intended to leave the United
Nations.'[1]

One of the most serious impediments for all English-language
journalists in South Africa has been the increase in legislation affecting their activities, which was discussed in the previous chapter. The
Criminal Procedure Act of 1955 which allowed for the subpoena of a
witness to answer questions before a magistrate had a particularly
marked effect on the daily work of the political journalist. The information most frequently requested from journalists was the dis-
closure of their sources for any story they might have written. An
amendment to the Act in 1964 increased the penalty for refusing to
disclose information from ten days to twelve months. If the journalist
still refused to disclose the relevant information after serving his
sentence he could be re-sentenced repeatedly for further periods of
twelve months. Although only seven journalists had been committed
to prison under the Act, the 1964 amendment was intimidatory in
that fewer journalists were willing to write stories which would en-
danger both their sources and themselves. Many English Press
political journalists were questioned by police about their sources.
As often as not police questioning resulted from the most seemingly
trivial remarks in news stories, as for example when the political
correspondent of the *Sunday Times*, Stanley Uys, reported the opening
of the Transkei Parliament in 1964. The Speaker of the House in the
Transkei who was elected in December 1963, was a member of the
Opposition. The *Sunday Times* correspondent wrote that 'strange
things' had happened during the recess after which the Government
rallied its working majority and a new Speaker was elected. (The

[1] IPI Survey: *Government Pressures on the Press*, 1955, p. 87.

Chief Minister of the Transkei requested the removal of the Speaker (or Chairman) on the grounds that he had attacked the rules of the House during the Parliamentary recess.) Within hours of the article's appearance, the police arrived to question him and to ask him what 'strange things' had happened. The most significant effect of police inquiries about journalists' sources and intentions was severe reduction in the amount of information journalists maintained in their possession. This has been particularly true in relation to the non-Whites and their activities, and consequently journalists became increasingly ignorant about the political activities of the non-Whites.

The position of the Afrikaans lobbymen was quite different. In the first place they were all members of the National Party. The closeness of their association with the Prime Minister and his cabinet depended to some extent on the individuals concerned but under most circumstances they could have access to the Prime Minister or any of his ministers whenever the need arose. However, ease of accessibility varied from Prime Minister to Prime Minister. All Afrikaans lobbymen agreed though that whenever an important policy question arose, the Prime Minister would be interviewed. The aim of such an interview would generally have been to acquire background information and material to be used anonymously. It would be rare to obtain a formal statement from the Prime Minister in such a manner. On a particular issue, the political correspondent would follow the guidelines the Prime Minister laid down. When anything of interest happened, the Afrikaans lobbymen was invariably very well informed. On occasion he was specifically requested to publish certain facts and would generally do so though the Nasionale Pers journalists claimed that they would not always do so. Afrikaans lobbymen, as might be expected, also got the fullest co-operation from departmental heads and civil servants and were usually extremely well briefed for anyhing that might happen.

When Parliament was not in session the Afrikaans lobbymen would accompany the politicians to the Transvaal. The Cape and Cape-backed newspapers were invited to send their political correspondents to the Cape Nationalist Congress and the same was true in the Transvaal for the Transvaal newspapers.

Considering the almost complete lack of co-operation of Government MPs with the English-language journalists, it was perhaps not surprising that one of the most consistent complaints heard from Nationalist politicians and newsmen was that the English Press displayed remarkable ignorance about Government. The 'inaccurate reporting' – which on may occasions can be re-interpreted as critical reporting–of the English-language political correspondents was a reason given by many Nationalist MPs for refusing to talk to the English Press. When it was suggested to Nationalist politicians that one of the possible causes of English Press ignorance might be that information was deliberately withheld from them and that they had to operate under conditions of acute political and Government secrecy, the standard reply was that when the English journalist was benefited with information, he so distorted it as to preclude the likelihood of any future disclosures. This argument seems circular. On the other hand some backbench MPs claimed that they were rarely approached by the English Press (which was so accustomed to being rebuffed) and that if they had been approached they would willingly have talked to English journalists. There was at least some truth in this suggestion. On the other hand, the position of the English political journalist as constant critic, and the attitudes within the political system to serious criticism, make it likely that any newly acquired contacts would not have been of long duration.

Despite the largely critical presentation ministers received in English newspapers they complained continuously about the bias of the English Press in the amount of coverage given to them. Similarly members of the Opposition were dissatisfied with their coverage in the Afrikaans Press and generally speaking their complaints were more valid even when taking into account that the Government is bigger 'news' than the Opposition. The Press Gallery chairman suggested that one problem was the failure of some ministers to understand their newsworthiness and to take advantage of it. Dr Verwoerd, for example, as an ex-newspaperman appreciated the importance of 'news value' and he frequently announced new schemes on the same day on which the leader of the Opposition was to give a major policy speech and naturally succeeded in ousting the Opposition leader from the papers' page one lead story. Mr Vorster, on the other hand, failed to understand that he had this power and normally replied on the last day of a debate, seldom being prepared to break his schedule. But the real problem it seems was that the English Press had at best only the assistance of Opposition MPs in compiling its stories and until such time as this changes, greater coverage will continue to be given to the United, and in some instances, the Progressive Party, in the English-language Press.

Finally it must be said that not all of the lobby correspondent's day was used in listening to debates and speaking to politicians and civil servants. All lobby journalists, whether representing the English or Afrikaans Press, were issued with their own copies of bills before the House, white papers, special reports and other miscellaneous

Parliamentary papers which they had to analyse. They were not pre-briefed and were usually issued with copies of bills on the same day as they were to be read in the House. Although English journalists generally would not get the co-operation of ministers or their secretaries when requesting policy statements or expansions, the Government Information Office or the secretaries would assist them with 'technical' problems. Because the lobby correspondents of the English papers were usually the gallery correspondents as well, newspaper groups worked together in Parliament. For example, the Morning Group newspapers pooled their resources and for straight Parliamentary reports, newspapers relied largely on SAPA. The Afrikaans newspapers also worked together to some extent and *Die Transvaler* and *Die Burger* correspondents stood in for each other when one or the other was unavailable.

The differences between the English and Afrikaans Presses' political correspondents in their methods of acquiring information about Government reflect the attitudes of Government and the administration to the two groups of newspapers. This can be shown most clearly by summarizing, in point form, the channels through which the Parliamentary correspondents most frequently acquired information:

English Press	Afrikaans Press
· Through Opposition MPs	· Through Government MPs
· The Afrikaans Press	· Pre-Parliamentary briefings by the Prime Minister
· Occasional 'leaks' from Government MPs	· Interviews with Ministers and the Prime Minister on request
· Through Government Ministers when publicity in the English Press desired	· National Party Conferences
· Through 'exposes' in the English Press requiring Government elucidation	· Occasional Press conferences

· Debates, public statements and actions of Government members

· Papers of the House

· Civil service and departmental heads

· Government Information Office

· PGA luncheons and parties

144

THE PRESS AND GOVERNMENT

The Editors

(a) The Afrikaans Press

Within the Afrikaans Press, the lobbyman's role was sometimes shared by his editor. At different times different editors were influential, but the newspaper which was consistently the receiver and creator of information and policy, was *Die Burger*. For this reason it will be of value to discuss at some length the relationship of *Die Burger* with the National Party Government after 1948, particularly with reference to its earlier years.

Geographically the editor of *Die Burger* had an advantage over his counterparts in the other provinces, in that he was situated in the country's legislative capital, Cape Town. It might be argued that Transvaal editors had the advantage for at least half the year in that they lived near the administrative capital, and under certain Prime Ministers, this claim had some validity. But *Die Burger* as the first and oldest of the National Party newspapers, and furthermore the most financially successful in the Afrikaans Press, historically had the closest association with the party and had party intellectuals and policy-makers as its editors. Its first editor, Dr Malan, who at the time was the chairman of the party in the Cape, used *Die Burger* to discuss and publicise many of his policies. In a book published to celebrate the fiftieth anniversary of *Die Burger* in 1965[1], P. A. Weber an ex-editor of the paper, said that Dr Malan did not in any way separate his role as editor from that of party leader. He cites an instance when Dr Malan as party leader addressed a meeting one evening at Malmesbury. Dr Malan, the editor, in a leading article the following week, began: 'As we said last Friday night at Malmesbury . . .' According to Mr Weber, Dr Malan's special relationship with *Die Burger* was maintained up to and including the time when he became Prime Minister. He claimed that 'The *Burger* remained a confidant and a trusted adviser of Dr Malan's, indeed to the extent that a Minister once remarked, and not without good cause, that we at the *Burger* often know more about Dr Malan's plans than some members of his cabinet![2] Although this close association between Dr Malan and the *Burger* was maintained long after Dr Malan resigned his editorship, the relationship between the paper and the Prime Minister could obviously not be the same as when the party

[1] J. P. Scannel (ed.), *Keeromstraat 30* (Cape Town: Nasionale Boekhandel Bpk, 1965), p. 18.
[2] ibid., p. 19.

K 145

leader was the editor. As Mr Weber pointed out, under Dr Malan's editorship, 'Die Burger was Dr Malan'.[1]

By appointing a journalist as opposed to a party-politician to succeed Dr Malan to the editorship, Nasionale Pers established at an early stage the principle that the newspaper was to have an independent existence within the party.

After the death of Dr Malan, Die Burger's relationship with the Government underwent further changes, especially as the new Prime Minister, Mr Strijdom, was a Transvaal man, whose closest associates were fellow Transvalers. But contact between Die Burger and the Government continued at the highest level. No Prime Minister could afford to ignore the influence of Die Burger, particularly amongst his own supporters. Mr Weber describes the role of Die Burger at this time as that of 'pioneers, scouts and protagonists'.[2] He reveals that Mr Strijdom said to Die Burger that a Government cannot move too swiftly ahead of public opinion, and that the Prime Minister asked Die Burger to pioneer a new 'Bantu' policy, and to win the support of public opinion for such a new policy. At the same time, Mr Weber confessed, Die Burger 'went too fast' for the party and caused them some embarrassment as, for example, on the republican issue.

The ebb of Die Burger's direct influence with the Government began when Dr Verwoerd came to power for he too was identified with the Transvalers. More importantly he consulted less with his colleagues than any of his predecessors. He, as the party's leading ideologist, felt less need for the services of Burgermen, as they called themselves, and the Prime Minister and Die Burger's journalists increasingly came into conflict. Die Burger enjoyed its pioneering role and its influence in the party while Dr Verwoerd could brook no opposition. He wished the party line as laid down by himself to be strictly adhered to on all matters. After Dr Verwoerd was shot–and survived–Die Burger to a great extent lost the battle: a fierce loyalty to the person of the Prime Minister developed at the expense of support for Die Burger.

The coming to power of Mr Vorster marked the re-emergence of Die Burger and its editor, Piet Cillie, as a powerful political force. To the surprise of many party members, Mr Vorster chose to be guided by Die Burger, rather than by any of the Transvaal papers. To a large extent Die Burger, together with Die Beeld, saw itself and was seen by many Nationalist politicians and newsmen as the creator of 'verligte'

[1] ibid., p. 24.
[2] ibid., p. 33.

Vorster. Partly because of the 'verligte-verkrampte' split and partly because of his special relationship with *Die Burger*, Mr Vorster resigned as chairman of Afrikaanse Pers and Voortrekkerpers, a post which had previously been held by Mr Strijdom and Dr Verwoerd.

Die Burger's rift with Dr Verwoerd began in 1960, when *Die Burger* represented the Cape Nationalist 'intellectual' viewpoint that Coloureds should be represented by Coloureds in Parliament. Dr Verwoerd tried to halt *Die Burger's* attempt to discuss the issue publicly, in its news and letter columns. Eventually Dr Verwoerd was compelled to assemble the Federal Council of the party to force *Die Burger* to stop the discussion. The directive from the Federal Council in conjunction with a door-to-door campaign by Verwoerd loyalists enjoining subscribers to stop buying *Die Burger,* eventually forced *Die Burger* to halt the campaign.

The final rift came when *Die Beeld* was established in 1965 in competition with Dr Verwoerd's paper, *Dagbreek*. But then in a sense the establishment of *Die Beeld* was evidence that the rift had already taken place, for it was set up against the wishes of the Prime Minister. By the time Mr Vorster became Prime Minister, *Die Beeld* was established and very successful, and the 'verligte verkrampte' issue was being openly discussed. *Die Burger* quite deliberately ventured to win Mr Vorster to their way of thinking which they described as Cape and 'verligte'. The Cape Nationalists saw themselves as less brash, more tolerant, democratic and 'civilized' than the Transvaal Nationalists since the Afrikaners who remained in the Cape were not compelled to endure the insecurity and harsh conditions which confronted the 'Trekkers'. Furthermore, the Cape Nationalists, through a more constant contact with the British in the Cape, were more deeply imbued with British concepts of democratic processes as well as the idea of compromise. Many Nationalists feared that Mr Vorster had become *Die Burger's* puppet and accusations that the paper was trying to rule the party frequently reached its editor. His reply was 'It is not a newspaper's business to run the country, but we do try to introduce new ideas to the Government. We write for the policy makers; we propagate a way of thinking and an approach'. More important for the newspaper as a whole was the effect of this new intimacy with the Government both institutionally and on a personal level, for the editor had been at University both with Mr Vorster and with the editor of *Die Beeld* and all three were friends of long standing. Instead of using the newspaper as a vehicle for expressing criticisms of the party and policy, he would approach the Prime Minister and discuss his differences inter-personally. Several *Burger* journalists expressed their concern at the new relationship of the paper with the

Government and claimed that they felt the effects of it in their daily work.

In addition to the frequent formal and social contacts between senior *Burger* journalists and high-ranking Nationalist politicians, the editor of *Die Burger* attended the pre-Parliamentary meetings with other Afrikaans editors and while Parliament was in session he attended almost every day, making use of lobby and gallery facilities. Under Dr Malan, the editor of *Die Burger* attended the weekly party caucus meetings (a practice which arose in Opposition days), but when Mr Strijdom became Prime Minister, Mr Weber, then editor of *Die Burger,* advised the Prime Minister to discontinue the practice as he claimed it was unfair to other Afrikaans editors.

Mr Strijdom took Mr Weber's advice and consequently *Die Burger* began to rely more on its lobbyman to report on the day-to-day activities of the Parliamentary party. Prior to the exclusion of *Die Burger's* editor from the caucus meetings, the editor would determine the main points of news. Usually, however, the paper would not publish a story, until it had been established independently by their lobbyman.

When important cabinet decisions were reached, the editor of *Die Burger,* as well as other Afrikaans editors or lobbymen, would be called in and 'told what to avoid'. In certain instances, such as that of the lowering of the voting age, the editor disagreed and under such circumstances he generally refused to conduct any campaign at all. He said that although he would not campaign for something he disagreed with, he would not oppose it either as he would not wish to appear to support the Opposition. In other words, Mr Cillie saw himself as a forerunner and an initiator of policy, but once a positive policy decision was taken, he would rarely oppose it in public. However, his silence on an issue of any importance could thus be interpreted as disapproval.

Historically, *Die Vaderland's* associations with the National Party were the most tenuous of the Afrikaans papers. Prior to 1948 it supported the early Hertzog National Party, then the coalition and eventually the fusion United Party. From 1948 it supported Mr Havenga's Afrikaner Party until the Afrikaner Party fused with the National Party, at which point *Die Vaderland* became the voice of 'fundamentalist Afrikanerdom' according to its most recent editor (A. M. van Schoor). Under General Hertzog *Die Vaderland* was for a time an influential newspaper but it was never, after it became a fully fledged supporter of the National Party, an official organ of the Transvaal Party nor did it try to initiate policy in the party. Under Mr Strijdom and Dr Verwoerd, the paper reflected and enunciated the policies of its chairmen. When Mr Vorster resigned as chairman of the paper, at the height of the 'verligte-verkrampte' exposures, there was a great deal of uncertainty in the party and Press about where *Die Vaderland* stood. Mr Van Schoor denied that he was 'verkrampt' or that his paper permitted Dr Hertzog, before he was forced to resign from the board of APB, to influence the tone of the paper. But he affirmed that he supported fundamentalism, that he believed in Sunday observance, that the Afrikaner had still to fight for his language against the encroachment of the world-language and culture, English. He believed not in a South African 'nationhood', but in a South African state based on the separation of identities, including the separation of English and Afrikaans speakers. His views, which were in fact those expressed by the 'verkrampte' faction of the party were certainly in conflict with his Nasionale Pers colleagues.

During the months when the politicians were in Pretoria, Mr van Schoor saw them daily but the tendency was for him to communicate almost exclusively with Transvalers. He had little affinity with the more 'liberal' Cape. His contact with Dr Verwoerd was far more intimate than that with Dr Vorster whom he thought young and inexperienced. As a Nationalist editor, Mr van Schoor maintained that the possibility of his disagreeing with Government policies did not arise but he admitted that he sometimes disagreed with the implementation of policies and on occasion he was known to hold the Government accountable for its actions. It is interesting that despite the more liberal claims of *Die Burger* for itself, *Die Vaderland* sometimes carried stories which the Cape paper refused to publish. This is explained partly by the fact that Mr van Schoor did not edit his paper with the same degree of control as Mr Cillie. Mr van Schoor remained primarily a leader-writer and concerned himself very largely with political comment rather than with the general running of the newspaper. In the 1960s the key man in *Die Vaderland* was the news editor, who allowed his staff some measure of freedom to write what they liked, resulting in the expression of a range of political attitudes within the Nationalist spectrum. Mr Cillie, on the other hand, kept a tight control on his entire paper, deciding personally on the front page leads and vetting all stories which appeared in his paper. Even billboard headings had first to be referred to Mr Cillie before being displayed.

Die Transvaler was the official organ of the National Party in the Transvaal but unlike *Die Burger* was unable to free itself from the party's shackles and create an original role for itself within the party. Under Dr Verwoerd—who as the paper's first editor had a special regard for *Die Transvaler*–and to some extent under Mr Strijdom, *Die Transvaler* managed to oust *Die Burger* as the Government's prime confidant. *Die Transvaler* and its editors had the ear of Dr Verwoerd, but as Dr Verwoerd was the most independent of the Nationalist Prime Ministers, their ability seriously to influence the direction of Government policy was never as great as that of *Die Burger*.

The Transvaal editors had to rely much more on their lobby correspondents to keep them in touch with the opinions and attitudes of the Parliamentary party. Like all other Afrikaans editors, *Die Transvaler's* editor went to Cape Town at the beginning of each Parliamentary session to attend the meetings with the Prime Minister. During the recess he had easy access to the Prime Minister in Pretoria if he wanted to discuss matters of policy as well as having frequent contact with ministers and Transvaal party officials. His Cape contacts would have been relatively fewer, although through a traditional association with Nasionale Pers–NPB is a shareholder in *Die Transvaler*–he had more contact with Cape Nationalists than *Die Vaderland*. Through his lobby correspondent the editor of *Die Transvaler* received information and instruction from the cabinet, when he was not available in person.

Die Transvaler did not see itself in the same role as *Die Burger* though it shared some of *Die Burger's* aspirations. The editor of the paper in 1970 said that it was not the function of the Press 'to guide the party and hence the Government into accepting new roles, principles or policies, but rather to scout around the existing problems and to inform the party itself about new possibilities. You can never really lead people if you move too far away from them.' In other words *Die Transvaler* came to see itself as the Government's public opinion pollster rather than as a policy-directing Press. This had not always been the newspaper's role, for under Dr Verwoerd's editorship, *Die Transvaler* was indeed a policy-making paper, whose editor used the paper to enunciate his own very personal and frequently original attitudes, with the intent of influencing the development of the National Party. Although a Southerner, or Cape man, Dr Verwoerd soon revealed himself as much closer to Mr Strijdom and the Transvalers than to Dr Malan, and during his years as editor played up such contentious issues as the Republic and the race question.

Die Volksblad and *Die Oosterlig,* as NPB papers, were dependent largely on the political staff of *Die Burger* for their 'orders' and information: The voice of *Die Volksblad* was that of the Orange Free State National Party although its views were somewhat tempered by its Cape backing. Neigher *Volksblad* nor *Oosterlig* had their own lobby correspondents but relied for their information on *Die Burger's* correspondent. They suffered by having to share such an important service, especially as the group's correspondent confessed that his first loyalty was to *Die Burger*, for which he always tried to 'hold back' good stories.

Die Beeld's editor on the other hand would never have tolerated such second-hand treatment and insisted on a full and independent staff with which to run what became the most controversial Afrikaans paper in the country. Most of *Die Beeld's* staff were drawn from *Die Burger*–the training ground for most NPB journalists–though their lobby correspondent was not an NPB man at all. After *Die Burger*, *Die Beeld* became the most important Afrikaans newspaper in the country. It did not use the methods of the parent paper to acquire influence with Government or the Party. *Die Beeld* was prepared to go much further than *Die Burger* in ferreting out undesirable facts about the Government. Particularly, its editor claimed responsibility for revealing the 'verligte-verkrampte' factions in the party. *Die Burger's* editor suggested that *Die Beeld* had the traditions of an NPB paper's independence and outspokenness and chose to adopt the 'brash Transvaal method' of expressing these qualities.

At the outset the creation of *Die Beeld* was involved in provincial Nationalist politics. As early as 1953 Nasionale Pers had decided to start a Sunday paper in the Transvaal, but were opposed by the Transvaal National Party and the then Prime Minister Mr Strijdom, who arranged instead for *Dagbreek* to be funded by the Transvaal party. For one thing a Nasionale Pers paper would not have been as enthusiastically pro-Strijdom as *Dagbreek* proved to be. It was not until 1964 that Nasionale Pers decided to try again to enter the Transvaal with a Sunday paper. They were met with ferocious opposition from the Transvaal party, the Prime Minister and even the Church, which suggested that it was a sin to publish a Sunday newspaper.

The spirit with which *Die Beeld* came into the Transvaal continued into the working policy of the paper, which embodied a belief in its 'mission' to propagate Cape Nationalism in the Transvaal and undermine the ever-growing dominance of Transvaal Nationalists in the Government. Thus, for example, *Die Beeld's* editor stressed the need for the paper to do what it could to influence the leadership succession. He claimed that 'one of our most important tasks is to influence the choice of Mr Vorster's successor. The Cape leader of the party is a candidate and we would like to see him at the helm. Our support of the Cape candidate is seen as an attempt from the South to increase

Southern political influence and as such has caused a fair amount of pressure to be exerted on us.' Mr Pienaar was, however, used to pressure by then. In addition to the initial opposition to *Die Beeld*, the revelation of a 'verkrampte' faction in the party resulted in numerous attacks on the paper and on the editor himself. The editor commented: 'We were accused of undermining the party leadership, and of spreading liberalism. But we pointed out that the "verkramptes" were the people trying to create division and their end view was a party takeover. They were infiltrating Afrikaner institutions and attempting to take them over. At the time there were high-level attempts to boycott *Die Beeld* and I was on occasion made to feel physically afraid.'

The kind of sanctions to which the editor was exposed, included not being invited to attend pre-Parliamentary meetings with the Prime Minister and being extensively ignored when he appeared in the Parliamentary lobby. He was also not permitted to attend Transvaal National Party Congress though in later years he was invited. Unlike most other Afrikaans editors, the editor of *Die Beeld* had very little contact with his fellow Afrikaans editors and journalists in the Transvaal (though this was largely a result of his own choice; pressure of work and 'differences in personality' were the reasons he gave for choosing to remain aloof from the editors of the other Afrikaans papers in the Transvaal). Once he was based in Johannesburg, *Die Beeld's* editor also saw very little of Government ministers and relied heavily on his lobby correspondent to keep him informed. Once a week he spoke to the lobby correspondent when he was in Cape Town, to get the lobbyman's 'minutes' on party caucus and cabinet meetings and the activities of individual ministers and politicians.

As Minister of Justice, Mr Vorster was actively neutral in his attitude to *Die Beeld* and by the time he became Prime Minister, *Die Beeld* was already established. Mr Vorster and *Die Beeld* were, according to the editor, on a good footing from the start. He had few doubts that Mr Vorster would turn out supporting the 'verligtes', though 'the verkramptes thought that Mr Vorster would be their man and as such supported him for Prime Minister. As Minister of Justice they saw in him the Nazi gauleiter as depicted by the English Press'.[1]

[1] It is interesting to speculate on the extent to which the English-language Press has unwittingly acted as kingmaker to the Nationalist Government. It is arguable, that by isolating and attacking, it has hailed the 'strongmen' for Government supporters. For example, Dr Verwoerd, as Minister of Native Affairs and the architect of apartheid, was identified during Mr Strijdom's rule as prime 'villain' by the English Press. He was invariably introduced at Nation-

According to the editor, the coming of the Republic was the single most important event which made *Die Beeld* possible. 'We grew up under the British umbrella and that umbrella has disappeared. We are now busy creating the opinions and the way of looking on the world which makes it possible for South Africa to follow the independent line which keeps us going. The party needs its Press even more than ever before to bring home to the Afrikaners the complete change that has come over South Africa.'

Before the Republic became a reality the Afrikaans Press was largely united by the 'great ideal of a republic'. Afterwards, it was only natural that differences of opinion in other matters would come to the fore and that *Die Beeld* should then feel free to be 'a bit reckless' in its criticisms of Government.

Perhaps the most important point to be made about the editor of *Die Beeld* and the policy of his paper was that he more than any other Afrikaans editor, distinguished between the National Party and the Government. He did all in his power to influence the course of Government, and used brasher methods of doing so than any other editor. He publicly exposed them to criticism if more subtle techniques were not available or proved ineffectual. And frequently he went further than the English papers who were much more vulnerable to Government retribution. After all, it must be remembered that the chairman of the N P B Board was, in 1968, also the country's Minister of Defence.

(b) The English Press

The basis of the relationship between the English Press and the Government was antagonism, varying in intensity according to the policies of individual newspapers and their editors. In contrast to Afrikaans editors, very few newspaper editors in the English sector had ever met a Nationalist Prime Minister. Sometimes they might have attended official functions together and possibly might have been introduced to each other. But then this was also true for the lobby correspondents who were after all 'living' in the same building as the Prime Minister for at least six months of the year. Mr Vorster was the

---

alist Party meetings as 'the man the English Press hates'. The day he became Prime Minister, a new 'villain' was identified, the Minister of Justice Mr Vorster. For, as Prime Minister, the mystique of being 'White leader' subtly sanctifies the man. It is, of course, quite impossible to measure the influence of publicity in the English-language Press on the ascendancy of Nationalist politicians in the party, but in the prevailing conditions of antagonism between the English Press and the Government, it seems at least possible that the hostility of the English Press can be advantageous to a Nationalist politician's career. Even if it is only because he is constantly in the news.

first Prime Minister after 1948 to agree to a meeting with selected English editors and at least one English editor, the editor of the *Natal Mercury,* developed an acquaintanceship with the Prime Minister, as the policy of his newspaper occasionally showed.

In general, though, the English Press continued to be uniformly and sometimes violently, opposed to the National Party Government and its policies. The Government in turn brought great pressure to bear on a Press which it invariably saw as un-South African and frequently 'dangerous and subversive'. The kinds of pressures which a powerful Government can bring to bear on a newspaper Press have already been discussed in earlier chapters, but some further aspects of Government pressures on the Press will be dealt with here. Although the English Press had no direct influence on Government in the sense that the Afrikaans Press had, it was a force in the society as a whole which the Government could not ignore. There were broadly two ways in which the English Press could bring pressure to bear on Government: first, by directly attacking Government, its individual members and their policies; and second, by making constant criticisms in the social realm, which inevitably had political repercussions. By attacking what they saw as the failures of the political policies in coping with social problems–and most importantly by giving them wide publicity–they frequently presented a view of the world and of South Africa which was wholly opposed to the Nationalist viewpoint. Although they had no measureable influence on the electorate the existence of a constantly opposing voice in the society could not be a wholly negative force. The English Press was after all the only written medium through which a sizeable percentage of the country's population got a picture of itself as a whole. And even if, as an English-language, establishment Press it presented a fractured view of that society, it still presented a vision almost totally opposed to the vision of the society's rulers.

The pressures upon English language editors to keep silent on contentious issues were in almost all cases great and increasing, though their experiences of these pressures varied quite considerably.

The editor of the *Evening Post* in Port Elizabeth, who was one of the harshest critics of Government, was exposed to more than the normal legal and political pressures that his colleagues had to endure. The more severe pressures on him began in 1960, shortly after the declaration of an emergency in the country. Mr Sutherland and his newspaper were charged with contravening the emergency regulations and the case went on for nine months and through three courts. He was eventually fined £5 but the costs of the case ran into thousands.

Other editors experienced more subtle forms of pressure. The editor of one opposition newspaper told the story of a raid on his offices by detectives from the Special Branch. They gave no reasons for their presence but significantly they arrived three-quarters of an hour after the post had arrived. The day's mail had contained a communist weekly which it was illegal to have in one's possession. The editor finding the unexpected arrival of such a journal suspicious, had ordered his secretary to destroy it immediately. There was thus no trace of the banned journal when the Special Branch arrived. The implication was, of course, that the publication was 'planted' by the police in an attempt to convict the editor of an offence.

These pressures built up an atmosphere of fear with the result that less and less politically contentious news was carried by the paper and the editor found it increasingly difficult to find reporters prepared to take on risky assignments. Despite these difficulties and the pessimistic view of his own role taken by this particular editor, his newspaper continued to be an articulate critic of South African society and Government. In consequence certain types of stories were simply being eliminated from the spectrum of possible news selection. In addition, the paper no longer employed a political correspondent but had to rely on the occasional 'anonymous' story from another newspaper's correspondent.

Mr Raymond Louw, who succeeded Laurence Gandar as editor of the *Rand Daily Mail,* which was more exposed to Government wrath than any other establishment newspaper, claimed that his newspaper was as much a crusading paper as ever, but that he had acquired a certain ingenuity in dealing with Government pressures. Things were kept out of the paper, but simply to comply with the law and no situation had yet arisen which was so serious that the paper felt it had to break the law and publish. There was, however, a certain ambiguity in Mr Louw's claim, as one of the major problems in working as an editor in South Africa was that the laws were frequently so loosely defined as to make it impossible to know when one was breaking them. Mr Louw admitted that while he himself had not been intimidated by Government pressures, at the level of the paper's reporters there was a growing feeling of intimidation, which was even more marked amongst the paper's African reporters. (The *Rand Daily Mail* published a 'township' edition for a period of time, which was run by a largely African staff.) The paper dealt with this in much the same way as the lobby correspondents coped with intimidation and the closing up of sources, namely by demanding the highest standards of accuracy and the most rigorous documentation of all stories which were likely to antagonize Government. An illustration of the techniques and style of social criticism which the *Rand Daily Mail* continued to pursue was the 'Morsgat' revelations in October 1969. As a result of the Government removals policy, it came to the attention of the *Rand Daily Mail* that in Morsgat, a non-White area in the Northern Transvaal nearly two thousand people had been living in tents for at least a year without being rehoused, after being forcibly removed from their original homes. The editor recognized that the Government would be angered by such a revelation and suspected that they might attempt to deny the facts. Further, the paper knew that residents of the tent-town would be afraid to talk to the Press for fear of Government reprisals and might, under Government pressure, withdraw their statements at a later date. The *Rand Daily Mail* did several things. First, it sent several African reporters and one White reporter into Morsgat with formally printed questionnaires, to interview the residents. All reporters were given documents to prove that they were employed by the *Rand Daily Mail,* a precaution intended to protect reporters from the police rather than to identify them to interviewees. Shortly after their first visit, the reporters were detained by the Special Branch and questioned for several hours but their investigations continued for nearly three months. The *Mail* then checked with some officials about the facts of the case and there appeared to be general agreement with the facts presented in the replies to the questionnaire. The *Rand Daily Mail's* next step was to draw up a list of sixty-four questions which it submitted to the relevant Government department. After sixteen days and approximately five requests to the Department for answers to their questions, the *Mail* published all the evidence they had accumulated, including aerial pictures of the tent-town.

The evidence which the *Rand Daily Mail* had accumulated was presumably sufficiently substantial to deter the Government from prosecuting the paper. For the *Rand Daily Mail* was correct in expecting Government denials and the paper alleged that it was only after the questionnaire had been submitted to the Department that attempts were made to clean up the environment and to provide latrines. Once this had been done a party of journalists from other newspapers were conducted round the site in an effort to disprove the *Rand Daily Mail's* claims. But Mr Louw believed that the paper was so overwhelmingly right that it was believed by its readers.

Other pressures put upon the editor and his staff included most commonly the tailing of reporters by the police and even of people seen to be visiting the editor. Because of the extensive ramifications of the Defence Act, the editor admitted that it had become common practice to contact the Minister of Defence when in doubt about reporting matters relating to defence.

Finally Mr Louw saw his paper and the English Press as a whole, as bringing pressure to bear on major Government issues and policies by informing the public of those policies and their ramifications. He said: 'The *Mail* leads minority opinion. We are concerned about the deprivation of rights, with the underprivileged, with the well being of the whole community and with apartheid.'

The Natal Mercury was one of the most conservative English-language newspapers in the country and remained more concerned with the rights of the English South Africans than with any other problem. The editor in 1970, John Robinson, who claimed to be a personal friend of the leader of the Opposition, accounted for his growing acceptance of the Nationalist Government, particularly under Mr Vorster, 'because Mr Vorster promised to introduce a more outward policy, which would be beneficial to the economy, and because he is the first Nationalist Prime Minister to stand up for the equality of rights between the English and the Afrikaner'.

Mr Robinson kept a tight control over the policy of his newspaper and spoke to his lobby correspondent daily. 'I tell him how he should report and what he should report. If I feel that he is not following the lines I want, I will tell him'. Despite the greater conservatism of the *Natal Mercury*'s policy, the editor still shared some of the ideals of all other English-language newspaper editors. He believed it to be his duty to ensure that the interests of the unrepresented non-Whites were brought to the attention of the Whites, though he was prepared to risk very little in representing those interests. The *Natal Mercury* went much further than the *Rand Daily Mail* in consulting the Minister of Defence, when in doubt about defence stories. For the editor issued a general directive to his staff to obtain 'authority' to publish any delicate stories. He said: 'Whenever I got a story that I feel might be a breach of regulations I refer it straight to the relevant minister. If he says we can publish, we do, if he says not, we don't.' And quite evidently the *Natal Mercury* journalists got a good deal more co-operation from the minister than most other English-language journalists.

The editor of the other major Durban newspaper, the *Daily News*, took it upon himself in 1969 to request a meeting with the Prime Minister. He had never met a Nationalist Prime Minister but thought it would be of value to try and establish some direct link with Government sources. He met no cabinet ministers but the Prime Minister granted him a forty-minute interview, during which Mr Vorster complained that the *Daily News* was against Bantustans and that the paper, in line with other English papers, wanted the National-ists to fail. But Mr O'Malley in his reply to the Prime Minister simply stressed what he saw as 'Our great responsibility of taking up the cudgels for the millions of voteless people'. The greatest pressures upon him, as he saw them, were the massive body of constricting laws, the difficulty of acquiring information from Government sources and intimidation by members of the Special Branch who occasion-ally 'tailed' his reporters.

'If I was told (and I knew it to be true) that a prisoner was "bumped off" in prison, I would not be able to publish it.' This and many other stories like it were daily censored at source, according to Victor Nor-ton, the editor of the *Cape Times*. He confirmed that 'there is little we can do about it, except continuously to protest against the law', and this, of course, brought the paper into conflict with Government. Because Mr Norton was based in Cape Town, he came into frequent contact with Afrikaans newspapermen and politicians through at-tending the many social functions which centre around Parliament when in session. But his contacts were not sufficiently meaningful for him to feel any freer of Government pressures than other English editors. At the most his contacts brought him a little closer to an understanding of the Nationalist and his policies.

Mr Norton was not by nature a campaigning journalist but he gave support to senior members of his political staff who were. When Anthony Delius was the paper's lobby correspondent, Mr Norton was called upon again and again to defend Mr Delius, whose views were invariably far more radical than his own. Government pressures were put upon Mr Norton 'to do something about Delius' but he refused to withdraw his support from Mr Delius or even to quieten him down. In 1956, for example, Mr Norton was reprimanded by the Senate bar for his paper's attitude to the Constitutional crisis, a rap he had to take largely on behalf of Mr Delius. Interestingly, while Mr Delius was the paper's political correspondent he had some in-fluence on the whole policy of the paper and was frequently able to persuade Mr Norton to his own point of view. After Mr Delius' de-parture, when he was no longer exposed to his political correspond-ent's views, Mr Norton adjusted the paper's policy to his own more conservatively critical approach to Government.

The East London *Daily Dispatch* in the 1960s took advantage of the backwater nature of the paper to criticize the Government in a way that few other papers in the country would consider. It was, for example, not realized, except by a very few outside of East London itself, that the *Daily Dispatch* had, at the same time as the *Rand Daily Mail,* published the prison condition articles which had so many serious repercussions for the *Rand Daily Mail*. Like the *Rand Daily Mail*, the *Daily Dispatch* saw itself as a crusading newspaper, but unlike the *Rand Daily Mail*, the *Daily Dispatch's* editor, Mr Donald Woods, believed himself to be playing some kind of 'dangerous political game'. 'You must,' he said 'have a personal relationship with the people you are criticizing.' He claimed to befriend political leaders so as to be able to attack them more informally and more vigorously. He suffered few repercussions, mostly because the paper was so small. On the other hand, attempts by the *Daily Dispatch* to increase its non-White readership in the Transkei are likely to make its policies more radical as well as to bring it under closer Government surveillance. In the meantime the greatest pressures upon Mr Woods were social pressures: 'vicious anonymous telephone calls, combined with pressures at the club or golf course', which in a relatively small community put strains upon an editor in the performance of his job.

Mr Rene de Villiers, the editor of the *Star*, the largest daily paper in the country, believed that Government pressures over the last twenty years had taken their toll; that the English-language Press became a little less aggressively political, a little less committed than they were at the beginning of the Nationalist's rule. He suggested that there was a growing acceptance of the political facts of life. 'We know that the political situation is desperately unfluid, and that we now have to try to get as much modification within the existing framework, though without accepting that framework.' Like other English newspapers, the *Star's* methods were to draw attention to some of the 'grosser injustices' and to the importance of 'values, standards and principles in politics'. Mr de Villiers saw one of the most serious repercussions of Government pressures on the Press as the clamming up of Africans, who were growing more cautious about talking to newspapers, with the result that White South Africans had less and less knowledge of what was going on in the minds of Africans. This silence was a direct result of Government legislation affecting newspapers themselves, which were unable to quote banned persons, were forced to disclose their sources, and which were extensively threatened if they ventured into the African world.

Mr de Villiers believed that English editors gave each other courage to continue their public opposition to Government, and, partly with this in mind, he had frequent contact with other English-language editors. Also, he had the occasional 'not very meaningful' contact with Afrikaans Press editors. Despite the fact that the *Star's* editor visited Parliament for the opening of each session he never met the Prime Minister or any members of the cabinet, though he believed that any meeting with them would not have resulted in the Government being more responsive to the needs and demands of the independent Press.

The editor of the *Sunday Times* on the other hand valued his contacts with Nationalist politicians and newspapermen, though his contacts with opposition MPs were very much more frequent. Joel Mervis, the *Sunday Times'* editor, laid great stress on his paper supporting a 'middle of the road' politics, though his clearly correct notion–if circulation is anything to go by–that politics is 'big news' in South Africa, brought him into frequent conflict with both Government and individual MPs. This resulted partly from his permitting individual political commentators and correspondents a fairly free hand in their handling of subject matter, and as his staff represented a relatively broad spectrum of political attitudes, the variety of socio-political or political stories published in the *Sunday Times* was wide. Most notably, the paper's lobby correspondent, Stanley Uys, had few restraints imposed on him by his editor although he was considerably less middle-of-the-road than Mr Mervis. Most MPs–and frequently both Government and Opposition members–regarded Mr Uys as the most 'undesirable' man in the lobby, a role he assumed when Mr Delius was expelled. The fact that Mr Uys was so very unpopular was indicative of his personal political attitudes rather than the attitudes of his newspaper, which were less offensive to many Nationalists than the politics of most other English-language newspapers. But it does indicate too that Mr Uys was permitted to express his views through his newspaper, and thus contributed to his own unpopularity.

The very large readership of the *Sunday Times* accounted for some of the Government's antagonism towards it, for finally, no matter how unimportant the Government may have felt the English Press to be, they retained a fear of the influence of the written word. And the fact that two million South Africans saw the *Sunday Times* each week–more readers than the Government had votes–resulted in a hypersensitivity to what that paper published. It also explains why the Prime Minister instructed the editor of *Dagbreek* to write a weekly column in the *Sunday Times* when Mr Mervis suggested his doing so.

The success of the *Sunday Times* made it both more exposed to and yet more secure from attack. Although not an official organ of the United Party, the *Sunday Times* claimed still to support that party, a fact which further strengthened its hand against Government attacks. But finally it was classed together with the English Press in the mind of the Government, with a Press which, with a single occasional exception, was opposed to it.

Conclusion

It will have emerged by now that the personality and attitudes of individual editors and journalists, and the traditions of individual newspapers influenced the nature of the Presses' relationship to Government. Further, every editor had his own interpretation of the Presses' actual or ideal role within the political process; yet there was an underlying pattern which made it possible to incorporate their various views into a broader generalization. There were in fact two distinctive generalizations to be made, relating to the two very different Press ideologies: side by side there developed a 'libertarian' theory of the Press, as expressed collectively by the English-language newspapers, and an 'authoritarian' Press ideology, to which the Afrikaans Press conformed.

The 'libertarian' theory incorporated a belief in the maximum independence of the Press from Government, to enable the Press to be an observant critic of Government and its officials; the notion that the Press should provide an arena for political debate of the widest possible spectrum of views, so that the Press could be an effective channel of communication between the 'people' and the Government, and the idea that the Press, as an instrument of publicity, should be the guardian of the 'public interest'.

The 'authoritarian' ideology on the other hand contained the idea that the Press ought to be a part of the Government's political communication machine, propagating a viewpoint which maintained the *status quo* and made the Government more, not less, secure. As a matter of policy, views and attitudes which seriously opposed the principles of the ruling group, were excluded.

The co-existence of two such opposing views of society and the role of the Press, reflected the contradictions within the political system; the reiteration of democratic principles in the face of blatantly authoritarian practices, the determination to work within and through a framework created by a White *élite* for the purpose of its own preservation, which enabled the Government increasingly to act outside that framework.

It is from these contradictions in the political system that further anomalies emerge: first, that Government only partially controlled the communication system; and second, that the 'libertarian' theory of the Press started from the assumption that the 'people' and the electorate were synonymous.

Thus the ideological gap between the English and the Afrikaans Press was accompanied by a discrepancy in the assumptions upon which both groups of newspapers based their claims. The English

Press in claiming rights of access to Goverment information–through officials and politicians–did so in the 'classic' democratic belief that the 'people' made decisions and in order to make those decisions they needed extensive information which it was the Presses' responsibility to provide. But in the South African situation none of these assumptions was true; there was no democracy and the electorate were not synonymous with the people.

The Afrikaans Press, on the other hand, saw itself and was seen by Government as a specialist extension of the Government's communication system, as the communication arm of a political party which claimed to represent an entire people. Hence Government's messages were directed primarily and often exclusively to the 'Volk' whose interests it represented and to whom it was responsible. In making decisions about what information to disclose to the independent Press, the Nationalists were both ideologically and instrumentally motivated. Ideologically, Government did not recognize the 'rights' of the independent Press to information, for the English Press did not represent the interests of the 'Volk' nor could it be trusted to communicate the political message. At the same time Government attempted to use the independent Press as a device for sustaining itself in power and more importantly to prevent that Press from undermining its political position. Simultaneously, the Nationalist Government concluded that the continued existence of an independent Press was evidence that the political system was democratic.

The explanation of these contradictions is to be found in the organization of political power: in the fact that four-fifths of the population are excluded from participation in the political process; and in the manner in which the conflict between the two White groups and their competing traditions, was settled.

The democracy which after 1948 the English Press claimed it was protecting was all along conceived as a White democracy. While the English-language Press had until the 1950s concerned itself primarily with the rights of English-speaking South Africans, its interpretation of its role as 'neutral' reporter meant that a spectrum of views were carried in the paper; even though the 'alternative' view was rarely applauded. The first mission of the Afrikaans newspapers was, initially at least, to propagate a set of ideas and attitudes to a limited audience defined by their ability and willingness to use the Afrikaans language as a means of communication, and participate in the creation of a self-conscious group. The Afrikaans Press never sought to win a wide, general audience, or to provide a comprehensive 'news' service. Its prime source of news was the party and its audience, party members.

In one sense the Nationalist Party did not complete the transition from Opposition to Government: but failure to account for policy-decisions to groups outside party circles whilst in Opposition was of less importance to the workings of the political system than a Government's refusal to offer explanations of its policy to all groups in the society. Thus despite twenty years of Government, the Nationalists did not radically alter their views about themselves and their responsibilities to the nation as distinct from the 'Volk' or the party. While there was evidence of change–as will be shown in the following chapter–the habit of accounting exclusively to 'members' of the group did not alter significantly. The changes that took place were centred on questions of re-defining the 'group' rather than considering that a national Government must be accountable to all groups. This goes some way in explaining why Nationalist journalists and politicians saw little cause for concern in the blatantly preferential treatment given to Nationalist newspapers by Government agencies. After all, the argument went, the Opposition party gave equivalently preferential treatment to the English-language Press.

Most importantly, what this attitude failed to take into account was the fact that as modern Governments have extended their areas of influence, they have become the source of vastly increasing amounts of political information. By refusing to co-operate with the independent Press, the Nationalist Government was capable of controlling the quantity and quality of information about itself that was made public. In practice however, this did not prove to be the case; for finally, the existence of an independent Press, with a strong free-Press ethic, and to a lesser extent the growth of rivalry within its own Press-ranks, meant that the Government was publicly exposed to the constant criticism of a hostile and prying Press.

In summary it can be said that the political attitudes of Government and Press to each other determined what information was readily available to the Press. Further, it was possible to determine through which channels individual journalists and newspapers were likely to acquire information according to whether they belonged to the English or to the Afrikaans-language Presses. The importance of this was that the methods and the channels through which journalists acquired information were closely reflected in what appeared in their newspapers. Where information was sparse, or when the Press was ideologically committed, the political opinions of the Press assumed a greater importance in the selection and presentation of news.

7

The Press in Opposition:
What the Newspapers Say

It is generally accepted that newspapers have a limited influence on how people think but are extremely influential in determining what people think about.[1] In South Africa this was of exaggerated importance because of the divided nature of the society, which prevented communication between individuals or groups of different races. Even within the White group, separation between the Afrikaans and English-speaking was enforced from an early age through an Education Act legally demanding schooling in the mother-tongue.

Because of these divisions and the almost total lack of inter-group contact, South Africans were wholly dependent on the media of communication for information about other groups within their society. Yet the divisions within the society were reflected in the Press which was also divided broadly on racial and linguistic lines. However, the Press had its own view of society and was simultaneously an observer and a participant in the political process. This was true for both groups of newspapers although they interpreted their roles very differently, observing and participating at quite different levels.

The Afrikaans Press never tried to convey a picture of the total society to its readers, but was concerned exclusively with representing the interests of the Afrikaner–whether political or cultural–and conveying to the Afrikaner a picture of himself. The English-language Press on the other hand, recognized the existence of the total society, despite its strong sectional bias. Furthermore, as readership figures show, the English Press conveyed its picture to a sizeable percentage of all racial groups.

The English Presses' recognition of the existence of all groups in the society, did not mean that it conveyed a picture of the parts or the whole acceptable to all or even to any of the groups about which it communicated. Nor did it convey an equality of information about

[1] See, for example, Joseph T. Klapper, *The Effects of Mass Communication* (Illinois: The Free Press of Glencoe, 1960).

the groups in the society; its primary concern was the English-speaking group whose interests it duly represented.

But through its recognition of all groups in the society, the English Press greatly increased the 'inputs' into the political system. As Black South Africans had no means of voicing their interests, they were effectively not a part of the political system at all. For it is only when interests are 'translated into a claim on the use of "public authority" that they enter the political system'.[1] Thus, by communicating non-White claims and representing non-White interests as they saw them, the English Press forced an entry for the non-White into the political system.

The Afrikaans Press operated well within the political system, serving as political communicator for party and Government and in later years, as an extremely powerful pressure group for change within the party. But always its concern was with the Afrikaner and with institutions within the political system rather than with defining the boundaries of that system.

The importance of this distinction can best be illustrated by asking the question, 'Would the South African polity be very different if the English-language Press did not exist?'. The answer is an unequivocal 'yes'. Without the English-language Press, discord of any sort would simply have ceased in the minds of White South Africans, except perhaps at times of severe political or economic crisis when the validity of the 'swart gevaar' (literally 'black danger') could best be brought home to the White electorate through the Government media. Nationalist newspapers only barely acknowledged the existence of Black South Africans and when they did so, it invariably was to provide evidence of the need for the continuing dominance of the White man. To take just one example, the *Evening Post* did an analysis of a week's reporting by Nationalist newspapers of assault cases across the colour line,[2] and found that there was a suppression or minimization of cases of White assaults on Blacks, while cases in which the accused were non-Whites were played up. An example cited by the *Evening Post* was that leading Nationalist newspapers did not print a single word about a long case in Heidelberg (in the Transvaal) in which two White farm foremen were found guilty of brutal assault on African labourers. Most of the Afrikaans Press also ignored the Johannesburg case of four White youths who went in search of Africans 'to beat up'. Yet all these papers gave bold headlines during the week to cases in which Blacks or Coloureds assaulted Whites.

[1] Gabriel A. Almond and James S. Coleman, *The Politics of the Developing Areas* (Princeton: Princeton University Press, paperback edition, 1970) p. 8.
[2] *Evening Post*, October 2, 1958.

Thus when the English Press publicized the existence of non-White poverty, or poor housing conditions, or the 'iniquities' of the pass system, or the growing lists of banned people, or the existence of Black nationalists, or that a protest march had taken place, it was extending the South African political environment. For if there had been no English Press, none of these facts would have 'existed' (other than in the minds or experience of the individuals immediately concerned) for no Afrikaans newspaper would choose to communicate such discontents.

The Afrikaans Press, whether addressing its 'mass' or political public, was always much more concerned with what its audience thought than with what it thought about. It tended to use political information as ideological evidence, to use 'news' as a weapon with which to change or maintain political attitudes. The English-language Press always insisted that there should be a sharp distinction between the provision of 'neutral' information in its news columns and the opinions it expressed and the inferences it drew in its editorial and feature columns.

Yet the distinction between news and opinion is less clear than it might seem for the content of each day's newspaper is the end product of innumerable choices of omission and commission from ever-increasing volumes of information available to the Press. However, the fact that the English Press always insisted that the distinction between fact and opinion be made was itself a part of the Presses' ideology and affected the content of its newspapers as surely as the Afrikaans Presses' failure to distinguish affected its content.

Hence an understanding of the Presses' political role is best exemplified by a study of the content of the Press between 1948 and 1968. This chapter deals with the main trends and changes which occurred in the attitudes of the South African Press between 1948 and 1968 and observes the growth of the Press as opposition.

Between 1948 and 1968 important changes occurred in the relationships of the Press to Government as a consequence of changes in the political system itself. In 1948, the English-language Press supported the governing United Party, the Afrikaans Press the opposition Nationalists. The effects of their reversal of roles after the Nationalists' 1948 victory were not seriously felt during the first ten years of Nationalist rule. For neither Press made any significant adjustments to the changes in their relative positions. The English Press still believed that a United Party victory was feasible whilst the Afrikaans Press was still wholly engaged in consolidating the victory of its party and in communicating its ideology.

The disillusionment of the English Press and the growing confidence of the Nationalists in their own staying power after the elections of 1958 shifted the intentions and actions of both Presses. The creation of the Republic in 1961 brought about further changes. English-speaking South Africans were finally cut off from Britain whilst the Republic, which had for so long been the primary goal of the Afrikaner Nationalists, ceased to be a unifying rallying point for Afrikanerdom.

As a result of these changes, conflicts which inevitably always existed in a part claiming to represent an entire people could no longer be contained and 1966 witnessed the public emergence of the major 'verligte-verkrampte' crisis within the National Party. Afrikanerdom, in freeing itself finally from what it saw as Britain's shackles, also freed itself to approach English-speaking South Africans to join with them against the common 'enemy', the African. But in so doing, Afrikaner nationalism faced a crisis; its strength derived from its exclusive self-consciousness, from its ability to draw for its support on a people speaking a unique language and sharing a common race, religion, culture and experience. In seeking to accommodate English-speaking South Africans, without conceding its exclusive political control, the National Party had to rely on an imperfectly implemented political ideology to hold both 'Volk' and White South Africa together.

For both the English and Afrikaans Press these changes had important consequences. The Afrikaans Press began to acquire an identity separate from that of the party, and in the 1960s the Afrikaans Press became embroiled in party conflicts and itself became both the source and the centre of controversy. Changes within the English-language Press and in its relationship to the society as a whole, came about more because of the refusal to change than because it was engaged in any re-definition of its role. The English-language Press in large measure alienated itself from all groups in the society, including that group whose interests it for so long represented that is to say, White, English-speaking South Africa. During the crisis following the Rhodesian unilateral declaration of independence, for example, all but one of the English-language newspapers supported Britain in its stand against Smith, despite the obvious support of White South Africa for the White Rhodesians. The only newspaper to support UDI was the stalwart *Natal Mercury*.

The English Press

(a) The Nationalist Interpretation

The attitudes of the Nationalists and the English Presses' to each

167

other have been intricately linked to the problems of English-speaking South Africans. Two factors traditionally dominated Afrikaner attitudes to English-speaking South Africans: British policy towards the non-Whites and the Afrikaners' own struggle for independence from the British and the establishment of a unique cultural identity. The changing attitudes and status of English-speaking South Africans *vis-à-vis* Britain and the Afrikaners did not wholly dispell the old fears. Rather, the English-language Press alone came to symbolize all the traditional antagonisms: its 'liberalism' implicitly and sometimes explicitly endorsed racial equality, its cultural links to Britain and through the English language its associations with a world culture persisted as a threat to the Afrikaner; the English Presses' unabated antagonism towards the Afrikaner and his ideals was held responsible for keeping English-speaking South Africans from converting to the 'Volk' and equally important, the English Press was held responsible for the unfavourable presentation of the Afrikaner to the outside world.[1] Lastly, the English Press through its associations with big business and industry was identified with English capitalism (and British Imperialism) which historically had been so hostile and oppressive to Afrikanerdom; and its greater financial success (than the Afrikaans Press) served as a constant reminder of the English South Africans' continuing domination of the economy.

With this interpretation of the English Press, it was only to be expected that after coming to power, the more militant Nationalists demanded that the English Press be silenced. Instances of such demands are too numerous to reference but a selection of statements by leading Nationalist spokesmen reveals the source of Nationalist disquiet in regard to the English Press.

In 1959, Eric Louw, then Minister of External Affairs, commented at a meeting at Roodepoort that 'a great deal of South Africa's internal trouble is due to political articles in the English Press. The writers are spreading liberal ideas and the trouble is that these seeds are being sown among Afrikaans-speaking people as well'.[2]

During the campaign leading up to the 1961 General Election, W. van Heerden, then editor of *Dagbreek*, said that the Government's most powerful opponent in the election was the English-language Press. He claimed that the Opposition supporting Press had understood the implication of multi-racialism long before the Progressive Party revolt and that it was 'pro the Progressive Party before the

[1] See F. A. van Jaarsveld, in *The Afrikaner's Interpretation of South African History* (Cape Town: Simondium Publishers (Pty) Ltd., 1964) p. 8, et seq.
[2] *Rand Daily Mail*, December 8, 1959.

Progressive Party had arisen' [September 17, 1961]. A more extreme point of view was expressed by the Nationalist MP, Jaap Marais in an interview with *Die Transvaler* published on March 27, 1964, when he said that the real opposition was the English Press, with its historical links with the gold-mining companies and financial institutions and hostile overseas bodies. Thus the weaker the Parliamentary Opposition became, the more dangerous the true opposition could become by joining up with foreign hostility and extra Parliamentary action against the Government and the National Party. *Die Burger* in an important leading article in April 1964 affirmed that

> 'Under the pressure of external and internal forces, it is becoming increasingly clear that the real tension and friction of political ideas no longer lie between the Nationalists and the United Party as such. They lie between the Nationalists with their idea of a freedom of its own for a White or predominantly White nation of Africa, and those who regard Black majority rule Government as ineluctable and believe that the transition can take place gradually, in an orderly manner and according to plan. The latter school of thought weak at the White polls but strong in journalistic and other intellectual circles, has replaced the United Party as the real challenger of Nationalism and is now struggling against it for the support of South Africa, both White and non-White'.[1]

And lastly *Die Vaderland*, in expressing its concern about the content of the English Press, said:

> '. . . a section of the Press in South Africa quite unconsciously often strengthens the cause of our own enemies. So-called Native leaders are immediately news, unknown agitators escaped, and the mere fact that the people and events appeared in the Press gave them importance' [February 8, 1961].

Thus *Die Vaderland* pinpointed the manner in which the English-language Press had come to constitute the opposition, had become in Nationalist eyes a fifth column rather than a fourth estate. When the struggle had been between the Afrikaners and the English, the English Press had represented the Nationalists' White opponents. Once the English ceased to be the major opponents – because the Afrikaners had proved their dominance and because the Nationalists believed the English to be less hostile to them – the English Press became a more serious opposition, which at times represented the interests of the non-Whites.

[1] As quoted in the *Rand Daily Mail*, May 2, 1964.

(b) *The Presses' View*

For its part the English-language Press no longer saw itself as an extension of the British Press, no longer employed editors and journalists directly from Britain, or gave British news priority over South African news in its news columns. Yet in its traditions and values, in its style and choice of content the English-language Press retained its links with the Western Press in a way in which English-speaking South Africans no longer retained their associations with Europe.

In its defence of 'British' values, the English-language Press continued to express its fears about the Afrikanerization of South African life (and its belief in the superiority of English cultural life) its beliefs about the effects of Nationalist politics on the country's reputation abroad and hence its economy at home, and its deep-seated repugnance for the ideological nationalism of the Afrikaner. In opposing apartheid, the English Press stressed the economic impracticability and expense of implementing the doctrine. In representing the interests of the African, the English Press expressed its concern for the 'underdog', a concern based on a paternalistic desire to guide the development of the African and ensure his commitment to the values it upheld.

Thus a continuing vision of the 'good society', based broadly on a belief in the 'rule of law', 'justice for all' and the urgent need continually to represent and defend the 'underdog' whoever he might be, ensured the continuing opposition of the English Press to the Nationalist Government and its policies. Determinedly, the English Press kept the vocabulary of democracy, and the concept and fact of dissent alive, and in so doing helped ensure its own continued existence. It was unable to stop the advance of repression in the society and was virtually impotent in respect of influencing Government policy and the functioning of the State apparatus. It was an extra-Parliamentary opposition but also part of the English-speaking establishment with vested interests in maintaining law and order and a stable economic system. Yet after an extended period of Nationalist rule the English Press was forced into an often unwilling awareness that its choice of content and the views it expressed were intrinsically inimical to maintaining the *status quo*. For it was not the content alone which determined the English Presses' political role, but equally Government's interpretation of that content, an interpretation which was based on an ideology which excluded the non-Whites from the White political system. The English Presses' recognition of its dilemma was expressed clearly by the *Natal Witness* which said [June 29, 1962]:

'... in the South Africa of today, to speak out in favour of fair-mindedness, of human sympathy and of plain common-sense is to be boldly (perhaps treasonably) political. To be non-political, on the other hand, is to be content with the *status quo*, with the constant movement towards the death of our society'.

(c) Content of the Press

The 1961 General Election was an important indicator of changes that had taken place in the Press since 1948. It was the first General Election to be contested by the Progressive Party which was formed in 1959 when eleven M Ps broke away from the United Party. They advocated a qualified non-racial franchise, a policy which was rejected by the White electorate who returned only one Progressive Party M P in 1961. It was also the first election in which the English Press as a whole did not fight to win a victory for the U P (whatever it felt its shortcomings to be) 'but to elect an opposition'.[1]

The *Rand Daily Mail* was one of the first newspapers to declare its interests a few days after the announcement of the election date and said that Progressive policy offered the best hope of fruitful co-operation among the races. However, the *Rand Daily Mail* was sufficiently pragmatic to say that in the prevailing state of public opinion, the Progressive Party did not enjoy the necessary support to offer itself as an alternative Government. Thus in contests between the U P and Progressive Party the *Rand Daily Mail* said it would support the latter but against the Nationalists it would support the U P [August 14, 1961]. Other newspapers too, notably the East London *Daily Dispatch*, the Port Elizabeth *Evening Post* and the *Natal Witness* came out in favour of the Progressive Party.

The important shift in the position of the English Press was that support was given to the U P only because the Press saw no practical alternative and not because of any sincere belief in the party or its policies. The electoral alliance between the U P and the National Union Party (formed by Japie Basson in 1959 on his defection from the National Party and led by ex-Chief Justice Fagan) was received critically, though latterly with resignation. The *Star* said [August 9 and 12, 1961] that the alliance 'brings into co-operation with the U P leadership a number of people who are basically Afrikaner National-ist', and a 'Fagan–Graaff administration would by African, even by Rhodesian standards be deeply conservative'. The *Daily Dispatch*

---

[1] *Rand Daily Mail*, September 20, 1961.

commented [August 8, 1961] that the fact that the UP could contemplate a pact with a staunch Nationalist like Fagan was evidence of the party's weakness and lack of principle. After the pact was sealed the *Daily Dispatch* confirmed its earlier judgment by saying that 'On all important issues of Black–White relationships, the UP remains anchored to discrimination' [August 17, 1951]. The *Rand Daily Mail* took the view that 'it is . . . the most advanced policy that our highly conservative White electorate is likely to accept at present' [August 17, 1961]. The *Natal Mercury*, while describing the pact agreement as one of 'unashamed expediency' necessary to attract dissident Nationalists, still felt that it was a stepping stone to the abandonment of hurtful methods of race discrimination [August 17, 1961]. Like most other English-language newspapers, the *Natal Mercury* also expressed some sympathy with the policies of the Progressive Party and said that the time would come when South Africa would recognize the wisdom of many of the Progressive Party's arguments, 'but the day is not yet come. The task is to get rid of Verwoerd and this can only be done if the voters support the Graaff–Fagan plan' [August 19/24, 1961].

The *Sunday Times* was virtually the only newspaper to give uncritical support to the United Party in the 1961 election. It said that 'the salient feature of the present election is the emergence of a great moderate coalition in the centre, flanked on the one hand by a National Party which shamelessly flouts non-White aspirations; and on the other, by a Progressive Party which appears to pay scant attention to White opinion. The one extreme is as bad as the other [September 24, 1961].

What emerged from the English Presses' expressed attitudes in the 1961 elections was that the English Press was as strongly anti-Nationalist as it had ever been. Despite its disillusionment with the UP and its anger at the UPs impotence, the English Press still felt compelled to support the UP against the Nationalists. Importantly, though the 1961 election marked a shift in the English Presses' emphasis in demanding rights for the English to calling for the recognition of non-White interests.

There was an added significance in the English Presses' stance in 1961, for events which had preceded it provided a stiff test of the English Presses' staying power and its willingness to oppose a powerful Government. The events of 1960 had exposed the English Press to vicious Nationalist attacks. Sharpeville had brought home to the Nationalists their extreme unpopularity in the international community and the English Press was blamed for providing unpatriotic and distorted reports to the world's Press. Racial disturbances before and after Sharpeville, on a scale previously unknown in South Africa, forced White South Africans to reappraise their positions. Where the Nationalists (and probably the majority of Whites) concluded that White South Africa should unite to defend their rights, the English Press inferred from these events that South Africa should modify her racial policies. Again this was a view which cast the Press in the role of a threatening opponent of White privilege and power. There was also the fact that the African nationalist organizations and many individual opponents of the Government had been banned, thus preventing the expression of their viewpoints. This left the English-language Press as the major articulator of anti-Nationalist and non-White opinion.

From the end of 1961, political sabotage, aimed primarily at Government installations and inspired by offshoots of banned African Nationalist organizations, was beoming a regular feature in South Africa. The Government's answer to this sabotage was the General Law Amendment Act of 1962, commonly known as the 'sabotage' Act. The Act equipped the Minister of Justice with sweeping new powers, and created provisions for placing opponents of the Government under house arrest. Less than a year later the Government introduced another General Law Amendment Bill, this time providing for the detention of persons without trial for ninety days. Despite widespread protests throughout the country by churches, the Black Sash, the Institute of Race Relations and other such organizations, the UP voted with the Government in 1963, leaving the sole Progressive Party MP, Helen Suzman, to cast the only opposing vote in the House.

The entire English Press united to oppose both Bills, and as a body, attacked the UP for its failure to oppose the Government at such a crucial moment in South Africa's history. Not only did the English Press oppose the Bills, but it gave extensive coverage to protest meetings and to other extra-Parliamentary opponents of the Bills.

The UP had opposed certain provisions of the 1963 General Law Amendment Bill in the committee stage but had supported the second and third readings of the Bill. The UPs leader, Sir de Villiers Graaf, said that the party supported the Bill only because the safety of the state was paramount. He registered the party's protest against the '90-day' clause and the 'Sobukwe clause' which (allowed for the extended detention of a prisoner after a sentence imposed by the courts had been served) and stressed that a concession had been gained by the UP in that the right of the Minister to detain prisoners due for release would have to come up for annual review before Parliament. But the right of habeas corpus was lost.

173

The English Press condemned the Bill as the most drastic piece of legislation ever placed before a peace-time South African Parliament. With varying degrees of virulence, the English newspapers registered their own opposition and also provided a platform for institutional opponents of the Bill.

The *Friend* said [April 24, 1963] 'Everybody agrees that order must be maintained. But the necessity of maintaining order with this kind of law is an indication of the inner sickness of a country which should be peaceful and prosperous'. The *Eastern Province Herald*, one of the more conservative of the English-language newspapers, said [April 25, 1963] 'It is clear that the Government regards South Africa as having entered a state of permanent emergency . . . This measure . . . finally does away with the principle of liberty of the subject as understood in every country that abides by the rule of law'.

The *Cape Times* warned [April 24, 1963] that in every country where a minority has tried to maintain governmental control of an unwilling majority, 'the authorities have been reluctantly forced to these wretched measures. And in every single solitary case, the measures have failed miserably'.

The Johannesburg *Star* advised [April 24, 1963] that 'the real road of our security' lay in passing 'constructive and conciliatory reforms' in housing, wages, pass administration and liquor laws. The *Natal Mercury* too felt that 'a sensible modification of restrictive and discriminatory racial laws' would eliminate the need for the 'executive to usurp the judiciary's powers and to permit an individual Minister . . . to apply no law but his own will . . . This Bill marks South Africa's compulsive entry into a valley of tears behind the leadership of men who have lost their vision in a fog of fear, [April 25, 1963].

Many of the opposition newspapers also predicted that more drastic measures would lead to a stronger reaction, that 'Black extremism thrives on apartheid extremism [*Evening Post*, April 24, 1963] and that 'in politics as in physics, every action has an equal and opposite reaction [*Cape Times* April 25, 1963].

The most remarkable feature of the English Presses' opposition was that despite the events which precipitated the legislation (events for which the English Press was again blamed), English-language newspapers continued to use such uncompromising language in expressing their views.

The role of the English Press in opposing the General Law Amendment Acts of 1962 and 1963 was clear cut: it expressed a genuine repugnance at the increase in repressive legislation and the decline of constitutionalism and it acted as an extra-Parliamentary opponent when the Parliamentary system failed to produce any opposition within itself. But the English Presses' response to ready-made issues was not the only way in which it opposed Government policies and values. Of equal importance were the issues it 'created', by focusing attention on unpopular ideas and on what it saw as 'malfunctions' in the administration, or on the aspirations of the Africans. The nature of the political system in which it operated transformed all criticism, whether socially or economically based, into a political attack. An editorial decision to focus attention on the 'unpleasant' or to provide a public platform for alternative ideas, became in effect a defiant political act.

There were marked variations in the extent to which individual newspapers were prepared to fulfil the role which the English-language Press had come to play. But most newspapers sympathized with those of the English Press who had become more rather than less outspoken in the years after the Nationalists came to power. Most notable amongst the 'crusading' newspapers were the *Rand Daily Mail* and the *Evening Post* and to a lesser extent the *Daily Dispatch*, the *Natal Witness* and the *Cape Times*.

The editor of the *Rand Daily Mail*, Mr. Gandar, in a statement of policy in *174*, the house journal of SAAN, said of his newspaper, that 'We have a clear and unambiguous political policy which is liberal in content and contemporary in spirit. In the twilight of South African traditionalism, we are a paper of vigorous dissent and social protest . . . In a continent in the throes of change, we endeavour to serve as an instrument of change. We fought the last election on the slogan of "Adapt or Perish" and I still think this fits the clamant needs of our time . . .'[1]

This was by far the most radical statement to be made by any editor of an Establishment newspaper, for it openly admitted a desire to be an 'instrument of change'. The *Rand Daily Mail* had already introduced the theme in the 1961 election, but it became an increasingly harsh and defiant critic of Government. In October 1962, Vorster, the then Minister of Justice, in a Kruger Day address in Pretoria, sounded a sharp warning against liberalism and the 'liberalist spirit', the 'precursor of communism' – which, he said, was a greater enemy than communism, for without always knowing it, 'we admit it into our homes and nurture it.'[2]

The *Rand Daily Mail* responded by confronting Vorster directly and telling him he knew perfectly well the difference between communism and liberalism and said [October 12, 1962], we are not

[1] As reported in the *S A Journalist*, Oct/Nov 1962.
[2] As reported in *Die Transvaler*, October 11, 1962.

disconcerted by Mr. Vorster. He can make a note of the fact that the *Rand Daily Mail* is a liberal newspaper and is not proposing to change.' The paper was attacked by the Afrikaans Press and a further warning was given by the Minister of Justice. Undeterred, the *Rand Daily Mail* responded with a front-page article signed by the editor [October 23, 1962] captioned 'Take Care, Mr. Vorster'. Gandar warned Vorster that he was playing a dangerous game by linking liberalism and communism and advised him that to combat communism it was essential to eliminate 'social wrongs', to satisfy some Black aspirations, and to make Western culture attractive to the non-Whites. 'Accordingly, we say to you, Mr Vorster, and your colleagues in the Cabinet: Take care, for you are playing with fire.' Vorster replied to the *Rand Daily Mail* through *Die Vaderland* that afternoon [October 23, 1962] by reiterating his belief that liberalism was the slippery slope to communism, and warned that 'The *Rand Daily Mail* is most definitely on a dangerous path . . . not only for itself, but also for South Africa'.

Although the implications of the *Rand Daily Mail*'s stated policy were self-evident, it was not until 1964 that the paper explained that multi-racialism meant 'going the whole hog', that the Nationalists were right, that integration meant mixed schools, mixed hospitals, Black neighbours and even mixed marriages. 'Indeed it does,' said Mr Gandar and 'there could scarcely be a greater challenge, a more stimulating mission than this – the uplifting of our own underprivileged peoples and sharing with them the rewards and values of Western civilization.' Mr Gandar argued in his column 'Viewpoint' that as integration was in the long run inevitable, it would be easier to guide the forces of change by working with them rather than against them [April 4, 1964].

Gandar's statement was remarkable in how far it went. Only the Liberal Party (and even its supporters arguably had not accepted these consequences) and the banned Communist Party and Congress movements had even implied such conclusions. As such the paper was providing a platform for views which by 1964 were largely outlawed. Thus by that time only the Press could have argued such a point as most others who might have done could not be quoted. The Afrikaans Press, somewhat startled, confirmed that 'never before has it been so clearly and frankly stated that liberalism is out to destroy utterly the traditional way of life of the Whites, both Afrikaans and English speaking [*Die Transvaler*, April 7, 1964]. *Die Vaderland* pointed out [April 14, 1964] that no echo had been heard from the Progressive Party, underlining the English Presses' alienation from even a 'liberal' minority.

The Afrikaans Press, politicians and newspaper readers (through the letter columns) attacked Gandar and another round of demands for rigorous Press censorship was set into motion. *Dagbreek* printed a report headed: 'Steps Against the Editor of the Mail?' [April 26, 1964], reminding Gandar of a warning by the Minister of Justice in 1962, though in his political column the paper's editor expressed the alternative argument that in view of the decreasing influence of the English papers on the political life of the country, Press censorship would perhaps be unnecessary. Nationalist politicians did not share the resigned 'tolerance' of some members of the Afrikaans Press and produced extremely hawkish statements. But still no action was brought against Gandar and the *Rand Daily Mail.*

Undeterred by the threats, and on the same day as a bomb explosion on the Johannesburg station outraged white South Africa, Gandar called for a multi-racial convention, representative of all races and 'all those, of goodwill who are hoping for a just solution in a non-racial South Africa' [July 24, 1964].

Die Transvaler replied [July 28, 1964] that it was beyond its comprehension how such a dangerous proposal could be made and asked what other result it could have 'than the sowing of confusion and bewilderment and suggesting demands to people which they have not even thought of themselves?' Addressing himself directly to the editor of the *Rand Daily Mail, Die Vaderland's* editor said [July 28, 1964] that the proposing of a national convention left only one choice, a non-racial society 'which you full well know means a Black dominated society' and this 'is typical of the liberal denial of free thought and choice within a democratic society'. The editor also reminded Gandar that this 'solution' had first been proposed by the African nationalist Nelson Mandela, 'now in jail on a life-sentence for sabotage', and by South Africa's enemies abroad.

It seemed impossible that Gandar and the *Rand Daily Mail* would not be prosecuted under one of a series of laws which could so easily have been invoked against him and the paper. But it was not until July 1965 that the Government acted when the *Rand Daily Mail* published its series of prison condition articles. All the English-language newspapers in the country supported the *Rand Daily Mail* in its demand for an immediate Government inquiry. The Government, which had responded by raiding the offices of the *Rand Daily Mail* and banning the informant on whose evidence the articles were largely based (thus immediately silencing him) was also severely criticized by the English-language Press for its response to the *Rand Daily Mail's* revelations. Government spokesmen were themselves silent for some time though the Afrikaans Press was an indicator of

Government thinking. *Die Vaderland* asked the *Rand Daily Mail* if it was of 'no concern to the editor . . . that just at this very time his self-extolled revelations can be embraced by South Africa's enemies abroad to resume their smear campaign against the Republic? . . . Such action demands explanation before the South African public will examine the merits of the *Rand Daily Mail*'s story [July 6, 1965].

Two rival claims were being made about the prison condition articles. On the one hand, the English Press in general and the *Rand Daily Mail* in particular saw the articles as a serious social criticism. As such they demanded that a full-scale official inquiry should be set up, and that in the event of the evidence proving true, something radical should be done about improving conditions. The Afrikaans Press and Government on the other hand, saw the *Rand Daily Mail*'s articles as a wholly political attack on the Government itself and immediately dismissed them as untrue; furthermore the attack was interpreted as unpatriotic in the sense that it would blacken South Africa's name abroad.

The *Rand Daily Mail* again and again repeated its claim that it was acting ' in the public interest', and assured the authorities and the public that it would not be deterred by 'threats or browbeating or angry noises from the Government or its Press and radio minions'. The paper concluded with a threat to publish further evidence unless prompt and effective action was taken to deal with the deplorable prison conditions which had been shown to exist.

Shortly before the *Rand Daily Mail* enforced its threat to publish new evidence, another English-language newspaper published its own prison condition revelations. On July 27, 1965, the *Sunday Times* carried a banner headline report that a head warder had revealed serious breaches of prison regulations by senior prison warders. By then, both the United and Progressive Parties had joined with the English Press in calling for a full judicial Commission of Inquiry into prison conditions, ensuring that the controversy over conditions in South Africa's prisons developed into a major political issue.

There was no official statement as to what action was being taken and it was left to *Die Transvaler* to report [July 24, 1965] that a departmental inquiry was being held. The pressure groups advocating an independent inquiry regarded this as a 'ludicrously inadequate response to these shocking allegations' [*Rand Daily Mail*, July 26, 1965].

One of the first official responses to be heard was that of the Commissioner of Prisons, who was reported in the *Star* [July 31, 1965], as saying that he would resist pressure for an inquiry, as would the Minister of Justice. The following day [August 1, 1965], the Minister of Justice gave a statement to *Dagbreek* in which he referred to the 'agitation waged in certain English-language newspapers about alleged shocking conditions in South African prisons'. He said, 'I will not have myself badgered into any overhasty action', and that what would probably follow the allegations was that members of the service would instigate actions for libel; that incidents of alleged contraventions of the Prisons Act would be referred to the Attorney-General, including possible actions against newspapers and that several charges of perjury would also be referred to the Attorney-General.

The Government's refusal to respond to pressures, particularly pressures from outside its own ranks, was based on the belief that to respond would be to show weakness and thus to encourage a host of intolerable demands from non-Whites and their representatives.

The first court case, in which the young prison warder, van Schalkwyk, was found guilty of perjury, further incensed the English Press, which strongly attacked the court's methods and its findings. The prison warder had not been defended, there was no cross examination of State witnesses (most of whom were State employees) nor was the *Rand Daily Mail* permitted to be represented. Yet it was recognized by the *Star* [August 18, 1965] that 'in these and other cases . . . it is the newspapers that gave publicity to the prisons "scandals" that are really on trial'. The *Sunday Times* went even further [August 22, 1965] and said that an examination of the documents in the van Schalkwyk trial made it clear that the prosecutor–the Deputy Attorney-General–had misled the court. The Afrikaans Press on the other hand, used the van Schalkwyk trial as further ammunition against the English Press, as proof of the unreliability of its evidence and confirming its belief in the political nature of the *Rand Daily Mail*'s attack. There was also speculation in the Afrikaans Press that Gandar had gone too far and might be dealt with by his own board of directors. When this did not happen, Dirk Richard, the editor of *Dagbreek*, suggested [August 22, 1965] that 'the fact that the *Rand Daily Mail* goes its way unhindered must be interpreted by the outsider as full support from its directorate'.

In its own defence the *Rand Daily Mail* said it accepted full responsibility for everything it had published about the prisons, that in spite of the sentence imposed on van Schalkwyk it was convinced that it had not broken the law and that it had acted in the public interest. The paper expressed its deepest concern about the Government's interpretation of its motives in bringing to light social injustices as 'dishonest and reprehensible' as well as 'politically motivated–to the benefit of the communist cause . . . Indeed one of the most significant developments in recent history has been the determined use made by the Nationalist Government and its supporters of anti-communism as a barricade against necessary social change' [August 21, 1965].

The actions and reactions of both Press and Government to the prison condition articles, revealed more effectively than almost any other single issue, the nature of the conflict between the English Press and Government. It also highlighted the unique position of the English-language Press in the South African political structure. Under equivalently restrictive or repressive regimes, the likelihood of such revelations being made about prison conditions is almost unthinkable. On the other hand, should accusations be made in the British Press about British prisons, it would cause few to reflect on the desirability of a free Press or to conclude that the articles were in the nature of a political attack on the Government of the day, though there might well be political repercussions.

The contradiction of a 'free' Press in a 'repressive' regime becomes clearer. The English Press concentrated its attention on prison conditions and on defending itself against Government attacks. Nationalist politicians and the Afrikaans Press concentrated their attack on the English Press itself, and all their subsequent actions were aimed at undermining the credibility of that Press and at intimidating the English Press into 'disciplining itself'.

The *Rand Daily Mail*'s editor, supported by most other English-language newspapers, had repeatedly claimed that in exposing atrocities in prisons, he had simply done his duty, that the criticism was a social criticism, not aimed at discrediting the Government at home or abroad, especially if subsequently prison conditions were improved. But this claim was only partially true, and for two reasons. The first was that the *Rand Daily Mail* had at least some awareness of the likely interpretation that the publication of the articles would produce. The second reason, which follows from the first, was that the nature of the political system, and the role of the English Press in that system, ensured the immediate politicization of any concerted criticism of the institutions in the society. And implicit in the *Rand Daily Mail*'s criticism was its intention to represent particularly the interests of non-Whites who constituted the bulk of the country's prison population, and for whom no alternate means of expressing their grievances existed. Thus regardless of the *Rand Daily Mail*'s intentions, by pitting itself against the Government and by representing non-White interests, directly, or indirectly, its actions were political.

What Nationalists said about the articles was thus a clear statement of their understanding of the political role of the English Press within the political system. The charges that the paper had behaved unpatriotically, a charge frequently levelled at the English Press, was consistent with a Nationalist interpretation of patriotism, which relied on the postulate that the 'common good' would be self-evident to all true patriots.

The Afrikaans Press

(a) The Republican Question

The National Party had come to power and stayed there by providing Afrikanerdom with a united leadership. The knowledge that historically, divided Afrikanerdom had been defeated or forced to share political control, still influenced Nationalist thinking. Thus provincial and attitudinal differences, which always existed, were rarely expressed prior to 1958. But after ten years in office–and with the comfort of having won three elections with increased support–a section of the Nationalist Press believed that the party and Government could tolerate a limited public exposure to differences within the ranks. By 1958 the Transvaal Nationalists were already asserting their dominance in national politics and still believed in the maintenance of rigid party discipline to ensure unity in private as well as in public. But the Cape Nationalists, dissatisfied with the diminishing importance of their province in national politics, attempted to assert themselves by extending the debate within the party to the Press.

The Cape Nationalist move was spearheaded by the Nasionale Pers newspapers who effectively forced the Transvaal Press to participate in the discussion. The first issue the Cape Press chose to focus attention upon was hardly a contentious point in Nationalist thinking; but the fact that it was the Press rather than the party which broached the subject of the republic immediately after the 1958 elections, disconcerted the party leadership.

Nasionale Pers began its campaign on April 22, six days after the elections, with an article published in both *Die Burger* and *Die Volksblad* (and the following day in *Die Oosterlig*) in which it was said that the result of the election could be interpreted as a mandate to the Government to continue on the republican path. By April 28, *Die Burger* and *Die Volksblad* were advocating a republic to be established as a member of the Commonwealth and without any important changes in the structure of the State.

The Cape Presses' insistence on forcing the republican issue so soon after the elections was (in addition to asserting the rights of their province) intended to extend the role of the Press itself in the structure of Nationalist politics. The editor of *Die Burger* confirmed[1] that the

[1] From an interview with *Die Burger*'s editor in January 1970.

Press (rather than the party) wished to open up a serious debate in public, so that in a short time a republic would be at least tacitly accepted by English-speaking South Africans, who traditionally were so opposed to the idea. Its second and more important intention was to 'win the Transvalers over to the idea of a "British-type" president and not a Kruger-type president'. By this the editor meant a president without executive powers, whose role would be roughly equivalent to that of the Governor-General.

Although Nasionale Pers did not have a Transvaal newspaper, every major daily and Sunday paper in the country gave prominent coverage to the re-emergence of the republican issue through *Die Burger*. Initially, *Die Transvaler*–the mouthpiece of the then Prime Minister, Strijdom–though more cautious in entering the discussion affirmed that the election had brought a republic very much nearer but added that intensified conversion work would have to be carried out in the next few years, as a stable republican government could only be obtained if a considerable majority were in favour of change.

The English Press uniformly opposed the creation of a republic and predicted dire consequences for South Africa. But *Die Burger*, by assuming the inevitability of a republic, forced the discussion even in the English Press to rotate around questions of what form the republic would or should take. Thus the *Cape Times* [April 29, 1958] challenged the Nationalists to 'give some detailed and realistic proposals for making it acceptable'. The *Cape Argus* [April 29, 1958] doubted the ability of *Die Burger* and the Cape Nationalists to influence the form the republic would take and felt that the Transvaal Nationalists would have it all their own way. The *Star* [May 2, 1958] invited supporters of republicanism to state what they believed to be the practical advantages of a republic in South Africa.

By the end of May, the more conservative Transvaal Nationalists clearly felt that the campaign was moving too fast, but more importantly they resented the authoritative claims of *Die Burger* in defining the constitution of a future republic. This resentment was expressed in an exchange between *Die Burger* and *Die Transvaler* at the end of May. *Die Burger* reported [May 30, 1958] that much would be heard about the republic in the coming Parliamentary session, and that the National Party were engaged in clarifying the precise form in which to present the republic to the country. The following day, *Die Transvaler's* political correspondent contradicted *Die Burger* and insisted that it was improbable that the republican issue would be raised in the coming Parliamentary session 'as has been held in prospect by certain newspapers'. Further reprimanding *Die Burger* journalists, without directly naming them, *Die Transvaler* said that future action by the Government regarding the republic was a matter for the Prime Minister 'and no one else' to decide.

The climax of the 1958 campaign was a 'referendum' held by *Die Burger* and several other newspapers. The voting form listed several alternatives: no republic, republic as a member of the commonwealth, not a member of the Commonwealth, a president without executive powers, and a president with executive power. *Die Vaderland*'s referendum, held before *Die Burger*'s, most strikingly revealed the differences between north and south within the Nationalist ranks, particularly on the question of presidential powers. A majority of readers in the Transvaal where memories of the old Kruger Republic were strongest, voted for a president with executive powers (70·0 per cent) whilst the Cape readers (67·1 per cent) voted for a 'British-type' president. Both referenda showed a majority of readers in favour of a republic within the Commonwealth though the majority was considerably larger in the Cape.

It was largely through the persistent campaigning of *Die Burger* from April 1958 onwards that the republic became 'practical politics' in 1960, and that in most particulars it resembled *Die Burger*'s prescriptions for the republic.

There were three phases in *Die Burger*'s campaign. At first *Die Burger* played the role of initiator, in re-introducing the republican theme immediately after the General Election. The fact that it was the newspaper, independently of the Government and party which had initiated the campaign caused some concern, but was then seized upon by Strijdom as an opportunity to sound out public opinion. By the end of May however, it was evident that *Die Burger* was 'uncontrollable' and was insisting on creating its own pace, a pace some party members felt to be too fast for the country as a whole. After the various referenda, however, the republican issue was dropped, to be replaced by the leadership struggle, in which divisions between Nationalists from the north and south were once more to be revealed through the Afrikaans Press.

Die Burger and its sister newspapers were less successful in their attempt to influence the leadership succession in August 1958 than they had been in forcing the republican issue. During the Prime Minister's illness, C. R. Swart, the leader of the Orange Free State National Party, was acting Prime Minister, but there was clearly disagreement within the party as to whom should succeed Strijdom. A front page announcement in *Die Volksblad* [August 25, 1958] that the new leader of the National Party would be elected on September 2 by the Parliamentary caucus of the National Party, said that there were three contenders for the leadership: Swart, T. E. Donges, Leader of the Cape National Party and Verwoerd, then Vice-Chairman of the Transvaal National Party.

The following day. *Die Burger* carried the story under the heading, 'Premier: Differences Within the National Party'. It was not until August 27 that *Die Transvaler* carried the story, saying that for the first time in the history of the National Party, a vote will 'perhaps' have to be taken to elect a successor to the Prime Minister. In informed Nationalist circles, said *Die Transvaler*, 'it was pointed out that such a vote is a pure democratic process and must not be interpreted in any sense as "differences" or even a "clash" in the Parliamentary ranks of the National Party, as certain newspapers are intimating . . . Nationalists place unity of their party above any preference for a person'. Further reprimanding Nasionale Pers, *Die Transvaler* continued that allegations of disunity 'are not only inappropriate now that the people are in deep mourning for the deceased chief leader but can only lead to a whispering campaign from which opponents of the National Party will try to draw an advantage'.

Die Burger did not hide its disappointment at the election of Verwoerd, a Transvaler, while *Die Transvaler* was jubilant and again and again stressed that the Prime Minister had once been the newspaper's editor. Dawie, *Die Burger*'s political columnist, said after the election of Verwoerd that it did not help to pretend that there were not some bruises after the election and he expressed sympathy with the two losers. Of Verwoerd, Dawie said [September 6, 1958] that 'he has it in him to be one of South Africa's greatest Prime Ministers. His critics say that he also has it in him to precipitate crisis. It is a natural difficulty with brilliant men in positions of power: they have the power to make certain people shudder'.

(b) *Die Burger against Verwoerd: The Coloured Question*

Die Burger's first major clash with Verwoerd and the Transvalers came in 1960. The opening shot in the battle for a change in Nationalist policy towards the Coloured population of the country, was fired by *Die Burger* in July 1960. Dawie claimed [July 23, 1960] that the pressure for a 'forward movement' in Nationalist policy for the Coloureds was growing stronger. 'The most dramatic idea is that the principle of the representation of Coloureds by Coloureds in Parliament must be recognized or in other words that the Coloured voters must be permitted to elect White or Brown members . . . My impression is that the National Party is already more than half way in agreement with the principle, and can be completely won for it by strong leadership. The time for a decision is approaching.'

For the next five months – interrupted for a short while by the republican referendum – *Die Burger* carried article after article presenting the case for a reappraisal of Coloured policy. Readers were invited to express their views and a great deal of space was given to letters sympathetic to a new deal for Coloureds. Finally on November 24, 1960, *Die Transvaler* carried Verwoerd's reply to the Cape Press, pointing out that allowing the Coloureds to 'merge' with the White group was wholly inconsistent with the apartheid ideology and could only lead to claims from other racial groups for similar inclusion.

Verwoerd's extreme anger with *Die Burger* and its supporters was left in no doubt. The aim of this 'surrender to limited integration' he said, was to create the idea that a 'larger group than the Whites will form the bulwark against Bantu domination . . . the truth is otherwise. The world will welcome such signs of surrender to the integration policy, infer from it that its pressure helps to get more surrenders.'

He went on to say that the suggestion was in direct contradiction to everything for which the National Party had fought through the years and was nothing other than the integration policy of the United Party and in some of its consequences even the policy of the Progressive or the Liberal Party. And again on December 1, *Die Transvaler* reported that Verwoerd, addressing a Rand conference of the National Party in Johannesburg, had said that renewed economic and political pressure on the Government regarding its colour policy 'perhaps even from our own ranks' could now be expected. He promised that the Government and leaders would stand 'like walls of granite' because the survival of a people was at stake.

Die Burger commenting on the Prime Minister's statement, said [November 25, 1960] that the Prime Minister was obviously immovably opposed to the idea of Coloured representation by Coloureds as the thin edge of the wedge, a dangerous step in the direction of integration leading to the engulfing and destruction of the White nation. 'It was certainly not seen in this way by its Nationalist protagonists . . .'

The following day, Dawie quoted at some length a statement made during a senate debate, by the Minister of Bantu Administration, M. D. C. de Wet Nel in which Nel had asked how members could imagine that the Africans would be content always to be represented by a few Whites in Parliament. It was this sort of logic, said Dawie, which led supporters of the Government and of separate development to the idea of Coloured representation by Coloureds, especially as the Coloureds had no large homelands of their own. Nel was also quoted in an earlier interview with *Die Transvaler* in which he had said that the question of Coloureds being represented by Coloureds largely depended on the growth of their political responsibility.

Thus instead of the question of Coloured representation being dropped by *Die Burger* after Verwoerd's statement through *Die Transvaler*, the conflict escalated still further. Nel wrote a letter to *Die Burger*, categorically denying that the interview referred to had ever taken place. He said that 'Dawie knows that I am not *persona grata* with him and his "advanced friends" precisely because I–true to my conscientious convictions–have consistently upheld my standpoint and that of my party on the issues in question'. *Die Burger* reprimanded Nel in the same issue [November 28, 1960] for accusing the columnist of 'an untruth and of attributing incorrect statements to the Minister', and by publishing a facsimile of the report of the Nel speech in *Die Transvaler* of September 20, 1960.

The editor of *Dagbreek* commented [November 27, 1960] that Verwoerd's view had always been NP policy and represented the outlook of the great mass of the NP members and supporters and a considerable percentage of UP people. 'On the other hand it is a fact which must equally be accepted that many Nationalists, and unshakeable supporters of separate development feel that the time has come for the party to think of representation of Coloureds by their own people.' Separate development, he explained, envisaged for the 'Bantu' a political realization which did not in present circumstances exist for the Coloureds, and placed the latter in an unfavourable position compared with the African. 'This is a position which the National Party sooner or later will have to face even if there is, as the Prime Minister rightly shows so much to be done at the moment in the Coloured population's economic and educational development that the political aspect can still be regarded as subordinate.'

While *Dagbreek* was trying to cool the divisions in party ranks, *Die Burger* published a second letter from Nel, in which he again criticized *Die Burger* [November 30, 1960]. In a leading article on the same day, *Die Burger* in effect exposed the argument that was going on within the party about the debate being held in public. It reminded Nel that he had free access to the paper and 'we to him ... along other roads than public statements and letters about which no one except political opponents rejoice'. The paper asked why Nel was insisting on expressing 'all sorts of grievances against *Die Burger* publicly', and on denying earlier statements. It concluded that Nel foresaw some kind of Nationalist witch hunt which he wished 'to divert to a loyal and doughty champion of our common cause and its so-called liberal friends, whoever they may be ...' In fact great pressure was building up against *Die Burger* and repeated requests and threats by high-ranking politicians had failed to silence the paper. Verwoerd had personally asked the editor to refrain from airing contentious issues at this time – it was after all the year of Sharpeville. But then it was also Sharpeville and the political passivity of the Coloureds after Sharpeville which had inspired *Die Burger* to embark on its campaign.

Defiantly, Dawie berated Nel [December 3, 1960] for accusing *Die Burger* of liberalism and of undermining the Nationalist Government. He pointed out that many Afrikaaners favoured direct representation for the Coloureds and that 'if we begin to abuse them as liberalists and integrationists ... it will be the beginning of the end of our National Party. Still worse there will be catastrophic gulfs within the Afrikaans people and all its institutions, including its Church.' A witch hunt would not end with a few intellectuals, warned Dawie, 'I have referred to the case of Oom Daan (Nel). I could mention other names, big names in Government, the Church and the general life of the people.' And again on December 5, fighting hard for its freedom, *Die Burger* repeated that 'To suggest that deep-rooted differences do not exist is foolish. To prohibit their discussion is impossible and positively harmful.'

On December 4, *Dagbreek*, one of Verwoerd's staunchest allies, expressed its positive disagreement with Verwoerd that direct representation for the Coloureds would be a first step to integration. 'It seems to me,' said the editor, 'that the value of separate representation for Coloureds precisely lies in its offering them the opportunity to develop full political dignity without there having to be integration ...'

Three days later, in a statement published in *Die Vaderland* [December 7, 1960] the Prime Minister announced a 'new deal' for Coloureds, which consisted of the appointment of a Minister of Coloured Affairs, extension of the Coloured Council and other economic and educational programmes. To all intents and purposes the discussion within the party was over.

The reaction of *Die Burger* to the Prime Minister's 'new deal' policy for the Coloureds revealed most starkly the pressures the paper had been exposed to and the efforts that had been made to defend its Coloureds policy, and its freedom to express that policy. Welcoming Verwoerd's programme, *Die Burger* said [December 8, 1960]: 'The Government's programme is a serious matter for us and probably the beginning of our last opportunity to lead the Coloured people to permanent and reliable co-operation with the White people.'

In a second even more illuminating leader, the paper said that

'As we now understand the position ... it is not the official agreed Nationalist point of view that the Coloureds will necessarily be always represented by White people. It is not the official Nationalist point of view that criticism of such a prospect is liberalist or betrayal of the National Party. It is not the official Nationalist point of view that direct representation would be necessarily the beginning of integration and bastardization ... The official agreed point of view is merely that the Coloureds should continue to be represented in Parliament by Whites and that it will be possible in the future to request the reconsideration of this in the light of changed circumstances through the proper channels, without anybody being exposed to an automatic condemnation because of treachery to the National Party, the Nationalist Government or the White race. If this is where we now stand, all reason for vehement argument between Nationalist on this matter disappears although perhaps not for calm discussion.'

By the following day, *Die Burger* had unconditionally surrendered. Verwoerd's programme was described as 'one long series of positive steps towards the uplift and development of the Coloured in our midst' [December 9, 1960].

Die Transvaler commented [December 8, 1960] that if the Government had given in to all these demands, 'a truly chaotic situation would have arisen'. It would have been a 'backward step' whereas the Government's programme was a 'forward step'. The Coloured issue was for the present at an end; the Cape rebellion had been quelled.

The extent to which *Die Burger* had extended itself beyond the bounds of acceptability, even to the Cape National Party, was evidenced in a statement by the leader of the Cape Party, Dr T. E. Donges, to *Die Volksblad* [December 12, 1960]. He said that differences of opinion were not solved by coming to blows in public. He warned too against divisions within the party and affirmed that 'Our accepted policy of separate development for the Coloureds is now being continued with new energy by the positive programme of the Government as announced by the Prime Minister ... I earnestly hope that we will not destroy what we have already built up by overhasty steps and particularly not through bitter polemics in the public press'.

Beaten and disappointed, *Die Burger* recognized [January 23, 1961] that advocacy of direct representation had never been a popular movement and that such a policy could only have been made acceptable to the broad strata of the National Party by 'decisive leadership from the highest circles. The decisive leadership had rejected that school of thought' and the policy had thereby lost virtually all influence within the party. 'Yet an idea with inherent validity did not die forever and if direct representation was such an idea, it would recur in the future.'

Die Burger's real bitterness was revealed in this last statement, for it was felt by senior journalists that Verwoerd alone could have brought about such a change in the Coloureds policy, and that an opportunity had been lost, 'perhaps forever'. One senior journalist, Louis Louw, said that 'No Prime Minister ever had so much power or was ever so strong as Verwoerd was at that time. After the shooting – and his survival [in April 1960] – his charisma was so fantastic, he could have done anything and carried the party with him. He could have brought the Coloureds back into the fold.' Instead, Mr Louw said, Dr Verwoerd listened to his Transvaal advisers, the very people *Die Burger* had hoped Verwoerd would carry with him.

One important result of *Die Burger*'s stand against the Prime Minister and the officially stated policy of the party, was that *Die Burger* ceased to be the official mouthpiece of the Cape National Party, though the significance of this was mainly symbolic. Such continued insubordination, even after receipt of an order to be silent from the infrequently constituted Federal Council, could not be tolerated. Regardless of the Cape Party's own views on the matter, it was virtually certain that the dropping of *Die Burger* as the official organ of the Cape party resulted from instructions from the Prime Minister himself.

'Verligtes' and 'Verkramptes'

Prior to 1966 conflicts in the Nationalist Party centred around single issues and policies, with divisions roughly on a north–south basis. At no time was the party itself seriously threatened, though relationships between individual journalists and politicians did become very strained. The formation of *Die Beeld* in 1965, as outlined in earlier chapters, further strained the relationship between Nasionale Pers journalists and Verwoerd's Government. But it took the campaign to 'smoke out' the 'verkramptes', begun in earnest in 1966, finally to split the party in 1969 when Dr Albert Hertzog headed a small group of Nationalists to form the Herstigte Nasionale Party. Although *Die Beeld*, followed by other Nasionale Pers newspapers bore the brunt of party acrimony during the initial stages of the campaign, it was supported by *Die Transvaler* and less surely by *Dagbreek*. In other words only *Die Vaderland* of the major Afrikaans daily Press did not participate in the campaign, though the paper's editor denied that he was ever a 'verkrampte'.

There can be little doubt that the Afrikaans Press brought about, or, arguably, speeded up the first split in the National Party for twenty years. Prior to the split there was a great deal of confusion, particularly amongst rank-and-file party members–though the uncertainty existed in the upper echelons as well–who exerted great pressure on the party to 'deal with' the Afrikaans Press. *Die Beeld*'s editor claimed that 'people who were not aware of what was going on fought a tremendous campaign against *Die Beeld*, with attacks 'on *Die Beeld* and on me personally. They accused us of undermining the party leadership and of spreading liberalism'. But they were not aware, he said, that the 'verkramptes' were infiltrating the Afrikaner institutions, attempting a takeover of the South African Academy of Arts and Science, and other such organizations, with the eventual aim of usurping the leadership of the party. 'It was they who were trying to create division within the party, not us.'[1]

It is impossible to know how events would have moved had Verwoerd not been assassinated at the start of the 'smoking out' campaign. He might well have been able to contain the dissenters within the party and to have kept up a united front. On the other hand, his inability totally to silence *Die Burger* over the Coloureds issue makes it seem unlikely that he would have been able to do so on this occasion. Besides the English Press had already picked up the story and were eagerly publicizing the 'split' in the Nationalist ranks. Vorster was initially 'actively neutral' but once he became involved in the strife he was unable to contain the dissenters and unwilling to take sides against the party Press which continued to make serious policy differences within the party public property. His resignation from the chairmanship of both Afrikaanse Pers and Voortrekker Pers was a direct result of the 'verligte-verkrampte' row and the contentious position of the party Press in the conflict.

The campaign against 'right wing' Nationalists was sparked off by a motion of 'thanks and appreciation to S. E. D. Brown and the *South African Observer*' by the Pretoria University Branch of the Afrikaanse *Studente Bond* (the Afrikaans student body).

As S. E. D. Brown, the publisher-editor of the *South African Observer*, was a 'verkrampte', and his paper had been consistently attacking leading Nationalists–editors, politicians and businessmen alike–this statement caused some concern, particularly as it was feared that the 'verkramptes' might be winning support amongst the younger generation of Nationalists.

In a front page news item on August 7, 1966, *Die Beeld* revealed that a 'long-brewing worry in Nationalist ranks has burst open and

[1] From an interview with Schalk Pienaar in January 1970.

has caused a stir in Parliament and political circles . . . It is actually an outburst of abhorrence of the methods of the English-speaking "Nationalist", S. E. D. Brown who in his journal, *South African Observer*, also acts as the mouthpiece for a little group of Afrikaner Nationalists.' Commenting on the news item in his political column, the editor accused Brown of sowing discord amongst Afrikaners and said that no Nationalist editor or newspaper had escaped attack by the journal. He warned fellow Nationalists to 'suffer them as nuisances' but not to accept them as political friends.

The following day [August 8], *Die Transvaler* splashed the news on its front page describing the journal's role as 'negative and divisive'. The report said that a study of the *South African Observer* revealed that it 'engages in attacks on Afrikaners in all walks of life'. Dawie had disclosed in his column in *Die Burger* [August 5, 1966] that the National Party had formerly subsidized the *South African Observer* but had withdrawn its subsidy a year or two earlier, because the journal had for some years been attacking prominent Afrikaners, 'on the lines of the American Senator McCarthy's method of "guilt by association"'.

Die Vaderland took a very different view in its main editorial [August 8, 1966] claiming that it was not Brown's blood Dawie was after, but 'that little group of Nationalists, the "little Northern circle" with their principled concept about the content and purpose of the National task and struggle . . . who are to be discredited through their association with that terrible fellow Brown'. Assuming that such a 'Northern circle' existed, *Die Vaderland* asserted that it would have the right to exist within the National Party. The paper safeguarded its interests by emphasizing that it did not defend Brown's 'editing, language or style' but simply questioned whether a lone Englishman's zeal should now be 'rubbed out as a tremendous national evil while suspicion-mongery against Nationalist statesmen . . . by a mighty English-language daily Press should be pampered as an untouchable part of our democratic process'. But *Die Vaderland*, on whose board Albert Hertzog (eventually identified as the head 'verkrampte') sat, deliberately missed the point being made by Nasionale Pers, namely that Brown was not a lone Englishman, but was being used by some high-ranking Nationalists to divide the party.

The following day [August 9], *Die Burger* discounted *Die Vaderland*'s attempt to brand the dispute as simply a north–south issue and supported its claim by pointing out that *Die Transvaler* had spoken out with the 'same voice as the newspapers of the Nasionale Pers Group'. And determined that the division should be taken seriously,

Die Burger emphasized that this was a 'national issue within Nationalist ranks ... There is no danger of a wedge between South and North, but possibly a danger of a wedge in the ranks of the Nationalists, especially in the North.'

For the rest of the week *Die Transvaler* and the Nasionale Pers papers continued to attack Brown and his journal, and assert that those who might have been sympathetic towards Brown would disassociate themselves, now that the issue had drifted to the surface. At the end of the week, Dawie concluded that the Brown episode was as good as forgotten, as 'no Nationalist of any standing had defended Mr. Brown'. But Dawie could not have been more wrong as he himself must have known. For the attack on Brown masked the more fundamental and ideological questions being asked in the party.

The 'verkramptes' as they came to be called, feared that the Afrikaner would not survive unless he continued in isolation. Thus the attempts, begun by Verwoerd, to follow an outward-looking foreign policy, and to accommodate sympathetic English-speakers in the 'Volk' were looked upon as a serious threat to the continued existence of the Afrikaner. The 'verligtes' on the other hand, saw the survival of the Afrikaner as dependent on an outward-looking foreign policy and felt that in order to preserve a White group on a Black continent, Afrikaner nationalism was compelled to relax at least some of its exclusiveness. The conflict was more than the old argument over the one or two-stream policy for White South Africa, though it certainly contained elements of the old argument. It also contained the fear that by permitting foreign Blacks to break South Africa's apartheid laws the policy of apartheid itself would be breached. The 'verkrampte' argument was finally an argument against change and the fear that a change in the means would bring about a change in the ends.

Die Oosterlig's political columnist described the 'trauma' some Nationalists might be enduring as a result of the visit of a Malawi ministerial delegation to South Africa [March 10, 1967]. He said there were those who applauded because they regarded the visit as a great diplomatic breakthrough and others who felt it was a breach of cherished principles, 'almost a kind of spiritual assault. What is astir among us is repugnance at the idea of a naked meeting with pitch-black people on a basis of equality ... It is the idea of equal value and identity behind different skin colours which some people feel as an annoying irritation of their personal dignity as Afrikaners and as Nationalists with a long history of exclusive own-sortness (eiesoortigheid) ...'. Grensboer, the political columnist, concluded by stating that there must, of necessity, be contact between South Africa and her Black neighbours.

Although the Nationalist Government felt sufficiently secure to adopt its new so-called outward-looking policies, it was not sure enough to tolerate such public questioning of its policies from within its own ranks. 'Verkramptes' were much more likely to be able to influence the direction of Nationalist policy as members of Government and party than as outsiders. Nasionale Pers clearly understood this possibility long before the division in the party was an accepted fact. Hence its repeated claims when under attack that it was serving party unity by exposing right-wing deviations, for by removing an offending faction, party unity could be maintained.

The 'verligte-verkrampte' issue was temporarily overshadowed by the assassination of Verwoerd and the election of a new leader. The second phase of the battle began with a speech delivered on October 4 at a Youth Congress of SABRA, the South African Bureau of Racial Affairs (an Afrikaner Nationalist version of the Institute of Race Relations). Addressing the meeting Dr W. J. de Klerk, son of the Minister of Education, Arts and Science, used the words 'verligte' and 'verkrampte' for the first time. In the original version of the speech, which had been released to the Press, de Klerk said that the 'known enemies' communists, liberals, progressives and others had been unmasked. But two dangers remained: On the one hand, there were 'enlightened Afrikaners, responsible for the infiltration of liberalism into Afrikaner institutions. On the other, there were "bigoted" Afrikaners who rejected all forms of change'. Dr de Klerk extolled the 'positive' Afrikaner, who recognized and appreciated tradition, yet was a man of today with a vision of tomorrow. When de Klerk delivered his address, however, he omitted all reference to the 'bigoted' Afrikaners, at the request of certain 'high office-bearers'.

Lest there should have been any doubts, *Die Beeld* informed its readers [October 9, 1966] that the 'entire matter is strongly connected with the affair in August over S. E. D. Brown and his ultra-right pamphlet'. Other Afrikaans newspapers were critical of de Klerk for suppressing his comments on 'bigoted' Afrikaners while *Die Vaderland* [October 7, 1966] allied him with the Cape Nationalist papers and the English Press amongst whom, it said, it was fashionable to divide Afrikaners into groups.

The next step in the campaign was an attempt by both sides–the Afrikaans Press versus Brown–to identify Verwoerd with their cause, in other words to make it seem that theirs was the mainstream of Afrikaner nationalism. By now there was a great deal of confusion and uncertainty within the National Party, for it was not at all clear who the victors would be. Nor was it obvious just how much support the 'verkramptes' had amongst the public, or for that matter who amongst the MPs privately supported the 'verkrampte' stand. And clearly the political futures of all concerned depended on being on the right side at the right time.

The most obvious outlet for this uncertainty was to criticize the Press, especially the Afrikaans Press which was forcing the whole issue to be discussed in public. A nervous Minister of Bantu Administration and Development (and Bantu Education) M. C. Botha, said that the Afrikaner must be wary of attacks from within his own circle against conservatism; 'it is not sensible to begin a hunt against those who are ultra-right ... Unhappily–and I say this with a weeping heart–columnists of Afrikaans newspapers have made attacks upon extreme Rightists or Conservatives [November 14, 1966].

Die Beeld [November 20, 1966] gave Botha the benefit of the doubt and said that the differences between itself and the Minister was one of 'words' and not thoughts, and that both sides should clarify their terms. While *Dagbreek* called yet again [November 20, 1966] 'for an end to this disparagement'.

But the end to the disparagement was not nearly in sight. Throughout 1967 and most of 1968 and 1969, the battle in the party raged furiously, and the Afrikaans Press was at the very centre of it. It was a fight for the control of the National Party, in the first instance by the 'verkramptes' and in the second by individual members of the Nationalist Press to gain the most influential position in the party. Nasionale Pers particularly wanted to ensure that Vorster was their man; they were justified in believing that he might be, for it was his foreign policy, immigration policy and attitude to the English-speaking sector which was under attack. Yet they feared that he might feel compelled to submit to 'verkrampte' pressure, and alter the direction of his policies, for which *Die Burger* believed it had been largely responsible in the first place. It was thus as much a bid for its own ascendency in the party–and it had suffered a serious falling off in influence under Verwoerd–as a fight against the 'verkramptes'.

Attacks on the 'verligte' Afrikaans Press and individual editors came from all quarters: S. E. D. Brown's *South African Observer, Die Vaderland*, Provincial Party congresses, Piet Meyer, the head of the South African Broadcasting Corporation, numerous Afrikaans cultural organizations and societies, and individual Nationalist politicians. In turn Nasionale Pers and its protagonists attacked critics of the Afrikaans Press and those organizations who opposed their views. In all its years in office, the National Party Government had never faced such a debate in public, and the publicity itself affected the nature of the conflict.

Early in 1967, the Minister of Defence, P. W. Botha, felt compelled to defend Nasionale Pers of which he had become a director in April, so serious were the pressures upon the Cape National Party to take action against *Die Burger* and *Die Beeld*. He said, at a conference of Peninsula constituencies, that as long as he was leader of the Cape National Party, he would expect every supporter of the party in the Cape to accept Nasionale Pers and its publications as courageous fellow fighters in 'our efforts to lead our country to a great and glorious future. The National Party and Nasionale Pers do not attempt to dominate one another. They are equal partners who fertilise each other'. He pointed out that 'attempts to play off the Nationalist Party against the Nasionale Pers will fail like similar attempts in the past', a reference to the Coloureds issue discussed earlier in this chapter.

The controversy in the party and the Press extended outwards to include the Afrikaans churches and Afrikaans cultural organizations. In the middle of 1967 the Afrikaans Press publicly exposed that the Afrikaner cultural organizations were involved in the political struggle. Minister Botha, the Cape Leader of the National Party, warned against 'over-organisation' and 'overlapping' of cultural organisations, which *Die Burger* explained [June 19, 1967], 'lent themselves only too easily to the activities of political and semi-political advisers who carry too little weight on the actual political front, that of the National Party'. *Die Vaderland* disputed *Die Burger's* interpretation [June 19, 1967] and said that the National Party 'lives and grows through the virility of organised Afrikaner National life', and the new method of 'inferences' and 'interpretations' was upsetting Afrikaner ranks and not the cultural organizations.

The *Sunday Times* [July 23, 1967] provided the explanation of the concern over the proliferation of Afrikaans organization in an article disclosing who some of the 'verkramptes' were. It alleged that the Afrikaner Orde headed by Hertzog was the main 'verkrampte' organization and gave details of twenty-seven of its 'front' organizations and also of twenty other organizations within which 'verkrampte' members acted as pressure groups.

Despite the fact that the English Press was throughout giving extensive coverage to the 'verligte-verkrampte' battle, and that the *Sunday Times'* political correspondent frequently disclosed more than

---

[1] *Die Transvaler*, March 10, 1967.

the Afrikaans newspapers themselves, only *Die Vaderland* and the *South African Observer* concerned themselves with the English Press. Again and again *Die Vaderland* argued that the English Press was responsible for sowing discord amongst Afrikaners and not S. E. D. Brown, and used this argument to berate *Die Burger* and *Die Beeld*, insisting that they were not directing their attacks against the 'real' enemy.

Up until July 1967, the Prime Minister had not made a single statement about the disturbances in Afrikaner ranks. Eventually on July 28, the Prime Minister gave a statement to *Die Burger* in which he said that the present quarrel in Afrikaner circles was unedifying and unworthy of all who took part in it. 'I sincerely hope,' he said, 'that we have seen the end of a vacation episode which has brought no credit to any of the participants nor secured any advantage to our party.'

The fact that the Prime Minister gave his statement to *Die Burger* rather than to any of the other Afrikaans newspapers, was interpreted by some newspapermen as an indication of which side he was on. But *Die Burger* was clearly not satisfied that it had convinced the Prime Minister of the seriousness of the split, for the following day [July 29, 1967], Dawie said that the activities of Brown went further than a 'vacation episode'. It had been going on for years, Dawie claimed, and the joint action of a series of Nationalist newspapers 'towards the middle of last year did not end it'. Dawie added that 'venom' was being spread orally throughout the country and that 'our evidence is in the hands of the Cape leadership'. He expressed serious doubts that the Prime Minister would be able to leave the matter at a single expression of disapproval.

The week-end brought confirmation that the dispute went deeper. Both *Die Burger* and *Die Beeld* carried further attacks on the 'verkramptes' while *Die Vaderland* which had welcomed the Prime Minister's call and promised to desist from further disputation, rejoined the fray with undiminished vigour [July 31, 1967].

The Prime Minister's first positively supportive statement for the 'verligte' Press came in August, following a four-page attack in the *South African Observer* on the editors of *Die Burger*, *Die Beeld*, *Die Transvaler* and *Dagbreek*. In a speech at Koffiefontein, Vorster condemned Brown and liberal-hunters in the National Party. He declared that the directors of Nationalist newspapers were all honourable Afrikaners and good Nationalists and would not employ 'liberalists' to edit their newspapers. But the Prime Minister still said that there was no quarrel amongst Nationalists and no split threatened the National Party.

196

It was expected that the Provincial Party Congresses would finally settle the 'verligte-verkrampte' row, either by forcing the 'verkramptes' to declare themselves, or by rendering them totally impotent. Instead the conferences, held in August and September, proved to be the source of even greater disruption, and the Afrikaans Press assumed still more importance in the conflict. It was itself responsible for the greater escalation of the argument and became the subject of heated disagreement in the party, bringing cabinet ministers into public opposition with each other.

After the Transvaal National Party Congress, *Die Beeld* in an unprecedented fashion, disclosed [September 10, 1957] that a 'great secret' of the Transvaal Congress was that a motion of confidence in the Prime Minister and all the Nationalist newspapers had been taken by the executive committee of the party for submission to the Congress; but the motion was never put to the Congress. The reason for this, according to *Die Beeld's* political correspondent, was that the two Pretoria MPs, Jaap Marais and Willie Marais, found themselves unable to vote for the Press section of the motion, particularly as *Die Beeld* would be included in the confidence vote. *Die Beeld* said it did not know why the resolution had not been publicized.

The General Secretary of the Transvaal National Party, J. H. Steyl, replied through *Die Vaderland* [September 11, 1967] claiming that no motion was taken by the executive committee for submission to the Congress; he lodged the 'strongest objection to this kind of casting of suspicion against the Transvaal National Party, its leaders and MPs'. Ben Schoeman, the Transvaal leader of the National Party (and Minister of Transport), when speaking at the Orange Free State Party Congress, openly criticized *Die Beeld* for publishing its report, and asked why the Nationalist Press had to provide ammunition for their enemies by washing dirty linen in public.

The immediate outcome of Schoeman's remarks was to further increase the tension between the Press and party. *Dagbreek's* front-page lead story that week [September 17, 1967] was headlined: '*Die Burger* and *Volksblad* Attack Mr. Schoeman – Polemic Sharper', while on the same day *Die Beeld* itself carried the headline: '"Quarrel" hare goes on running – Schoeman Is in the Arena – Newspapers Hit Back Angrily.'

The issue was taken a step further when, at the Cape Party Congress, the Cape leader, P. W. Botha, praised Nasionale Pers newspapers and reaffirmed the indivisibility of the Cape National Party and its Press. The unity of the Cape National Party and Nasionale Pers enabled *Die Burger* and *Die Beeld* to go much further in its attacks than if it had been less sure of its support from the Cape Party. Thus Dawie was highly critical of Schoeman [*Die Burger*, September 16] and said that his attacks on Nasionale Pers papers had been 'too wild, in large measure undeserved and completely untimely'. Dawie claimed that there was a 'venomous distortion factory in Pretoria (a reference to S. E. D. Brown), and I regret that Mr Schoeman has apparently become a victim of the distorted information of that factory'.

Die Volksblad too joined in [September 15, 1967] and advised Schoeman that 'If one wanted to attack Nationalist newspapers, plenty of examples can be found for Mr Schoeman nearer home'. The paper said it would be expected that newspapers which at times speak the S. E. D. Brown language would rather have been singled out for the kind of attack 'we have had to suffer'. *Die Volksblad* further supported Nasionale Pers by quoting J. Fouche, Free State leader of the National Party and a member of the Nasionale Pers Board who had said that the National Party had no better allies than the newspapers of Nasionale Pers.

Die Beeld's editor returned to his paper's exposé by asking what the paper's crime was [September 17, 1967]. 'Was it not true that such a motion had been taken?' If *Die Beeld* had erred, the paper said, then it was in good company, for according to the editor, several members of the Transvaal executive had contacted him subsequently to confirm that they had 'had the impression' that the motion was to be announced at the Congress. Pienaar warned that in the process of supporting the National Party and the Prime Minister, *Die Beeld* would hit back if attacked 'more than ever before'.

At this point, *Dagbreek*'s editor, Dirk Richard, turned on *Die Beeld* and asked if Keeromstraat was really going to allow its less respectable sister paper to 'climb in' despite the erosion of Afrikaner unity, just so long 'as the paper sold' [September 17, 1967]. Richard claimed that the 'verligte-verkrampte' issue was deliberately being kept alive to exploit it for increasing circulation a suggestion prompted no doubt by a sense of grievance on *Dagbreek*'s part against a competitor, as *Die Beeld*'s more sensational approach to politics had boosted its circulation enormously. At the same time Richard made it clear that his newspaper was just as 'enlightened as was possible', but that he was simply opposing the 'methods of persecution' employed by *Die Beeld* which failed to take account of the conservative nature of the average Nationalist.

'Willem' in *Die Volksblad* [September 22, 1967] rejected out of hand *Dagbreek*'s assertion that *Die Beeld* was profit-motivated and said that Nasionale Pers had always followed conviction, even though it meant an indefinite period in the wilderness. 'Never let us hear again from Afrikaans circles that Nasionale Pers publications support for leader and party are a smokescreen for profit seeking, and that from circles who have not travelled the whole road with us.' (This was a reference to Malan's break from Hertzog to form the Purified National Party. *Die Vaderland* at the time supported Hertzog's National Party and later the fusion United Party, while *Dagbreek* in its early days was an independent newspaper.)

Heedless of the crisis it was causing in Nationalist ranks, Nasionale Pers persisted in its campaign against Schoeman. At a meeting in Wolmaransstad Schoeman had disputed the existence of a northern group conniving with Brown. He said he had made a thorough investigation and found that every one of the Transvaal Nationalist MPs were loyal to the National Party and challenged anyone in the republic to prove otherwise. He concluded by saying it was not the task of newspapers to formulate National Party policy, though he emphasized the importance of their support.[1]

Dawie, quite obviously with tongue-in-cheek, welcomed Schoeman's investigation and said [*Die Burger*, September 30, 1967] that 'we have the word of the Transvaal leader of the National Party that there is total separation between all Transvaal MPs of the National Party and Mr Brown and that he himself will see to it that it remains like that'. But he also said that he would be happier if the group of MPs who persisted in praising Brown had themselves spoken out against him. Dirk Richard was enraged and asked whether it was not necessary for P. W. Botha and Jim Fouche to have a word with the newspapers of Nasionale Pers on their persistence in the controversy.

The Schoeman affair revealed a new facet to the political power game Nasionale Pers was playing, which goes some way in explaining the unwavering support of the Cape Party leadership for Nasionale Pers newspapers. It would seem that at this point Nasionale Pers already felt confident that they had won the goodwill of the leadership, though they were perhaps less sure of their support amongst rank-and-file Nationalists. But Vorster was a short-term investment in an increase in Cape influence, and Nasionale Pers was looking for future profit too. In other words Nasionale Pers was trying to influence the selection of a future leader of the party, who in their terms was quite logically, the leader of the Cape National Party, P. W. Botha.

Schoeman (or rather his successor) as leader of the Transvaal

---

[1] *Die Transvaler*, September 30, 1967.

National Party constituted the greatest competition to the Cape leader, particularly as every Prime Minister after Malan was drawn from the Transvaal. Throughout its 'campaign' against Schoeman, the Nasionale Pers papers lavishly praised their Cape leader and supporter and repeatedly described him as one of the most powerful men in the cabinet, a loyal supporter of Vorster and his policies, and as a leader united with his Press. Thus it was not simply Schoeman who was under attack; Nasionale Pers was trying to create the impression–and with some success–that the Transvaal Party was divided within itself, unlike the Cape Party which was united within itself and with its powerful Press, which had newspapers representing its views in three of the four provinces (and some circulation in the fourth).

Dirk Richard and to a lesser extent, A. M. van Schoor of *Die Vaderland*, began to realize what Nasionale Pers, and by association, the Cape Nationalists, were aiming at. However, van Schoor's natural hostility to Nasionale Pers, and *Dagbreek*'s acknowledged resentment of the changes Nasionale Pers had forced in the balance of the Afrikaans Press, tended to diminish the impact of either editor's analysis of Nasionale Pers' tactics.

What *Dagbreek* said [October 15, 1967] was that the enthusiasm of the Cape to make Botha 'Congress champion' brought provincialism back into the picture. Further, that with a newspaper chain from the Cape to the Transvaal at its disposal, Nasionale Pers was trying to exercise countrywide influence, and 'prescribing and determining for the country what sound National and good Nationalists are'. *Die Vaderland* on the other hand, stressed the fact that Nasionale Pers, especially *Die Beeld*, was trying to cause a split in Transvaal Nationalist ranks [December 4, 1967].

Dagbreek had adopted a variety of stances through the 'verligte-verkrampte' crisis. Acting initially as referee–a role its traditions best equipped it for–*Dagbreek* variously applauded the more open approach to political debate, at all times spoke of the need for self-discipline, on occasion denied the seriousness of the divisions, pitted itself against Nasionale Pers and particularly *Die Beeld* and finally tried to compete with Nasionale Pers in defining the role of the Afrikaans Press in the political structure.

Notably, on November 26, 1967 Richard suggested in *Dagbreek* that if he could choose a cabinet, he would advise that four senior Ministers (whom he named and including Hertzog and Fouche) be dropped. Richard's efforts at king-breaking were virtually unprecedented and had to be interpreted as an attempt to prevent Nasionale Pers from having a monopoly in the field. (As later events proved,

Richard and Vorster were largely in agreement. Three of the four cabinet changes did take place.)

The second important and controversial statement by Richard, was an article in *Dagbreek* [January 21, 1968] outlining past 'failures' of the Afrikaans Press. He said that at the time of the Constitutional crisis over the removal of Coloureds from the voters' roll the Afrikaans Press should have warned its readers against the High Court of Parliament Act in 1952, which he described as 'nothing but a violation of our administration of justice. To ask politicians to give the verdict on a law they themselves made was a deviation from the pure legal path . . .' He also suggested that the Afrikaans Press had failed to point out the inflexibility of the original Group Areas Act, which unnecessarily chafed human relations and consequently required many amendments. He revealed that 'Few Afrikaans pressmen at the time were in a frame of mind or were willing to consider the difference between the principle and content of legislation or its implementation. Everything was tied up in the same package of unassailability.' Richard made three other important criticisms of the past showing of the Afrikaans Press: that it had failed to encourage immigration in the 1950s (in the face of 'wrong' Government policy) that it had not prepared the Afrikaner for his broader role in Africa, and that many years had been lost by its failure to appreciate the value of the Tomlinson Report of 1954. This Report had pointed out that the Reserves were seriously deteriorating and would require an expenditure of £10 million per annum for ten years and that White capital and enterprise would be necessary for carrying out the proposals. Verwoerd, as Minister of Native Affairs, had quashed the proposals in a White Paper, and Richard admitted that it was 'political taboo to propagandise Professor Tomlinson's recipe for development of the homelands . . .' Richard had come a long way from some earlier statements when he concluded that the 'Afrikaans Press will make its voice heard more and more and will not merely remain an echo of the party . . . but a partner alongside it . . .'

An important consequence of the ferment going on within the Afrikaans Press and the party was the Prime Minister's decision, announced in *Dagbreek* on October 22 1967, to resign the chairmanship of Voortrekker Pers (Transvaler) and Dagbreek Trust (*Vaderland* and *Dagbreek*) on the pretext that Press affairs were occupying too much of his time. *Dagbreek* expressed its disappointment on the grounds that Vorster had broken with a tradition begun by Strijdom and Verwoerd. Nasionale Pers newspapers could hardly suppress their jubilation and *Die Beeld* was quick to point out that Malan as Prime Minister had never held office in a Press enterprise, for despite Malan's close association with *Die Burger* once he became Prime Minister he severed all official ties with the newspaper. By associating Vorster's actions with Malan's, *Die Beeld* was implying that Vorster's future way would be Malan's (and the Cape's) way rather than that of any of Malan's Transvaal successors. One explanation offered by *Die Beeld* was that competing business interests between Afrikaans newspaper groups was placing the Prime Minister in an untenable position.

It would however seem that Vorster's overriding reason for resigning from the two newspaper companies was the acute involvement of the Afrikaans Press in the crisis in Afrikaner ranks. At this point he was still unwilling to commit himself totally to any one group in the increasingly complex divisions occurring throughout Afrikanerdom. By disassociating himself, he neither sanctioned nor opposed the views of any part of the Afrikaans Press. But a result of his withdrawal was to leave him free to give at least tacit support to Nasionale Pers.

At the beginning of 1968 Vorster was still not prepared to admit publicly that any serious divisions existed in the party, despite the fact that the Afrikaans Press was daily asserting the existence of such divisions. On February 6, the Prime Minister stated in the Assembly:

> 'There is not a single man sitting on this side in the Parliament who does not subscribe a hundred per cent to the entire policy of the Nationalist Party in all its respects.'[1]

Yet by August, Hertzog had been removed from the cabinet, and Vorster had publicly defended the 'verligte' policies on immigration, relations with the Black States, and the co-operation between the two White groups.

Victory for Nasionale Pers–who had identified the 'enemy' and antagonized the party in ferreting him out–came in 1969, when Hertzog and two other Nationalist MPs had their membership of the party cancelled. A third member, threatened with similar action, resigned. The 'verkramptes' were out of the party and could no longer threaten its 'unity': an enemy without could be dealt with but dissent within the ranks could be neither ignored nor disclosed.

After twenty years of unbroken and individed rule the National Party was far less likely to be threatened by groups prepared to go into the political wilderness, as General Hertzog and Malan had done. Dr. Hertzog recognized the importance of remaining within the ranks of the National Party and stated that he would not leave the party

---

[1] Hansard 1, col. 62.

unless he was driven out.[1] If there was to be change it had to come from within, as both Hertzog and the Nationalist Press believed.

Thus important changes occurred within both the English and Afrikaans Press. Prior to 1948, the English-language Press enjoyed a large measure of freedom, but it restricted itself to the jealous protection of the rights of English-speaking South Africans in the 'White democracy'. Faced with a Nationalist Government and the formalizing of the apartheid policy, the English Press believed that the 'democracy' was seriously threatened and that the non-White people were to be deprived of their few existing rights and freedoms. Events in the 1950s confirmed its fears but for most of the decade the English Press put its faith in the United Party to defend the interests of English-speaking South Africans and the non-Whites. After the 1958 elections, the English Press assumed a greater responsibility and despite increasing social and governmental pressure, showed a growing concern with the wider South African society and particularly for the interests of the unrepresented members of the society. Support for a Progressive Party would have been highly improbable in 1948. But the general sympathy expressed in 1961 reflected both the English Presses' dissatisfaction with the United Party and its increased concern for the rights of the non-Whites, as did its continuing opposition to the Nationalists and the values of a major proportion of the White society.

The Afrikaans Press started out to create a culture, a language, a political party and to unite a 'Volk'. By 1948 it had achieved all this and more; during the 1950s its task was largely one of consolidation and its role was to be an uncritically supportive arm of party and Government, to hold the 'Volk' together under an ideological umbrella it was in the process of creating and communicating. As for the English Press, 1958 was a year of change; the Afrikaans Press was demanding a more than simply supportive role in the governmental structure. *Die Burger* particularly, with its memories of the early years of equal partnership with the party, wanted a new role in relation to party and Government. Building up a party and supporting it whilst in opposition was not the same as providing unquestioning support for a Government. By 1960 the revolt was well under way, until in 1966 with the emergence of the 'verligte-verkrampte' issue, the Afrikaans Press was publicly debating differences within the party and Government and its own role within the Government structure.

These changes in the Afrikaans Press did not bring about any extension of interest in the greater society. In changing, the English

[1] *Rand Daily Mail*, April 30, 1969.

Press looked outside itself to the total society; the Afrikaans Press looked inwards. As a result of the changes which took place, both the English and Afrikaans Press can be said to have been forces of opposition: the English Press, in so far as it represented the interests of the 'voteless majority', posed the 'real' challenge to the Nationalist Government and White South Africa. The Afrikaans Press, on the other hand became the most powerfully organized opposition force within Government and party itself. Within the institutional framework of White South African politics, the Afrikaans Press became an opposition to be reckoned with.

Conclusion

Between 1948 and 1968 a single party, representing a single sector of a minority group in the population held office in South Africa. In that time all serious opponents of the Government were suppressed and in the process the range of views which might be conciliated or even articulated narrowed very considerably. Yet the overwhelmingly dominant Press, the English-language Press, was uniformly and sometimes vociferously opposed to the Government, its ideology and its supporters–by then a clear majority of the White population. On the other hand the Government supporting Press failed to compete with the English Press for readers, although, as an integrated part of the National Party and government machine, the Afrikaans Press was powerfully placed to influence and communicate Government policy.

The history of the two Presses explains the existence of the two quite different types of mass communication structures. The English-language newspapers began as business enterprises, run for profit; in style and content (and even personnel) they were fashioned on the British Press. The Afrikaans-language Press started out to create a language, a culture and a people and was an integrated part of the political organ of Nationalist Afrikanerdom, the National Party.

The two Presses reflected and helped to maintain existing divisions within society. Early in its history the ownership of the English-language Press passed to the mining industry and big business entrepreneurs and reflected the English South Africans' dominance in the economy. The Afrikaans Press, owned by numerous small shareholders, was intricately linked to the National Party through party-political editors, including Malan and Verwoerd, and through directorial boards dominated by Prime Ministers and cabinet ministers.

The evidence of the readership surveys confirmed the importance of the English Press' earlier start in producing urban daily newspapers and suggested too that newspapers with a strong profit (rather than political) motive were those most likely to win readers. The two most important features of newspaper readership to emerge from the surveys were: first, that in general the English-language newspapers had succeeded in maintaining their percentages of Afrikaans-speaking readers whilst the Afrikaans-language Press failed to do so. The seriousness of this failure was underlined by the fact that the Afrikaans Press depended almost exclusively on White Afrikaans-speaking South Africans to read its newspapers. Second, the English-language Press attracted readers from all racial groups and by 1968 more than 50 per cent of the readers of the *Cape Argus*, the third largest daily newspaper in South Africa, were non-White. Non-White readership of daily newspapers is likely to increase and it seems inevitable, according to present trends and remembering the numerical imbalances in the population groups, that non-Whites will constitute the majority of readers of many English-language newspapers in the future.

The accessibility of the English-language Press to all racial and linguistic groups has already had serious consequences for the Press. As one of the few racially non-exclusive institutions in the society, the opposition English-language Press offered an alternative and to the Government, an unacceptable view of society.

The Nationalist Government responded by attempting to intimidate the Press into exercising self-censorship. It did this by appealing to its patriotism, by making constantly repeated threats, by setting up a Press Commission of Inquiry which took fourteen years to report, by forcing the creation of a proprietorially regulated Code of Conduct and through a massive body of loosely defined, seldom invoked laws.

The Government also tried to control the content of the Press by refusing to disclose information about itself and by obstructing the English-language Press in its attempts to acquire political information from non-governmental sources.

The Afrikaans Press saw itself and was seen by the Government as the communication arm of a political party which claimed to represent an entire people. Hence the Government's messages were directed primarily and often exclusively to the 'Volk'. Ideologically, Government did not recognize the rights of the independent Press to information, for the English Press did not represent the 'Volk' nor could it be trusted to communicate the political message.

In one sense the National Party did not complete the transition from Opposition to Government. Failure to account for policy-decisions to groups outside party circles whilst in Opposition was of less importance than Government's refusal to offer explanations of its policy to all groups in the society.

The Afrikaans Press never tried to offer a picture of the total society to its readers, but was concerned exclusively with representing the interests of the Afrikaner and conveying to the Afrikaner a picture of himself. The English-language Press gave recognition to all groups in the society despite its sectional bias. As Black South Africans had no means of articulating their interests or communicating their claims, they were effectively not a part of the political system at all. But by representing non-White interests as they saw them, the English Press forced an entry for the non-White into the political system. The Afrikaans Press operated within the confines of White institutional politics, serving as a political communicator for party and Government and in later years as an extremely powerful pressure group for change within the party. But always its concern was with the Afrikaner and with the organization of structures within the party and the Government.

The English Press increasingly became identified with those interests to which it gave expression. When the struggle for political domination had been between the Afrikaners and the English, the English Press had represented the Nationalists' White opponents. Once the English ceased to be the major opponents, the English Press became a more serious opposition, which at times represented the interests of non-Whites. In Nationalist eyes the English Press became not a fourth estate but a fifth column.

The English Press' highly developed independent Press ethic and its vision of the 'good society' ensured its continuing opposition. The Government could have silenced the English Press; yet it did not do so and the English Press remained freer than any other individual or institution in the society to oppose the Nationalist Government.

Why has this been so? Perhaps the single most important reason was that the English-language Press was a White Press. The Nationalist Government was ruthless in its suppression of Black opposition or groups associated with the Black opposition. But it did little directly to suppress the White opposition, both because it did not constitute a serious threat and because the Nationalists continued to win elections. This is not to say that White South Africans did not suffer a serious decline in their civil liberties but this was a by-product of laws aimed at suppressing the non-White opposition, rather than the result of deliberate Nationalist policies. Thus the Nationalists were reluctant to be seen tampering directly with the 'freedom' of the English-language Press which, as a part of the White Establishment, was protected by the White democracy theory. It was easier to 'snuff out' individuals by imposing banning orders–and hence preventing the publication of their views–than to ban the financially powerful English-language newspapers if the Nationalists wished to maintain the 'myth' of *Herrenvolk* egalitarianism and White democracy. Instead the Government sought to persuade the English-language Press to censor itself.

The belief that the existence of a powerful independent Press was evidence of the democracy, weighed heavily in the Presses' favour. For in balancing the effects (as they saw them) of the free Press on the political system against the inevitably hostile response of an already hostile 'world opinion', were the Nationalists to eliminate the English-language Press, they chose to allow a measure of freedom to the independent Press. It seems reasonable to assume that the English-language Press was itself largely responsible for the persistence of the belief that a free Press was a necessary concomitant of democracy. The English Press was throughout its own strongest defender and clearly succeeded in maintaining a greater measure of freedom for itself than for the individuals in the society as a whole.

The third part of the explanation is to be found in the fact that the English-language Press was a 'responsible' Press. Like the United Party which it once wholeheartedly supported, the English-language Press believed that the political game ought to be played according to given rules. It came easily within the bounds of its responsibility to attack the rules, but never to flout them or deliberately to encourage others to do so. Thus the English Press would never, for example, have encouraged African strike action (partly too because of its vested interests in the country's economy) but it would deplore the fact that the machinery for non-White collective bargaining did not exist and discuss the likely effects of the system's unresponsiveness to non-White needs. The publicity that the English Press gave non-White activities and aspirations was regarded by the Nationalists as an identification with those aspirations and as such constituted a threat to them. For in focusing attention on what it saw as non-White needs, the English Press was believed to be creating those needs. The fact was however, that the radical opposition had already been suppressed and the extent to which the English Press could represent a spectrum of non-White aspirations was already circumscribed. Its 'responsibility' helped safeguard it from even more extreme Nationalist pressures, while freeing it to express views which would not otherwise be heard, even if an increasing range of political facts (as opposed to opinions) were precluded from publication.

Nationalist beliefs about the influence of the English-language Press on the different groups within the society and on 'world opinion' outside it, provide a further clue to the ambivalent behaviour of the Government *vis-à-vis* the English-language Press. Nationalists consistently believed that the English-language Press, through its hostile presentation of the Afrikaner, kept English-speaking South Africans from giving positive support to the National Party and Government. Simultaneously the belief grew that the English-language Press, had become 'alienated' from English-speaking South Africans. For a long time too, Nationalists feared the influence of values propagated by the English newspapers on the Afrikaner who in sizeable numbers read the English rather than the technically less expert Afrikaans-language newspapers. But fears about that influence were constantly palliated by the fact that the Nationalists continued to win elections. Nationalist fears about the influence of the English-language Press on the African, centred on the belief that in offering a public platform to the non-White it helped to create a hostile non-White opinion. It provided a focal point, helped unite non-White opinion by giving it 'status' (through the printed word) and allowed it to be communicated to an extensive audience. On the other hand the Nationalist Government was remarkably successful in suppressing united and hostile non-White movements or preventing their formation.

Thus there were contradictions in Nationalist attitudes towards the English-language Press. The Government believed that English-speaking South Africans had become alienated from the English-language Press (and therefore less hostile to the Afrikaner) and it had electoral proof that the Afrikaner remained impervious to the values expressed through the English Press. Also the non-Whites were under control, so the Government could afford to permit the English Press to continue in its opposition. At the same time the old fears about the influence of the printed word on men's minds persisted and the campaign to undermine the credibility of the English Press and to curtail its licence continued.

A final factor which contributed to the continuing freedom of the English Press was the failure of the Nationalist regime to make any attempt to relate to the total society. In so far as its Press policies were derived from a Nationalist ideology, they related almost exclusively to the Afrikaans Press. The Nationalist Government had no coherent policy which it consistently applied to the English-language Press. Rather, its English Press policies were dictated by the political circumstances at the time. Nationalist controlled information media were instruments for communicating and promoting Government ideology and as such were responsible for guiding opinion in conformity to that ideology. The Nationalist Government made few serious attempts to induce ideological conformity amongst groups outside its own community, although it certainly had the power to do so. It chose rather to rely on the fervour and commitment of its own supporters as members of a fiercely exclusive group, and was content with the acquiescence of outsiders. This helps explain both why an independent Press was permitted to exist and why the English-language Press appeared to make so little constructive impact on Government policy.

It also confirms and underlines the importance of the Afrikaans Press as an institution within the Nationalist ranks. By 1948 the Afrikaans Press had achieved most of its original objectives. Through the 1950s its task was largely one of consolidation and it was content to give uncritical support to party and Government. But after ten years in office and a third election victory, a section of the Nationalist Press believed that the party and the Government could tolerate a limited public exposure to differences within the ranks. The initial impetus came from the Cape Nationalist Press who opposed the shift in the balance of political power to the Transvaal. The feeling grew too that providing unquestionable support for a Government was not the same as building up an army and supporting it whilst in opposition. The independent Press ethic of the English-language Press had made its impact on the journalists of the Afrikaans Press.

During the 1960s, after Sharpeville and the creation of a republic, the Afrikaans Press forced the discussion of serious differences in the party and Government to be debated in public, demanding, in the process, a new role for itself within the Government structure. Within the Government and the party the Afrikaans Press became the most powerfully organized force of opposition. In large measure the Afrikaans Press must be held responsible for the occurrence of the first split in the National Party for twenty years.

Note on Sources

Throughout this study reference has been made to a number of books written about the South African Press. Yet none have attempted a serious analysis of the complex inter-relationship of the Press and the Government and the role of the Press in the political system. H. Lindsay Smith's *Behind the Press in South Africa*, written in 1947, is probably still the best account of the Press in the pre-1948 years. It is a slight book and was conceived as an attack on the structure of the Argus Group and particularly on John Martin, the *eminence grise* of the group for nearly twenty years. Another book on the Argus Group, L. E. Neame's *Today's News Today*, relates the history of the company. But as the book was commissioned and published by the Argus Company and written by an ex-Argus employee, the result was an uncritical and favourable recording of the company's history.

Morris Broughton's *Press and Politics of South Africa* is a turgid and very personal account of the English-language Press. The author is an ex-editor of the *Cape Argus* and as such the book is enlightening in so far as it reveals the attitudes of an English newspaper editor. Theo Cutten's *History of The South African Press*, written as a Ph.D. thesis at the University of the Witwatersrand in 1936, provided some useful information on the early history of the two Presses. There are two good chapters on the South African Press in Rosalynde Ainslie's book on *The Press in Africa*. Scott Haigh's anecdotal account of the Press in Parliament provides some useful insights but as it was written in 1951 it could not encompass the important changes which occurred after the Nationalists came to power.

The most adequately covered aspects of the South African Press is that which describes the legal framework within which the Press operates. There are two good factual books on the subject: Blackwell and Bamford's, *Newspaper Law of South Africa* and Stuart Klopper's, *The Newspaperman's Guide to the Law*. A third publication, a pamphlet by Alexander Hepple, *Censorship and Press Control in South Africa*, covers the legal and non-governmental pressures on the Press. On the Afrikaans Press, there is only *Die Burger*'s fiftieth anniversary publication, *Keeromstraat 30*, which contains some

211

revealing articles by past and present journalists and editors of the newspaper. Nasionale Pers also published a collection of 'Dawie's' articles between 1946 and 1964, which is useful for following developments in *Die Burger*'s thinking during those years.

The Jewish Board of Deputies' *Press Digest* is an indispensable weekly guide to the contents of the Press. The Government's publication, *Weekly Press Digest*, is also useful but not nearly as good as the *Press Digest*. The Institute of Race Relations and SABRA also produce publications through which it is possible to follow events in the newspapers over the years.

One of the most useful sources of information is the fourteen-volume Press Commission Report, which unfortunately is not available outside South Africa as only a few copies of the Report were published. The report is rich in facts about the histories and financial structures of the Presses and other related organizations up to 1956.

The International Press Institute in Zurich has a small but growing file on the South African Press and some interesting information on governmental pressures on the Press. Some of these findings appear in the Institute's monthly Bulletin. The MRA surveys, commissioned by the Newspaper Press Union and the biannual circulation figures of the Audit Bureau of Circulation were indispensable for the chapter on readership. These figures have not been generally available for public scrutiny as the NPU has insisted on keeping the information confidential although the *Financial Mail* has in recent years begun to publish some details of circulation.

The South African newspapers themselves are available in Britain at the British Museum's newspaper library at Colindale. Finally this study draws heavily on discussions with the newspaper editors, journalists, and proprietors as well as politicians.

Bibliography

1. South Africa

Heribert Adam (ed.), *South Africa: Sociological Perspectives* (London: Oxford University Press, 1971).

Rosalynde Ainslie, *The Press In Africa* (London: Victor Gollancz Ltd., 1966).

Arthur G. Barlow, *Almost in Confidence* (Cape Town: Juta & Co., 1952).

M. Ballinger, *From Union to Apartheid* (Cape Town: Juta & Co., 1969).

L. Blackwell and B. Bamford, *Newspaper Law of South Africa* (Cape Town: Juta & Co., 1963).

Alexander Brady, *Democracy in the Dominions: A Comparative Study in Institution* (Toronto: University of Toronto Press, 2nd ed., 1952).

Edgar H. Brookes (ed.), *Apartheid, A Documentary Study of Modern South Africa* (London: Routledge & Kegan Paul, 1968).

——, *South Africa in a Changing World* (Cape Town: Oxford University Press, 1953).

Edgar H. Brookes and J. B. Macaulay, *Civil Liberty in South Africa* (Cape Town: Oxford University Press, 1958).

Morris Broughton, *Press & Politics of South Africa* (Cape Town: Purnell & Sons (SA), 1961).

James Bryce, 'Two South African Constitutions' in his *Studies in History and Jurisprudence* (New York: Oxford University Press, 1901).

Brian Bunting. *The Rise of the South African Reich* (London: Penguin African Library, 1964).

D. E. Butler (ed.), *Elections Abroad* (London: Macmillan & Co., 1959).

G. H. Calpin, 'South Africa in Afrikaner Hands', in *Foreign Affairs,* April 1951.

Peter Calvocoressi, *South Africa and World Opinion* (London: Oxford University Press, 1961).

Gwendolen M. Carter, 'Can Apartheid Succeed in South Africa?' in *Foreign Affairs*, January 1954.

—— (ed.), *Five African States* (London: Pall Mall Press, 1964).

——, *The Politics of Inequality* (London: Thames & Hudson, 3rd. ed., 1962).

——, 'Union of South Africa; Politics of White Supremacy' in *The Annals*, March 1955.

George Clay and Stanley Uys, 'The Press: Strijdom's Last Barrier' in *Africa South*, October–December 1957.

213

Theo E. Cutten, *A History of the Press in South Africa* (Johannesburg): The National Union of South African Students, 1936).

K. Danziger, 'Ideology and Utopia in South Africa: A methodological Contribution to the Sociology of Knowledge', in the *British Journal of Sociology*, March 1963.

——, 'Modernization and the Legitimation of Social Power' in Heribert Adam (ed.), *South Africa: Sociological Perspectives* (London: Oxford University Press, 1971).

C. W. de Kiewiet, *The Anatomy of South African Misery* (London: Oxford University Press, 1956).

——, *A History of South Africa, Social and Economic* (London: Oxford University Press, 2nd ed., 1966).

R. de Villiers, *The People and the Press* (Johannesburg: South African Institute of Race Relations, Topical Talk Series, 1964).

G. V. Doxey, *The Industrial Colour Bar in South Africa* (Cape Town: Oxford University Press, 1961).

R. Farquharson, 'South Africa' in D. E. Butler (ed.), *Elections Abroad* (*London: Macmillan & Co., 1959*).

A. J. Friedgut, 'The Non-European Press' in Ellen Hellman (ed.) *Handbook on Race Relations in South Africa* (London: Oxford University Press, Published for the South African Institute of Race Relations, 1949).

H. R. Hahlo and E. Kahn, *The Union of South Africa: The Development, of Its Laws and Constitution* (London: Stevens & Co., 1960).

Scott Haigh, *Strangers May be Present* (London: G. Allen & Unwin, 1951).

Ellen Hellman (ed.), *Handbook on Race Relations in South Africa* (London: Oxford University Press, Published for the South African Institute of Race Relations, 1949).

Alexander Hepple, *Censorship and Press Control in South Africa* (Johannesburg: Published by the Author, 1960).

——, *South Africa: A Political and Economic History* (London: Pall Mall Press, 1966).

——, *Verwoerd* (London: Penguin, 1967).

Thomas Hodgkin, *Nationalism in Colonial Africa* (London: Frederick Muller, 1956).

Tom Hopkinson, *Drum: In the Fiery Continent* (London: Gollancz, 1962).

Muriel Horrell, *Days of Crisis in South Africa, A Fact Paper* (Johannesburg: South African Institute of Race Relations, 1961).

——, *Legislation and Race Relations* (Johannesburg: South African Institute of Race Relations, 1963).

——, *Non-European Policies in the Union and the Measure of their Success* (Johannesburg: South African, Institute of Race Relations, 1954).

Institute of Social and Economic Research, *Daily Dispatch Attitude Survey* (Grahamstown: Rhodes University, 1967).

BIBLIOGRAPHY

International Commission of Jurists, *South Africa and the Rule of Law* (Geneva, 1967).

——, *Erosion of the Rule of Law in South Africa* (Geneva, 1968).

Journal of Racial Affairs (Stellenbosch: Journal of the South African Bureau of Racial Affairs, quarterly).

Ellison Kahn, *The New Constitution* (Johannesburg: Juta & Co., 1962)·

T. Karis, 'South Africa' in Gwendolen M. Carter (ed.), *Five African States* (London: Pall Mall Press, 1964).

Arthur Keppel-Jones, *South Africa: A Short History* (London: Hutchinson, 1965).

D. W. Kruger, *The Age of the Generals* (Johannesburg: Dagbreek Book Stores, 1958).

—— (ed.), *South African Parties and Politics, 1910–1960* (Cape Town: Human & Rousseau, 1960).

Leo Kuper, 'Techniques of Social Control in South Africa' in *Foreign Affairs*, July 1958.

John Laurence, *The Seeds of Disaster* (London: Victor Gollancz Ltd., 1968).

Colin and Margaret Legum, *South Africa: Crisis for the West* (London: Pall Mall Press, 1964).

G. H. L. Le May, *British Supremacy in South Africa 1899–1907* (Oxford: Clarendon Press, 1965).

Julius Lewin, *Politics and Law in South Africa* (London: Merlin Press, 1963).

Colin Leys, *European Politics in Southern Rhodesia* (Oxford: Clarendon Press, 1959).

Louis Louw (ed.), *Dawie, 1946–1964* (Cape Town: Tafelberg Uitgewers, 1965).

I. D. MacCrone, *Race Attitudes in South Africa: Historical, Experimental and Psychological Studies* (London: Oxford University Press, 1937).

W. H. Macmillan, *Bantu, Boer and Briton: The Making of the South African Native Problem* (Oxford: Clarendon Press, 1928, 1963).

D. F. Malan, *Afrikaner Volkseenheid en My Ervarings Op Die Pad Daarheen* (Cape Town: Nasionale Boekhandel Beperk, 1959).

J. S. Marais, *The Fall of Kruger's Republic* (Oxford: Clarendon Press 1961).

Market Research Africa, *Readership Survey* (Johannesburg, 1962, 1968).

Leo Marquard, *The Peoples and Policies of South Africa* (London: Oxford University Press, 1952, 1969).

——, *The Story of South Africa* (London: Faber & Faber, 1955, 1966).

A. S. Mathews, 'Security Laws and Social Change in the Republic of South Africa' in Heribert Adam (ed.), *South Africa: Sociological Perspectives* (London: Oxford University Press, 1971).

Henry J. May, *The South African Constitution* (Johannesburg: Juta & Co., 1955).

Edwin S. Munger, *Afrikaner and African Nationalism: South African*

Parallels and Parameters (London: Oxford University Press, for the Institute of Race Relations, 1967).

——, *Notes on the formation of South African Foreign Policy* (Pasadena: Castle Press, 1965).

——, 'Self-Confidence and Self-Criticism in South Africa' in *Foreign Affairs*, July 1958.

——, 'South Africa's Prime Minister John Vorster' in *American Universities Field Staff Reports, Central and Southern Africa Series*, 1968.

L. E. Neame, *Today's News Today: The Story of the Argus Company* (Johannesburg: Argus Printing & Publishing Co., 1956).

C. R. Nixon, 'The Conflict of Nationalisms in South Africa; in *World Politics*, October 1958.

Alan Paton, *Hofmeyr* (Cape Town: Oxford University Press, 1957).

Sheila Patterson, *The Last Trek: A Study of the Boer People and the Afrikaner Nation* (London: Routledge & Kegan Paul, 1957).

——, *Colour and Culture in South Africa: A Study of the Status of the Cape Coloured People Within the Social Structure of South Africa* (London: Routledge & Kegan Paul, 1953).

S. Pienaar and A. Sampson, *South Africa: Two Views of Separate Development* (Cape Town: Oxford University Press, 1960).

Press Digest (Johannesburg: Jewish Board of Deputies, weekly 1948–68).

Report of the Commission of Inquiry in Regard to Undesirable Publications (Pretoria: The Government Printers, 1957).

Report of the Commission of Inquiry into the Press (Pretoria: The Government Printers (14 volumes), 1962, 1964).

R. Reynolds, 'Exit Malan' in *The Political Quarterly*, January–March 1955.

H. M. Robertson, 'Coloured Disfranchisement' in E. H. Brookes (ed.), *Apartheid, a Documentary Study of Modern South Africa* (London: Routledge & Kegan Paul, 1968).

M. Roberts and A. Trollip, *The South African Opposition 1939–1945* (London: Longmans, Green, 1947).

The Round Table: A Quarterly Review of British Commonwealth Affairs.

Edward Roux, *Time Longer than Rope: A History of the Black Man's Struggle for Freedom in South Africa* (London: Gollancz, 1948).

Anthony Sampson, *Drum: A Venture into the New Africa* (London: Collins, 1956).

J. P. Scannel (ed.), *Keeromstraat 30* (Cape Town: Nasionale Boekhandel Beperk, 1965).

G. D. Scholtz, *Het Die Afrikaner Volk'n Toekoms?* (Johannesburg: Voortrekkerpers, 1954).

H. Lindsay Smith, *Behind the Press in South Africa* (Cape Town: Stewart, 1947).

South African Press Board of Reference, *The First Periodical Report, June 28, 1962 to February 29, 1964* (Johannesburg, 1964).

——, *The Second Periodical Report, March 1, 1964 to June 30, 1968* (Johannesburg, 1968).

216

BIBLIOGRAPHY

South African Press Council, *Constitution, Code of Conduct and Rules of Procedure* (Johannesburg, no date).

K. W. Stuart and W. Klopper, *The Newspaperman's Guide to the Law* (Johannesburg: Mainpress Books, 1968).

N. M. Stults and J. Butler, 'The South African General Election of 1960' in the *Political Science Quarterly*, March 1963.

Survey of Race Relations in South Africa (Johannesburg: South African Institute of Race Relations, published annually).

L. M. Thompson, *The Unification of South Africa 1902–1910* (Oxford: Clarendon Press, 1960).

——, 'Constitutionalism on the South African Republics' in *Butterworth's South African Law Review*, 1954.

Stanley Trapido, 'Political Institutions and Afrikaner Social Structures —in the Republic of South Africa' in the *American Political Science Review*, March 1963.

Union Statistics for Fifty Years: Jubilee Issue 1910–1960 (Pretoria: Bureau of Census & Statistics, 1960).

Stanleys Uys, 'The Referendum and After' in *Africa South in Exile*, January–March 1961.

——, 'The White Opposition Splits' in *Africa South*, January–March, 1960.

Pierre van den Berghe, 'Language and Nationalism in South Africa' in *Race*, July 1967.

——, 'Racial Segregation in South Africa: Degrees and Kinds' in Heribert Adam (ed.), *South Africa: Sociological Perspectives* (London: Oxford University Press, 1971).

——, *South Africa: A Study in Conflict* (Berkeley: University of California Press, 1970).

F. A. van Jaarsveld, *The Afrikaner's Interpretation of South African History* (Cape Town: Simondium 1961).

——, *The Awakening of Afrikaner Nationalism 1861–1881* (Cape Town: Human & Rousseau, 1961).

W. H. Vatcher, *White Laager: The Rise of Afrikaner Nationalism* (London: Pall Mall, 1965).

Eric Walker, *A History of South Africa* (London: Longmans, Green, 1957).

Weekly Press Digest (Pretoria: Issued by the Government Information Office, weekly).

K. C. Wheare, *The Statute of Westminster and Dominion Status* (London: Oxford University Press, 1953).

Francis Williams, 'The Embattled Press' in *Africa South*, April–June 1960.

G. H. Wilson, *Gone Down the Years* (London: Allen & Unwin, 1947).

2. Communications and General

Gabriel A. Almond and James S. Coleman, *The Politics of the Developing Areas* (Princeton: Princeton University Press, 1970).

Gabriel A. Almond and G. Bingham Powell, *Comparative Politics: A Developmental Approach* (Boston: Little, Brown & Co., 1966).

Hannah Arendt, *The Human Condition* (New York: Doubleday Anchor Books, 1959).

——, *The Origins of Totalitarianism* (Cleveland: Meridian Books, 1964).

T. B. Bottomore, *Elites and Society* (London: C. A. Watts & Co., 1964).

Frede Castberg, *Freedom of Speech in the West* (London: Houghton Mifflin, 1959).

Zechariah, Chafee, Jr., *Government and Mass Communications*, Vols. I and II (Illinois: The University of Chicago Press, 1947).

Bernhard C. Cohen, *The Press and Foreign Policy* (Princeton: Princeton University Press, 1963).

R. A. Dahl, *Political Oppositions in Western Democracies* (New Haven & London: Yale University Press, 1966).

Bertrand de Jouvenel, *Sovereignty* (Cambridge: The University Press, 1957).

Karl W. Deutsch, *The Nerves of Government: Models of Political Communication and Control* (New York: The Free Press, 1966).

M. Duverger, *Political Parties* (London: Methuen & Co., 1964).

Richard R. Fagen, *Politics and Communication* (Boston: Little Brown & Co., 1966).

Oron J. Hale, *The Captive Press in the Third Reich* (Princeton: Princeton University Press, 1964).

W. E. Hocking, *Freedom of the Press: A Framework of Principle* (Chicago: The University of Chicago Press, 1947).

International Press Institute, *Press Councils and Press Codes* (Zurich: International Press Institute).

G. Ionescu and I. de Madariaga, *Opposition* (London: C. A. Watts & Co., 1968).

IPI Report (Zurich: The International Press Institute Bulletin, monthly).

IPI Survey, *Government Pressures on the Press* (Zurich: The International Press Institute, 1955).

——, *The Press in Authoritarian Countries* (Zurich: The International Press Institute, 1959).

E. Katz, 'The Two-Step Flow of Communication' in Wilbur Schramm (ed.), *Mass Communications* (Urbana: University of Illinois Press, 2nd ed., 1960).

Elie Kedourie, *Nationalism* (London: Hutchinson University Library, 1969).

J. T. Klapper, *Effects of Mass Communications* (Glencoe: The Free Press, 1960).

H. D. Lasswell and A. Kaplan, *Power and Society* (New Haven: Yale University Press, 1950).

Daniel Lerner, 'Communication Systems and Social Systems' in Wilbur Schramm (ed.), *Mass Communications* (Urbana: University of Illinois Press, 2nd ed., 1960).

BIBLIOGRAPHY

Walter Lippman, *Public Opinion* (New York: The Macmillan Co., 1954).

S. M. Lipset, *Political Man* (New York: Doubleday & Co., 1960).

Henry Mayer, *The Press in Australia* (London: Angus & Robertson, 1946).

Robert McKenzie, *British Political Parties* (London: Heinemann, 2nd. ed., 1963).

Lucian W. Pye (ed.), *Communications and Political Development* (Princeton: Princeton University Press, 1963).

Wilbur Schramm, *Mass Communications* (Urbana; University of Illinois Press, 2nd ed., 1960).

——, *Mass Media and National Development: The Role of Information in Developing Areas* (Stanford: Stanford University Press, 1964).

Colin Seymour-Ure, 'Policy Making in the Press', in *Government and Opposition*, Autumn 1969.

——, *The Press, Politics and the Public* (London; Methuen & Co., 1968).

Fred S. Siebert, Theodore Peterson and W. Schramm, *Four Theories of the Press* (Urbana: University of Illinois Press, 1956).

E. Lloyd Sommerlad *The Press in Developing Countries* (Sydney: Sydney University Press 1966).

Wickham Steed, *The Press* (Harmondsworth: Penguin Books, 1938).

UNESCO, *The Daily Press* (UNESCO, 1953).

——, *World Communications* (UNESCO, 1964).

Francis Williams, *Dangerous Estate* (London: Longmans, Green & Co., 1957).

——, *Press, Parliament and People* (London: William Heinemann, 1946).

——, *The Right to Know, The Rise of the World Press* (London: Longmans, Green & Co., 1969).

Raymond Williams, *Communications* (London: Chatto & Windus, 1966).

3. Newspapers

Die Beeld. Weekly Nasionale Pers Beperk, Johannesburg (Afrikaans).

Die Burger. Morning Daily, Nasionale Pers Beperk, Cape Town (Afrikaans).

Cape Argus, Afternoon Daily, Argus Group, Cape Town (English).

Cape Times, Morning Daily, Independent, Cape Town (English).

Dagbreek en Sondagnuus, Weekly, Afrikaanse Pers Beperk, Johannesburg (Afrikaans).

Daily Dispatch, Morning Daily, Independent, East London (English).

Daily News, Afternoon Daily, Argus Group, Durban (English).

Diamond Fields Advertiser, Morning Daily, Argus Group, Kimberley (English).

Eastern Province Herald, Morning Daily South African Associated Newspapers, Port Elizabeth (English).

Evening Post, Afternoon Daily, South African Associated Newspapers, Port Elizabeth (English).

The Friend, Morning Daily, Argus Company, Bloemfontein (English).

The Natal Mercury, Morning Daily, Independent, Durban (English).

The Natal Witness, Morning Daily, Independent, Pietermaritzburg (English).

Die Oosterlig, Afternoon Daily, Nasionale Pers Beperk, Port Elizabeth (Afrikaans).

Pretoria News, Afternoon Daily, mainly Argus Group, Pretoria (English).

Rand Daily Mail, Morning Daily, South African Associated Newspapers, Johannesburg (English).

The Star, Afternoon Daily, Argus Group, Johannesburg (English).

Sunday Express, Weekly South African Associated Newspapers, Johannesburg (English).

Sunday Times, Weekly, South African Associated Newspapers, Johannesburg (English).

Die Transvaler, Morning Daily, Voortrekkerpers Beperk, Johannesberg (Afrikaans).

Sunday Tribune, Weekly, Argus Group, Durban (English).

Die Vaderland, Afternoon Daily, Afrikaanse Pers Beperk, Johannesburg (Afrikaans).

Die Volksblad, Afternoon Daily, Nasionale Pers Beperk, Bloemfontein (Afrikaans).

Index

221